Policy Borrowing and F

Laura M. Portnoi

Policy Borrowing and Reform in Education

Globalized Processes and Local Contexts

Laura M. Portnoi
California State University
Long Beach, California, USA

ISBN 978-1-137-53022-6 (hardcover) ISBN 978-1-137-53024-0 (eBook)
ISBN 978-1-349-70843-7 (softcover)
DOI 10.1057/978-1-137-53024-0

Library of Congress Control Number: 2016942690

© The Editor(s) (if applicable) and The Author(s) 2016, First softcover printing 2019
This work is subject to copyright. All rights are solely and exclusively licensed by the Publisher, whether the whole or part of the material is concerned, specifically the rights of translation, reprinting, reuse of illustrations, recitation, broadcasting, reproduction on microfilms or in any other physical way, and transmission or information storage and retrieval, electronic adaptation, computer software, or by similar or dissimilar methodology now known or hereafter developed.
The use of general descriptive names, registered names, trademarks, service marks, etc. in this publication does not imply, even in the absence of a specific statement, that such names are exempt from the relevant protective laws and regulations and therefore free for general use.
The publisher, the authors and the editors are safe to assume that the advice and information in this book are believed to be true and accurate at the date of publication. Neither the publisher nor the authors or the editors give a warranty, express or implied, with respect to the material contained herein or for any errors or omissions that may have been made.

Cover Illustration © Pat Canova / Getty

Printed on acid-free paper

This Palgrave Macmillan imprint is published by Springer Nature
The registered company is Nature America Inc. New York

This book is dedicated to the students from the Social and Cultural Analysis of Education master's program at California State University, Long Beach, with whom I have had the pleasure to interact over the past ten years. They encouraged me to write this book and continue to serve as an inspiration every day.

Preface

No matter where we live, we experience international connections—through the foods we buy at grocery stores, the clothing we wear, and the everyday products we use in our homes. Global developments and trends influence sports, politics, economics, and just about every other aspect of today's society. Although education has historically been, and continues to be, governed by local jurisdictions, global developments and trends have a profound impact on education in today's interconnected world. Current global trends, such as the preponderance of standards-based education in schooling environments and the emphasis on rankings and competition in higher education, are affecting educational systems around the world. Globalization and its influences are not a 'given', however, and local responses to global trends vary based on the contexts involved. For all of these reasons, studying globalization and policy borrowing, as well as the global and local manifestations of educational reforms, is important for all types of educators as well as for those from affiliated disciplines.

Situating the Study of Globalization

As I explain more fully in Chap. 1, 'globalization' is a complex concept that has developed through a combination of academic and popular sources. The meaning of 'globalization' remains contested, as are its processes and impacts. The formal study of globalization is relatively new, beginning in earnest in the 1970s. Understandings of globalization continue to be developed in various areas and through a number of academic disciplines, and it is not uncommon to find globalization courses in sociology, political science, anthropology, education, and policy studies departments, among others. Indeed, the fact that globalization is tied to so many different areas of study serves as one of the foundations of this book, which takes into account that students or scholars of education may not have formal exposure to the history, theories, and concepts related to globalization.

In addition to its integration into traditional academic disciplines, globalization is studied as a central component of two interdisciplinary fields: Global Studies and Comparative International Education (CIE). Established in the late 1990s and early 2000s, Global Studies is a relatively new domain, which Global Studies scholar Manfred Steger (2013) describes as 'transdisciplinary' because it is not confined to a specific field within the humanities or social sciences. Instead, Global Studies—also referred to as 'Globalization Studies'—uses theories and ideas from multiple arenas and requires students and scholars to have an understanding of a variety of academic disciplines, including philosophy, modern languages, economics, and communication studies. Some Global Studies programs are housed in specific academic departments (e.g., political science or sociology), although most are offered as stand-alone, interdisciplinary programs, often as part of Global Studies Institutes. Global Studies curricula generally include thematic and/or regional course offerings, along with transdisciplinary Global Studies courses that allow for developing an understanding of how insights gained from various perspectives or disciplines fit together into an integrated whole. Many established Global Studies programs are offered at the graduate level, although undergraduate majors in Global Studies are growing in number as well.

Given that the field is still evolving, the Global Studies Consortium, which includes a variety of institutions from around the world, developed a set of five common areas of focus for Global Studies graduate programs: transnationality (occurring across national boundaries), interdisciplinary (drawing from multiple academic disciplines), both historical and contemporary perspectives (focusing on the here and now while recognizing historical roots), postcolonial and critical approaches (critiquing how Western[1] knowledge and countries are privileged), and connections to global citizenship (solving problems and operating on a global scale) (Juergensmeyer, 2011). Despite this concurrence regarding the emphases of graduate-level Global Studies programs, many within the field are still debating its parameters, which is not surprising because most faculty who teach within such programs come from other, more traditional academic disciplines. A consistent central aspect of Global Studies, however, is its emphasis on studying global trends, processes, and topics that cut across national borders and occur in multiple countries.

Like Global Studies, CIE has evolved as a field that draws upon multiple disciplines. It emerged as a formal area of study in the late 1950s and early 1960s, when the first comparative international education journal (*Comparative Education Review*) and graduate programs in CIE were established.[2] Many senior academics within CIE today were originally trained as economists, sociologists, or educators from other disciplines. This array of scholars has come together to study CIE and train master's and doctoral students in the field, using a wide variety of theories and constructs, many of which are drawn from other disciplines. Areas of study within CIE include international development education, study-abroad and international education, globalization, policy borrowing, area studies, and specific topics relevant to education in countries around the world (e.g., language policies in Russia or affirmative action in South Africa).

CIE covers the full range of educational levels, from preschool to higher and adult education, and much of its scholarly literature focuses on specific country case studies that employ qualitative research. Although large-scale cross-national quantitative studies are part of the field's literature base, the preponderance of country-based studies has led some CIE scholars to question how 'comparative' the field truly is (see, e.g., Cummings, 1999). Moreover, discussions about the boundaries of the field are continually present at annual meetings of the US-based Comparative and International Education Society, as is the question of whether CIE constitutes a field or a discipline (see, e.g., Arnove et al., 2006; Carnoy, 2006; Wilson, 1994).

Interestingly, Global Studies scholars would likely criticize CIE for an overemphasis on the nation-state as a key actor; indeed, using the nation-state as the unit of analysis tends to restrict scholars' ability to study developments and topics that occur at the global level (Shields, 2013). Nonetheless, numerous scholars within CIE take a broader perspective and have focused on topics such as globalization, the diffusion of knowledge across borders, educational policy borrowing and lending, and global competition in higher education (see, e.g., Chakroun, 2010; Jakobi, 2012; Portnoi & Bagley, 2014; Steiner-Khamsi, 2004, 2012; Tikly, 2001). In a certain sense, these scholars have added a Global Studies angle to their CIE lenses because they concentrate on the global aspects of education that cut across borders.

This book is situated within this area of CIE scholarship that focuses on globalization and educational reform, utilizing a global perspective.

Given that my doctoral training was in CIE, I continue to operate from a CIE approach, though my focus has extended beyond the nation-state as a unit of analysis and country-based studies. A great deal of my scholarship in CIE over the past several years, while working collaboratively with Sylvia Bagley, has centered on global competition within higher education (Bagley & Portnoi, 2012, 2016; Portnoi & Bagley, 2011, 2014, 2015; Portnoi, Bagley, & Rust, 2013). I provide this information on my training and where I situate this book within CIE so that readers have a general understanding of my approach. Nevertheless, as I explain in more detail below, this book was designed to appeal to a wide range of students and scholars from a variety of fields, and a key strength of the book is that it draws upon a variety of disciplines within education and beyond. Thus, this book was written with a broad, diverse audience in mind and is intended to be accessible to all readers, whether or not they have had exposure to CIE.

Purpose and Scope

This book addresses the intersections of globalization, policy borrowing, and educational reform. Using syntheses of diffuse literature drawn from education and other disciplines, I focus on the processes of educational reform in a globalized world. By emphasizing a critical perspective that highlights the geopolitical dominance of the Global North/'developed' countries,[3] this book offers a comprehensive understanding of how globalization and significant related developments, including the emergence of global governance organizations, have had an impact on educational reform worldwide. Throughout the book, I emphasize the manner in which local jurisdictions exercise agency and intervene to mediate the forces of globalization, thereby complicating the normative 'convergence' narrative—the commonly held notion that globalization promotes uniformity worldwide through employing the 'best' policies and practices—that permeates much of the discussion on globalization.

Several premises were inherent in the conceptualization of this book. First, globalization and key related developments have an impact on educational reform in local contexts. Second, everyone involved in education, from practitioners to scholars to policymakers, ought to be informed about globalization's impact on education and educational reform in local contexts. Third, despite the impact of globalization on education, local actors have agency to resist and mediate global trends. Fourth, historical developments have led to the current context in which the Global North's (or 'developed' world's) geopolitical influence is dominant. Finally, the current processes of educational reform cannot be fully understood without first having a strong understanding of the processes of globalization, various approaches to studying globalization, and key developments related to globalization. With these underlying assumptions in view, the overarching goal of the book is to provide a comprehensive discussion of educational reform processes in a globalized world, built upon fundamental understandings of globalization, its associated developments, and theories of globalization.

This book allows readers to explore the following questions: What is 'globalization', and how has it been conceptualized? What are the fundamental debates that surround globalization, and what are its benefits, costs, and dilemmas? What are the key trends and developments related to globalization, and what is the role of global governance organizations specifically? What contributes to the dominant influence of particular countries or regions in a globalized world? How have different approaches to globalization (theories and constructs) had an impact on the way that it has been understood and analyzed? More specifically, what is the connection between globalization and education, and what trends have occurred in the educational realm due to globalization? What are the parameters of the educational policy process, and what are the challenges to implementing public policies? How do educational borrowing and lending differ, and what are the politics involved in these processes? To what degree does policy convergence exist, and to what extent can nations and local constituencies exercise agency to resist global trends? What patterns are evident in research on educational reform processes in a variety of contexts? What lessons may be learned from studying globalization, policy borrowing, and educational reform?

The chapters in this book provide a synthesis of a diffuse set of literature from education and other disciplines[4] to provide a comprehensive foundation and context that serve to frame the syntheses of current scholarship on educational reform processes that follow in the latter portions of the text. The book draws upon diverse sources, including perspectives from the Global South and the East, wherever possible, which are not as prominent as are those of the West in terms of the existing globalization and education literature. Importantly, although the focus of this book is on synthesizing and understanding broad developments and trends, this does not imply that educational reform is a 'one size fits all' endeavor. On the contrary, the analyses and discussions I present throughout the book emphasize how dominant forms of globalization (or globalization from above) are interrupted and reframed in local contexts through vernacular globalization (or globalization from below).

Organization of the Book

After perusing the book's contents, readers may wonder why education is not explicitly the focus of the first three chapters. This book is designed for those who wish to gain a comprehensive understanding of the realm of globalization and educational reform. The structure of the book allows readers to develop knowledge of a wide range of historical and recent developments that have an impact on globalization's intersections with education and educational reform. Because the subject matter is multidisciplinary in nature, educational reform processes must first be situated within broader developments and theories related to globalization. Although I make connections to education in Chaps. 1, 2 and 3, it is important to provide this broad, multidisciplinary foundation before shifting to a focus on education, expressly because globalization and educational reform are intricately connected to wider developments and theories or constructs.

In Chap. 1, 'Understanding Globalization', I cover globalization comprehensively to provide a context for understanding this complex and contested concept prior to focusing on globalization and education, specifically. The chapter begins with a discussion of the origins of the concept of 'globalization', using a historical perspective to consider whether globalization is a new phenomenon and when it began. I also present terminology that policymakers, scholars, and global governance organizations use to describe different types of countries. This historical background is followed by an overview of varying conceptions of globalization as well as its dimensions: economic, political, cultural, social, technological, and ecological. I also present key debates within the study of globalization, including those that concern the formation of a world culture, the inevitability of globalization, and the role of nation-states. These debates draw from multiple disciplines, including globalization studies, political science, and education. I also consider the costs, benefits, and dilemmas of globalization. With its emphasis on understanding globalization, Chap. 1 serves to frame the in-depth analyses and discussions that follow in the remainder of the book.

Chapter 2, 'Why Study Globalization? Developments, Actors, Resistance', covers broad developments and trends that have been central to the heightened nature of contemporary globalization since World War II. Highlighted worldwide developments include technological advances, especially in the area of information and communications technology; economic globalization and the retreat of the welfare state; the shift from Fordism to post-Fordism; the development of a global knowledge economy; international mobility and transnational migration; and shifting cultural patterns. The launch of the aid and development regime is also an area of focus, followed by an overview of the historical emergence of global forms of governance, including intergovernmental organizations, regional organizations, bilateral organizations, international monetary organizations, and international non-governmental organizations. Other actors in the policy development and implementation process also are highlighted: transnational corporations; nation-states; communities, policy implementers, and individuals; and think tanks, special interest groups, and lobbyists. In the latter part of the chapter, I also explore the development of a Washington (and Post-Washington) Consensus that has guided international aid and development since the 1970s and discuss resistance movements to neoliberal globalization. Given all of these developments and the increasing interconnectedness of the world, the importance of studying global educational reform processes becomes clear. This broad overview of key developments related to globalization sets the stage for focused discussions on globalization, education, and educational reform throughout Chaps. 4, 5, 6, 7, and 8.

Before delving into globalization and education specifically, the discussion turns to the important realm of theories and constructs related to globalization. Chapter 3, 'Theorizing Globalization', provides an in-depth discussion of theories and constructs that have been used to study globalization, most of which originate outside the educational realm. Understanding theories and constructs related to globalization is critical to interpreting the globalization and education literature, which draws from an array of theories and constructs from a variety of disciplines. The first part of the chapter provides an overview of the broad theoretical domains of modernism and postmodernism before moving into specific theories. The theories covered in Chap. 3 include human capital theory; modernization theory; world-system theory; world culture theory (also known as world polity theory or neoinstitutionalism); the culturalist approach; theories of global capitalism; the theory of globalization as empire; theories related to flows and networks; theories related to time, space, and place; transnationalism and transnationality; global governance; poststructuralism; and postcolonial theory. In addition, I unpack several constructs associated with globalization, including deterritorialization, McDonaldization, neocolonialism, glocalization, and vernacular globalization. Overall, this chapter emphasizes competing and complementary theories and constructs and how differing perspectives on globalization lead to a variety of perspectives in the literature.

After establishing historical and recent developments related to globalization as well as the various lenses for studying this phenomenon, I turn the focus in Chap. 4, 'Globalization and Education', to how globalization and its related developments have an impact on education. This chapter covers key developments and trends within the educational realms of schooling and higher education. Specific trends in schooling discussed include marketization and shifting values; corporatization; decentralization, privatization, and choice; accountability and standardized testing; and the ICT Revolution, while the discussion of trends in higher education includes expansion; shifting funding patterns and privatization; corporatization and commodification; internationalization and student mobility; and university rankings and global competition. In this chapter, I also discuss how the aid and development regime relates to education specifically and introduce Post-Washington Consensus global declarations that have an impact on education (Education for All, the Millennium Development Goals/Sustainable Development Goals, and the Fast Track Initiative/Global Partnership for Education). Finally, I return to the key debate about convergence introduced in Chap. 1, with a specific focus on assessing whether convergence is occurring in education worldwide. A salient point of this chapter is that, despite global trends, most developments and reforms in education (and in other sectors) are localized through vernacular globalization.

In Chap. 5, 'Educational Reform Processes in a Globalized World', I move the discussion to a focus on educational reform (or policy) processes. After establishing what policy is and what its parameters are, I consider the ideological and political nature of policymaking. Public policies provide governments with the opportunity to publicly declare what their priorities are, while the absence of a policy indicates a lack of commitment to a specific issue. In this chapter, I also cover the field of policy studies, which evolved as a subdiscipline of political science in the late 1950s and early 1960s. This field includes research *for* policy, typically undertaken by governments, and research *of* policy, typically undertaken by higher education researchers.

Next, I outline theories and models related to the formation of public policies, including the influential policy process model and CIE scholars David Phillips and Kimberly Ochs' (2003) Four Stages of Policy Borrowing Model that directly connects to policies that transfer across borders. Other competing and complementary theories covered include rational choice, incrementalism, institutionalism/neoinstitutionalism, systems, group choice, public choice, and elite models or theories. I also outline three emerging approaches that have grown in prominence more recently: the streams model, the punctuated equilibrium model, and the advocacy coalition framework. The next section of the chapter covers implementation, including forward-mapping (top-down) and backward-mapping (bottom-up) approaches and the role of the 'street-level bureaucrats' who are charged with implementing policies. I also consider the question of coercion versus agency during the policy implementation phase. Finally, I reflect upon educational policymaking in a globalized environment, providing a bridge to the next chapter.

Chapter 6, 'Mapping Educational Policy Borrowing and Lending', provides an overview of educational policy borrowing and lending, highlighting the political nature of these processes. I distinguish between the concepts of 'policy transfer', 'policy borrowing', 'policy lending', 'policy attraction', 'policy learning', and 'policy diffusion' and outline the policy borrowing and lending continuum. This continuum, with coercive lending on one side and voluntary transfer on the other, provides a useful way for considering the influences and purposes involved in policy borrowing and connects to the motivations and rationales that countries employ when undertaking policy borrowing (and lending). When intentionally borrowing policies, countries often undertake 'quick fix' or symbolic reforms for political reasons (e.g., an upcoming election). The impetus to adopt policies for political legitimacy paradoxically leads to reforms' being adopted that may not have been successful in the country from which they are borrowed. In other cases, countries enact policies to comply with international norms or mandates (e.g., due to treaties or conventions). Lending countries also have political motivations because they gain cache as 'star' systems that others wish to emulate.

In this chapter, I also consider the normative nature of policy borrowing and lending, especially through policy diffusion and 'best practices' lending, which is often connected to neocolonialism and the influence of global governance institutions. Next, I provide five cases of policy borrowing and lending that serve to illustrate varying motivations and types of policy borrowing and lending. In the final section, I discuss the complexities of the policy borrowing and lending processes, including multiple directions of transfer, local agency to resist global trends, and indigenization of policies into the local context.

Chapter 7, 'Patterns of Educational Reform and Policy Borrowing', provides a synthesis of research on educational reform and policy borrowing in various international contexts. Rather than focusing on specific educational issues or countries, I place an emphasis in Chap. 7 on understanding *patterns* of educational reform. I discern five key interrelated patterns through a systematic review of the literature from CIE, other areas of education, and other fields. This set of scholarship covers all stages of the policymaking process and has expanded in recent years due in part to nation-states' increased use of reforms from elsewhere. The first overarching pattern in the educational reform literature is the manifestation of neoliberal, market-oriented principles. Given the impact of globalization and the dominance of neoliberal globalization in particular, many countries around the world have instituted neoliberal reform packages that include policies such as standards-based education, quality assurance, and decentralization. The neoliberal market orientation is also evident in policies designed to ready learners for the post-Fordist global knowledge economy.

A second pattern is that most reforms originate from external sources, and a great deal of these reforms stem from 'best practices' lending fostered by global governance organizations. The third pattern is that policymakers and governments typically overlook the importance of context, including three forms: the broad context, the culture of schooling, and the educational infrastructure of the receiving country. A fourth pattern is closely related: Limited attention is paid to the educators who will implement the policy. Many reforms are top-down and fail to consider the needs and experiences of street-level bureaucrats in either the policy formation or implementation stage of policymaking. The lack of adequate training and professional development to implement these policies is a key oversight. The final pattern is that global reforms are adapted into the local context through vernacular globalization. Throughout the discussion, I provide several examples that illustrate each pattern. I conclude the chapter with reflections on the educational reform lessons that derive from the literature on educational reforms in international contexts.

In Chap. 8, 'Assessing the Impact of Globalization on Education and Educational Policy Reform', I briefly synthesize topics covered throughout the book and reflect upon the impact of globalization on education and educational policy reform. I emphasize alternatives to globalization (from above), highlighting local adaptations and globalization from below. In this final chapter of the book, I also return to the importance of understanding globalization and its related developments in any consideration of educational reform in today's globalized world.

Audience and Key Contributions

Although this book is situated within the field of CIE, its comprehensive, multidisciplinary nature is designed to enhance its broad appeal to audiences in associated disciplines within and outside education, such as social foundations, educational policy, teacher education, higher education, global studies, sociology of education, and policy studies. The thorough and comprehensive nature of the book offers important contextual grounding and foundations for readers, especially those who have not studied education and globalization directly. The book is geared primarily toward graduate students at both the master's and doctoral levels and is intended to serve as a core text, with complementary readings to support it. For example, during a week when students are scheduled to read and discuss Chap. 6 on educational policy borrowing processes, an instructor might provide current case studies to supplement the text. Advanced undergraduate students also would find the text beneficial and accessible, as would faculty who are new to the study of globalization and education.

This book provides up-to-date analyses of the interconnected nature of globalization, policy borrowing, and educational reform, including contested notions of globalization, related theories/debates, and in-depth syntheses of existing literature on educational policy reform processes in a variety of educational and geographic contexts. This comprehensive synthesis of extant literature offers a solid contribution to the field in an area of needed scholarship. Most existing globalization-focused texts are edited volumes and/or emphasize particular issues or country case studies or contain theoretical and argumentative papers. This existing scholarship provides access to important contributions to the field, yet it tends to offer limited contextualization and background to situate the authors' analyses. Additionally, these volumes generally do not provide a thorough overview or synthesis of the full scope of the literature. Thus, readers who do not have a substantial background in the field may have difficulty accessing them fully, and those who do not plan to study CIE may not find them to be relevant. In contrast to existing texts, this book covers the existing set of literature as a whole rather than addressing specific topics or issues that may appeal to only some readers. It is a timely book that covers current debates, while emphasizing the *processes* and *patterns* of educational reform around the world.

Another significant contribution of this book is that it offers a critical perspective on globalization, policy borrowing, and educational reform. Much of the rhetoric on globalization operates, either explicitly or implicitly, from a normative point of view. In other words, scholars and others often write or speak from the assumption that there is an accepted, standard set of 'best practices' for education and other social arenas that all countries should emulate. Although often not stated explicitly, these practices that become taken for granted as the 'best' way of operating tend to derive from Global North/developed countries. This standard approach lacks a critical angle that questions the logic and motives of importing educational and other policies into Global South/developing countries. A critical perspective entails problematizing the relationship between Global North/developed and Global South/developing countries and considering the contributions that countries in the latter group bring to the table. Further, employing a critical angle exposes the possibility of nation-states' and stakeholders' operating in a globalized environment while simultaneously employing agency to resist dominant trends and forge their own paths. In this manner, the critical perspective that I take in this book acknowledges the presence of local adaptations of global trends from the outset.

In sum, this book provides a beneficial introduction to the major debates and scholarship related to globalization, policy borrowing, and educational reform for scholars and students, whether they are in CIE programs or from other education fields or associated disciplines. Emphasizing a critical perspective, the book problematizes the normative nature of much of the existing scholarship on globalization and education, highlighting agency and resistance to globalization from above. Through comprehensive syntheses of diverse literature, this book covers the history and contested conceptualizations of globalization and globalization theories and debates, along with educational policy reform processes and the politics of borrowing and lending comprehensively and presents them in an accessible way. Importantly, the book also includes a clear introduction to the vocabulary, terminology, and acronyms associated with globalization and educational reform, providing readers with a compendium of resources and literature related to the topics covered in the text.

Laura M. Portnoi
Long Beach, CA, USA

Acknowledgments

Seeing this book through to the finish involved a great deal of support and encouragement from a number of people, for whom I have a great deal of gratitude. My husband, Howard, who always has such a positive outlook on life, has been a constant source of inspiration. He has helped me to laugh often and to be 'present' and enjoy whatever I am undertaking. My parents, Tom and Peggy, have always been a significant source of encouragement—for this project and everything that came before it. Although my dad is no longer physically here, he has been with me every step of the way while I was writing this book. My mom has carried her familiar torch of serving as a cheerleader throughout the process. My entire family has been very understanding of the demands that this book has placed on my time, and they have supported me throughout the entire process. I cannot thank them enough for their support throughout all of my endeavors, including the work I completed for this book.

Several people within my professional realm also deserve my gratitude. Sylvia Bagley, with whom I frequently collaborate on research projects, has been a great sounding board for my ideas. In addition, one of the central premises of this book—that global trends and developments are mediated and reshaped within local environments—mirrors my continuing work with Sylvia on global competition in higher education. Sharon Bear has provided solid professional editing support that has pushed me to improve my work a great deal. I would also like to thank Nina Flores for her valuable review of my book proposal as well as three anonymous reviewers who provided feedback. Graduate student Paolo Varquez also contributed to this work through literature searches for Chap. 7. Finally, my co-workers at California State University, Long Beach, have provided constant encouragement as I completed this book. I am very appreciative of all of the support I have received.

Notes

1. See Chap. 1 for a description of the use of the term 'Western' and other terminology to describe various types of countries.
2. Comparative efforts in the realm of education began informally hundreds of years before CIE became an official academic field. For a full overview of the history of CIE, see David Phillips and Michele Schweisfurth (2014).
3. As noted earlier, see Chap. 1 for an overview of terminology used in globalization studies to describe different types of countries.
4. Sources consulted were limited to: (a) those that could be obtained online or via interlibrary loan or purchased in hard copy and (b) those written in (or translated into) English. Although I made every attempt to include as diverse a set of literature as possible, these limitations necessarily affect the contents of this book.

Contents

List of Acronyms

ARWU	Academic Ranking of World Universities
BCE	Before the Common Era
BRICS	Brazil, Russia, India, China, and South Africa
CBHE	Cross-Border Higher Education
CCTs	Conditional Cash Transfers
CIE	Comparative International Education
DFID	Department for International Development [UK]
ECSC	European Coal and Steel Community
EEC	European Economic Community
EFA	Education for All
EGM	Emerging Global Model
EPZ	Export Processing Zone
EU	European Union
FTI	Fast Track Initiative
GATS	General Agreement on Trades and Services
GATT	General Agreement on Tariffs and Trade
GER	Gross Enrollment Ratio
GMO	Genetically Modified Organism
GNI	Gross National Income
GPE	Global Partnership for Education
GRU	Global Research University
HDI	Human Development Index
HEI	Higher Education Institution
IBDP	International Baccalaureate Diploma Programme
ICT	Information and Communications Technology

IEA	International Association of the Evaluation of Educational Achievement
IGO	Intergovernmental Organization
IMF	International Monetary Fund
IMO	International Monetary Organization
INGO	International Non-governmental Organization
LCE	Learner-Centered Education
LLL	Lifelong Learning
MDGs	Millennium Development Goals
MNC	Multinational Corporation
MTL	Masters in Teaching and Learning
NAFTA	North American Free Trade Agreement
NATO	North Atlantic Treaty Organization
NGO	Non-Governmental Organization
NIC	Newly Industrialized Country
NQF	National Qualification Framework
NSS	New Secondary School
OBE	Outcomes-Based Education
OECD	Organisation for Economic Co-operation and Development
PIRLS	Progress in International Reading Literacy Study
PISA	Programme for International Student Assessment
PWC	Post-Washington Consensus
QS	Quacquarelli Symonds
ROI	Return on Investment
ROR	Rates of Return
SAP	Structural Adjustment Program
SDGs	Sustainable Development Goals
TCC	Transnational Capitalist Class
THE	Times Higher Education
TIMSS	Trends in International Mathematics and Science Study
TINA	There Is No Alternative
TNC	Transnational Corporation
TNPs	Transnational Practices
TNS	Transnational State
TRIPS	Trade-Related Intellectual Property Rights
UN	United Nations
UNDP	United Nations Development Programme
UNESCO	United Nations Educational, Scientific and Cultural Organization
UNICEF	United Nations International Children's Emergency Fund
UPE	Universal Primary Education

USAID	United States Agency for International Development
VET	Vocational Education and Training
WB	World Bank
WEF	World Economic Forum
WSF	World Social Forum
WTO	World Trade Organization
WWII	World War II

List of Figures

CHAPTER 1

Understanding Globalization

Globalization is a contested concept, and its processes and manifestations are complex. This term has been used in many different ways across various contexts, including both popular and academic realms. Although globalization is a 'buzzword' of our times, many who use the term may not be familiar with all that it entails. In addition, people assign different meanings to 'globalization' based on their perspectives and, in the case of scholars, their academic training (e.g., as economists, sociologists, or anthropologists). Although there is continual debate about when globalization began, what it involves, and to what degree it is beneficial or detrimental, what is clear is that changes have taken place worldwide that make it difficult for nation-states or individuals to operate from an entirely local perspective. An understanding of globalization provides a key foundation for learning about policy borrowing and educational reform both within our own contexts and across international environments.

This chapter presents several perspectives on the history of globalization (as both a process and a concept), various conceptualizations of globalization, the dimensions of globalization, and key debates related to globalization as well as its costs, benefits, and dilemmas. The central purpose of this chapter, in conjunction with Chap. 2's focus on heightened developments related to globalization since World War II (WWII), is to provide a context for understanding globalization prior to focusing on globalization and education specifically.

© The Editor(s) (if applicable) and The Author(s) 2016

L.M. Portnoi, *Policy Borrowing and Reform in Education*,
DOI 10.1057/978-1-137-53024-0_1

Unraveling the History of Globalization

When did globalization begin? Although this is a straightforward question, the origins and timeline of globalization are often debated in academic circles. Globalization is a gradual process that has occurred over time, although the question is often raised as to whether globalization is relatively new or whether recent developments and trends (see below) are extensions of a lengthy history of globalization. Some scholars trace globalization's roots only to the 1970s, when global connections seemed to expand dramatically, while others include nineteenth-century developments, such as the Industrial Revolution, and still others take the history back even further, to before the Common Era (BCE) (Steger, 2013). As described in more detail below, although the word 'globalization' did not appear until the 1960s,[1] most scholars agree that the process of globalization was well under way before a term was coined to describe it. Although scholars' breakdown of historical periods may differ, most historical accounts of globalization highlight the deepening interconnectedness of nation-states, characterized by increased trade and flow of goods and people, which represents significant changes from past historical eras. In addition, the spread of colonialism is key to unraveling the history of globalization, as is the resulting growth in economic inequality, both between countries and within them.

Global studies scholar Manfred Steger (2013) provides one of the most comprehensive conceptualizations of the history of globalization. According to Steger, the first historical period tied to globalization is the prehistoric (10,000 BCE–3500 BCE), in which hunter-gatherers spread to all five continents and began to establish informal settlements based around agricultural production. Steger's second historical period is the premodern (3500 BCE–1500 BCE), during which important social and technological advances, such as the invention of writing and the wheel, fueled globalization because they allowed for greater communication and flow of people and goods. The premodern period was also the age of the empire, in which some states established permanent rule over others (e.g., the Chinese and Ottoman Empires), and overseas trade routes flourished. During this time period, increased cultural and economic exchange led to migration. Steger posits that Europe and its social practices took center stage in fueling globalization during the third period, the early modern (1500–1750). Technological innovations improved and spread during this time. Importantly, new ideals of individualism, limited government, and rampant accumulation of wealth came about because the Protestant Reformation[2] served to reduce the role of the Catholic Church. At the same time, the Westphalian state system, in which independent nation-states serve as the bounding factors for societies, took root by 1648, while interdependencies between nation-states simultaneously grew.

During the modern period of globalization (1750–1970), the new ideals of the prior period were transformed into capitalism, an economic paradigm that involves free markets, competition, and private ownership of capital goods, which has become embedded in the social and economic systems of most countries around the world. World trade, especially of 'brand name' goods, such as Coca-Cola and Singer sewing machines, increased during this time. The modern period was also characterized by colonial expansion, coupled with a profound population increase that resulted in mass migration. Steger's contemporary period (1970–present) is punctuated by the creation of a single global market, coupled with advances in communication and technology and ever-increasing flows of capital, goods, and people.

Writing from a historical and sociological perspective, Charles Tilly (2004) would concur with Steger, asserting that humanity has been under a process of perpetual globalization for centuries, a process that has intensified since the end of WWII. He argues that there have been three main waves of globalization since 1500. The first wave involved increasing European influences as well as the expansion of the Ottoman Empire and merchant activity of Chinese and Arab traders. Overlapping with the end of the first wave, the second, from 1850 until the beginning of WWI in 1914, was characterized by long-distance migration, increased international trade and flow of capital, transportation and communication improvements, and increasingly uniform prices for trade goods, all of which resulted in prosperity for Western and more developed nations, including Japan and many countries in Europe and North America. According to Tilly, at the same time, disparities widened between these beneficiaries of globalization and their counterparts, particularly colonies.

The third wave of globalization began after WWII and was characterized by further increasing trade and flow of goods and capital, coupled with decreased migration as compared to the second wave (Tilly, 2004). Two parallel forms of migration were central during this third wave: (a) small numbers of skilled professional and technical workers from wealthier countries and (b) large numbers of unskilled workers from poorer counties who sought better livelihoods in wealthier countries or who were taken on as indentured servants. Tilly indicates that, during this latter wave of globalization, Asian countries have benefited financially, in particular, parallel to the continued dominant position of North American and European countries. Further, Tilly asserts that industries focused on technology and scientific innovation have flourished in this more recent period of globalization.

Another perspective on the history and origins of globalization cites the influence of colonialism more directly. John Coatsworth (2004), a social scientist focused on Latin America, posits that there have been four major cycles of globalization. The first was from 1492 to the early 1600s and involved Spain's and Portugal's conquest and colonization of the Americas and the establishment of several trade routes (trans-Atlantic, trans-Pacific, Atlantic to Indian Oceans, Acapulco to Manila, and between Europe and East Asia). In the second cycle of globalization, from the late seventeenth to the early nineteenth centuries, European colonization continued with the establishment of slave colonies that also served as settlements for Europeans. This cycle ended with major upheavals that included the French and Haitian Revolutions.

The third cycle occurred during the late nineteenth century into the 1930s (roughly corresponding to Tilly's [2004] second wave) and included significant increases in the flow of trade, capital, and technology. Mass migration from Asia and Europe to the Americas, along with a new wave of colonization, also took place during the third cycle. According to Coatsworth (2004), this cycle ended with the Great Depression of the 1930s. The fourth cycle, which continues today, began after WWII with the liberalization of the international trade of manufactured goods. Like Tilly, Coatsworth argues that East Asian countries benefited more from the economic aspects of globalization during this time period compared to 'protectionist' countries in Latin America and South Asia that maintained closed trade environments. Coatsworth also recognizes that, although 'globalization cycles have produced immense and measurable increases in human productivity' (p. 39) that involve improvements in standards of living in many countries, the inequality gap has widened between countries that have been heavily involved in globalization and trade liberalization and those that have not.

Education scholars Fazal Rizvi and Robert Lingard (2010) argue that, due to the complex and dynamic nature of globalization, it is difficult to determine historical time periods in which it developed. Concurring with the aforementioned scholars, they posit that globalization is not 'new' per se and that it is closely tied to colonial expansion in which dominant powers sought to unite disparate geographical areas into their economic and political domains. In the nineteenth century, colonial practices became more coordinated, and colonial powers developed integrated global financial systems and markets within their empires (Rizvi, 2007; Rizvi & Lingard, 2010). The increasing coordination of colonial regimes coincided with the emergence of capitalism.

Capitalism has increased the economic and social interdependency of countries around the world because it relies on growth, which produces more profits, expansion into new markets, utilization of cheaper resources and labor, and the speeding up of production (Sparke, 2013). The dominance of capitalism and the legacy of the colonial system have led to a hierarchy of countries, in which 'developed' countries (also referred to as Western or Global North countries, as discussed below), such as Japan and countries in North America and Europe, dominate the economic, political, and social spheres. The spread of capitalism is also linked to an increasing wealth and prosperity gap within countries, based on those who own goods and resources and those whose labor produces them. Given the profound influence of capitalism at a time when globalization also was developing, the term 'globalization' is often used nearly synonymously with capitalism, despite the fact that globalization has many dimensions beyond the economic, including political, cultural, social, technological, and ecological. After I provide an overview of country terminology, these various conceptualizations and dimensions of globalization will be the focus of the sections that follow.

No matter how the history of globalization is understood or whether we call the entire set of processes 'globalization' or confine it to more recent developments and trends, it is clear that many changes have occurred that have increased the interconnectedness of nation-states in terms of trade and other forms of exchange (e.g., cultural). It is also evident that the period from after WWII (or 1970, depending on whose version of history one uses) to the present marks an unprecedented era of globalization. For this reason, I use the term 'contemporary globalization' throughout this book to refer to the period of intensified global interconnectedness since WWII. Developments and trends in this contemporary period of globalization, such as communication and technological innovations and the emergence of global governance institutions, are the focus of Chap. 2.

What's in a Name? Navigating Terminology for Labeling Countries

Following a modernist perspective[3] that calls for a linear process of social and economic development that all countries should follow, scholars, policymakers, and the public typically use two broad terms to characterize different types of countries on the global stage: 'developed' and 'developing'. 'Developed' (wealthy) countries, which include those in North America and Europe, as well as Australia, New Zealand, and Japan, tend to be highly industrialized and have high standards of living along with high per capita income. These dominant countries of the world are also often referred to as 'Western' nations.[4] In this sense, the Western label is somewhat of a geographic misnomer, as it refers to countries that are not all geographically west per se. In contrast, 'developing' (poor) countries, such as those in Africa, Latin America (including Central America), and South and Southeast Asia, are generally less industrialized and have lower standards of living and per capita income; they are also more likely to be countries that were colonized in the past. This terminology of 'developed' and 'developing' is often conceived as connected to economic development in particular. Prior to today's common use of 'developed' and 'developing' to distinguish between country types, the favored terms were 'First World' and 'Third World'[5], with the latter aligned with the 'developing' countries.

Both sets of terminology are often critiqued due to their built-in assumptions that one type of country is superior to the other and that all countries should ascribe to the same manner and mode of development. Given the normative assumption of a linear, singular path to development that is inherent within this terminology and the way that these terms have been used, critics have argued that these terms suggest that developing, or Third World, countries are inferior not only in the economic sphere, but also in political, cultural, and social realms (Sparke, 2013). In other words, becoming developed is a status to which developing countries should ascribe because it is perceived as the standard and best approach. In addition, depictions between developing/developed or First/Third World fail to recognize the impact of colonialism and the reasons why and how countries have become positioned within these various categories. These terms also present a 'false dichotomy' because the reality is that a continuum of development exists beyond what these two binary (or opposite) terms connote (Phillips & Schweisfurth, 2014).

Although the generalized terms 'developed' and 'developing' are often used in both popular and academic discourse, finer-grained distinctions exist. For example, the United Nations Development Programme (UNDP) Human Development Index (HDI) compares development across countries. Three categories of development indicators are at the center of the HDI—income, health, and education—and progress is generally measured by higher incomes, longer life expectancies, and a more educated populace. Each year, UNDP's Human Development Report reviews where countries stand on the HDI, utilizing four categories: very high human development, high human development, medium human development, and low human development.

Over the past two decades, certain countries have been singled out for their rapid increases on the HDI, most notably Brazil, Russia, India, and China (also known as BRIC countries). Most recently, South Africa has been added to the list, now referred to as the BRICS countries. The World Bank[6] (WB) uses another classification scheme, focused solely on income. The WB (2015) utilizes countries' gross national income (GNI) per capita—the country's total value of goods and services plus all other assets, excluding net taxes, divided by the total population—to categorize countries into four groups: low ($1045 or less), lower-middle ($1046 to $8621), upper-middle ($8622 to $12,745), and high income ($12,746 or more).

Another common term used in economic circles that adds gradation to the simple binary classifications that are commonly employed is 'newly industrialized country', or NIC. Although there is no shared definition of a NIC, these countries generally have achieved a stable level of industrialization accompanied by an increasing standard of living that puts them ahead of their counterparts, yet behind industrialized (or developed) nations. The term 'NIC' arose in the 1970s when the so-called Asian Tigers (Hong Kong, Singapore, South Korea, and Taiwan) received attention because they had experienced rapid industrialization and had achieved exceptionally high growth rates over a number of years. Even though these nuanced classifications offer levels of development beyond two categories, they nonetheless continue to emphasize a linear pattern of growth or progress to which all countries can and should ascribe.

More recently, critically oriented scholars and activists have begun to use the terms 'Global South' and 'Global North' to differentiate between country type, based, to a large degree, on economic wealth and historic conditions. Unlike prior terminology, the use of 'Global South' and

'Global North' breaks from the notions that there is a linear path to development that countries must follow and that economically poorer countries also are impoverished culturally or politically. The Global South typically aligns with what have been known as 'developing' countries, while the Global North includes countries in North America and Europe as well as Australia, New Zealand, and Japan. Although not geographically accurate in some cases, these blanket terms have become preferred because 'Global South' is not subtractive; in other words, it does not connote the 'lesser than' notion that the terms 'developing' or 'Third World' do. In addition, the manner in which most of the countries in the Global South became part of this group is taken into account in conceptualizing the Global South and Global North. Specifically, the history of colonialism and the fact that most countries in the Global South were also colonized are considered (Escobar, 2011; Rizvi, 2007). Countries in the Global South are acknowledged to be poorer, in general, and the reasons for this are connected directly to colonization and continued forms of neocolonialism through the aid and development regime.[7]

All of the classifications that have been or are being used to differentiate between country types are imprecise and provide overgeneralizations of the types of countries that fall within the various categories. Most also ignore variations in wealth within countries (Sparke, 2013). Growing inequality gaps are prevalent in countries around the world, including those in both the Global North and Global South. Despite the problematic nature of these terms, it is often useful to distinguish between country type, not to further marginalize countries that are poorer and working through a colonial legacy but, rather, to explore inequities that exist between the countries that dominate the global arena versus those that have a less prominent geopolitical stature. Despite the limitations, for consistency and ease of discussion, I use the terms 'Global South' and 'Global North' throughout this book to refer to the two major groups of country types.

Conceptualizing Globalization

How should globalization be understood? The answer to this question is not simple because the processes of globalization are complex. Just as the history of globalization is debated, so, too, is the meaning of the term. The word has different connotations in various contexts and depends on how the discussion around globalization is framed and who is framing it. For these reasons, articles or books on globalization typically have sections or chapters that cover its meaning, while edited volumes that focus specifically on globalization often contain a chapter on debates about what globalization is, along with a description of the term in each contributed chapter (which may differ by author). The concept of globalization is not only pertinent to the academic realm but is also discussed in the popular and business worlds, adding to the difficulty in pinning down exactly what it constitutes. To help the reader to develop an understanding of globalization, this section provides a broad background of several complementary and competing conceptualizations of globalization—as a concrete set of processes, an ideology, and a social imaginary—while Chap. 3 provides a detailed discussion of the ways in which globalization has been theorized.

Three Complementary and Competing Conceptualizations of Globalization

1. Globalization as an empirical fact that involves a set of processes through which the world has become more economically, politically, and socially interdependent. These processes have evolved over a lengthy history, though they have intensified since WWII.
2. Globalization as an ideology in which neoliberal tenets reign, which acts as a proxy for the dominance of the Global South by the Global North. Steger (2013) calls this current ideology of globalization 'market globalism'.
3. Globalization as a social imaginary that involves people around the world becoming aware of their interconnectedness, leading to their changing identities and affiliations.

One of the key questions surrounding the term is whether globalization is an entity in and of itself. Globalization is not a 'thing' or an 'it', but rather a process (Robinson and White, 2007), which is a common way to conceptualize and understand it. This understanding of globalization recognizes that it is an empirical fact based on significant transformations that have occurred in the world that have resulted in greater economic interdependency as well as cultural and political interconnections (Rizvi & Lingard, 2010). Similarly, geography and international studies scholar Matthew Sparke (2013) posits that one of the central forms of globalization is the processes of economic, political, and social integration that have occurred and are continuing to occur throughout the world. Further, he sees these processes as long-standing developments that may go back to the influence of colonialism and the birth of capitalism. These processes involve interdependencies in which what occurs in one locale has a direct impact on what happens in another, and vice versa. Sparke points out that this set of processes and interdependencies has become increasingly integrated into a larger, more comprehensive system. Likewise, Steger (2013) maintains that globalization is a set of social processes that are leading to a state of 'globality' in which 'tight global, economic, political, cultural, and environmental interconnections and flows' become standard (p. 9). The interdependency and interconnectivity of places and people are generally thought to be deepening and accelerating due to technical innovations that began after WWII and increased in the 1970s (Ritzer, 2007). This version of globalization emphasizes the concrete and observable changes associated with the processes of globalization.

Aside from the concrete nature of globalization, it can also be understood as an ideology. 'Ideologies are powerful systems of widely shared ideas and patterned beliefs that are accepted as truth by significant groups in society' (Steger, 2013, p. 103). As an ideology that is often associated with capitalism and neoliberalism (Rhoads, 2003; Sklair, 2005), the term 'globalization' commonly acts as a proxy for the dominance of the Global South by the Global North. Neoliberalism is an economic paradigm that supports deregulation, privatization, and a shift away from government involvement in domestic economies. Neoliberalism favors free-market methods, fewer restrictions on business operations, minimal taxation, and property rights. In the free-market economy, neoliberals assert that the unrestricted flow of capital will produce the greatest social, political, and economic good.

The trend toward neoliberalism began during the Cold War period, becoming prominent in the 1970s and reaching its height in the era of the UK prime minister Thatcher and US president Reagan in the 1980s (Morrow & Torres, 2013). The paradigm is termed 'neo'liberalism because it harkens back to the days of classical liberal economic theory (e.g., Adam Smith's writings on the 'invisible hand' of the market), when the free-market capitalist system took shape. Critical scholars have criticized this neoliberal ideology of globalization because it equates globalization with capitalism and because neoliberal globalization has produced marked inequalities both between and within countries (Sen, 1999b;

Stiglitz, 2002). Despite continued criticism, however, the neoliberal ideology of globalization remains dominant.

Steger (2013) calls this dominant form of globalization—globalization as an ideology infused with neoliberalism—'market globalism'. Globalisms are the values and meanings that become attached, through ideology, to views about globalization. According to Steger, market globalism has become the codified 'business as usual' approach to globalization, especially economic globalization. Market globalism, which is tied to free-market principles and consumerism, is propagated by business and government leaders, the media, and many other political, cultural, and social entities. Steger posits that market globalism has five major claims: (a) economic liberalization and the global integration of markets is the basis of globalization, (b) globalization is a natural force that is both inevitable and irreversible, (c) globalization has no people in charge, as market forces govern, (d) everyone wins due to the supposed benefits of neoliberalism tied to economic conceptions of globalization, and (e) (economic) globalization spreads democracy because neoliberalism does. These viewpoints have become commonly accepted as the 'way things are' by global governance institutions, most nation-states, and the general world populace.

According to Sparke (2013), this second version of globalization—as an ideology—served instrumental political purposes during the 1980s, when neoliberalism gained ascendancy, particularly in the USA and the UK. Although Sparke considers this version of globalization to be political in nature, and, indeed, it may have had political origins, most scholars tend to classify it, instead, as essentially economic. This form of globalization is also referred to as 'globalization from above' because it is the dominant ideology of geopolitically powerful countries in the Global North and has an impact on economies throughout the world. Whether it is categorized as political or economic, it is clear that there is a profoundly 'common sense' version of globalization that is closely associated with neoliberalism.

Sparke (2013) argues, 'The buzzword usage of Globalization[8] has effectively made the word a synonym for a suite of pro-market policy norms and the wider influence of market forces in political, social, and personal relations' (p. 6). Therefore, those who identify with the market logic are often characterized as pro-globalization, while those who do not are characterized as anti-globalization. Whether they are proponents, skeptics, or critics,[9] commentators focus on neoliberal globalization in particular. Sparke contends that the two usages of globalization—as a concrete process and as an ideology (currently, market globalism)—have become muddied to a large extent in practice because the dominant ideological form of globalization has become closely connected to practice.

The dominance of market globalism as an ideology has not remained uncontested, however. Steger (2013) posits that two additional forms of globalism have emerged as alternative ideologies to market globalism. 'Justice globalism' is focused on altering the processes and impact of economic globalization to foster greater equality worldwide, particularly between the Global North and Global South. Steger states that justice globalism emerged in the 1990s, when progressive individuals and organizations began to rise up against the steady march toward, and entrenchment of, neoliberal globalization, using globalization from below.[10] Justice globalists reject the notion that neoliberal globalization and its free market principles lead to greater equality and stronger democracy. Justice globalists seek the redistribution of wealth and power within and among societies and often advocate for a return to increased nationally provided social welfare, reduction or elimination of debt for poorer countries, and increased focus on specific disparities, such as those of women, children, and people with disabilities. An additional form of globalism that has become increasingly salient in recent years is what Steger calls 'religious globalisms'. According to Steger (2013), this form of globalism is conservative, yet its proponents seek an alternative to market globalism. Religious globalisms are reactionary, and those who ascribe to them seek for their versions of organizational structures to supersede secular and state-based entities.

Although each form of globalism differs greatly, neither of the counter-globalisms completely rejects globalization. Indeed, rather than these counter-globalisms being 'anti'-globalization, they represent 'alter'-globalizations (Steger, 2013), connoting a rejection of globalization as it is now—in the case of justice globalism, due to its emphasis on neoliberalism and free-market principles. Certain *anti*-globalization forces do exist, although most scholars, leaders, activists, and citizens recognize that globalization is here to stay and cannot be completely avoided but, rather, can be altered.

In addition to concrete and ideological forms of globalization, a third way to understand the term is as a social imaginary (Rizvi & Lingard, 2010). Connected to Steger's (2013) notion of the 'global imaginary'—people's growing consciousness of being part of a global community—Rizvi and Lingard argue that globalization should also be understood as a social imaginary in which increasing awareness of the interconnectedness of the world around us has an impact on our practices and beliefs. Rizvi and Lingard states that globalization 'has produced not only material economic shifts, but also a changing sense of identities and belonging' (p. 34) as it becomes internalized and reshapes people's lives.

The social imaginary form of globalization is composed of both ideas and practices and has become an implicit, shared way of thinking and operating within a globalized world. In this way, the social imaginary form has a normative effect because it is has gained a certain sense of legitimacy as the taken-for-granted worldview. At the same time, it is a collective social force that is in a constant state of flux and one that should be considered with regard to how counter-hegemonic alternatives might develop. In other words, social imaginary globalization is influenced by the ideology that is in use at the time (currently market globalism), but this influence could be altered if the dominant ideology were to change. Indeed, Rizvi and Lingard (2010) argue that there is already a multiplicity of social imaginaries because not everyone ascribes to the normative view of neoliberal globalization that dominates the social imaginary currently.

Even with varying viewpoints about what globalization is and the various ways in which the term has been used, most scholars would agree that globalization is multidimensional and that it has multiple effects (Robinson, 2007). Recognizing the multifaceted and complex nature of globalization is the key to understanding it more fully. Using only one lens to understand globalization provides only part of the story. Therefore, both Sparke (2013) and Steger (2013) suggest a broader understanding that takes into account the multidimensionality of globalization.

Dimensions of Globalization

Although the economic aspect of globalization has become synonymous with globalization to a large extent, it goes beyond the economic realm. This section provides a brief overview of the various dimensions of globalization—economic, political, cultural, social, technological, and ecological—that comprise its multidimensional nature. I untangle each dimension for explanatory purposes in this discussion, although they operate together as an integrated set of layers in practice.

In the economic realm of globalization, the economies of countries around the world have become increasingly interconnected through the spread of neoliberalism, international trade in a free market world economic system, and the establishment of international monetary organizations.[11]

Economic decisions or maneuvers made in individual countries have an impact on the world economy through ripple effects not only on neighboring countries but also on countries in regions across the globe. As countries become increasingly interconnected in their manner of governance and policies, political globalization mirrors economic globalization. More specifically, as described in detail in Chap. 2, global governance organizations increasingly govern significant portions of national matters (e.g., through international declarations and treaties), which has led some to question the role of the nation-state in setting its domestic agenda and policies.

Although the evolving role of the nation-state in monitoring its own affairs is continually under debate, what is clear is that it is now less common for countries to act entirely independently without coordinating with other international players in the region or the world. The political dimension of globalization equates neither with powerful countries' being entirely restricted nor with the Global South's moving up to a level playing field with their Global North counterparts. Indeed, due to the ascendancy of neoliberalism as the dominant economic paradigm worldwide, the significant divide between the geopolitical power of the Global North and Global South remains and is being further exacerbated through globalization. Nevertheless, even the more powerful countries tend to collaborate and consult with their peers on significant policies and decisions that will have an impact on them and the rest of the world.

Just as economic policies and governmental practices have become more interconnected, so, too, have cultures. Cultural globalization relates to important aspects of everyday life, including the foods we eat, the languages we speak, and the books we read. Hyperglobalists and skeptics will continue to debate how significant these changes are and whether we are moving toward one world culture. Clearly, there has been greater mixing of cultures in the years since WWII than in any previous time. It is now common, for example, for the music of popular musicians (mostly from the USA) to be heard across the world at the same time, rather than albums taking years to make their way to another country. Enhanced technology and avenues for communication, such as social media, contribute to the exchange of cultural practices and information, as does the increasing ability to travel to other countries. We have intercultural interactions with immigrants in our communities, read books by international authors, and hear various languages spoken around us on a daily basis. In short, the exchange of cultures is happening in our everyday lives.

A related dimension of globalization that is often implied but not directly identified is the social (Rizvi & Lingard, 2010; Robinson & White, 2007). Social change is tied to increasing interconnections and an awareness of living in a globalized world—Steger's (2013) 'global imaginary'. In other words, changes that happen socially within a given country may very well reflect changes that happen around the world. The recent increase in policies and legislation that allow same-sex marriages in numerous countries is a poignant example of how social processes within local jurisdictions are affected by what happens in other parts of the world.

Technological aspects are another dimension of globalization and are seen in the rapid changes in the way information is exchanged, people and products travel across and between borders, and everything from business to medical innovations is executed. Advances in technology increase the impact of globalization, which is one of the reasons that some authors often cite the post-WWII era as a key break between past and contemporary forms of globalization. The rapid changes that have taken place, and continue to evolve, in the ways that we communicate and live in today's society have a profound global impact.

Finally, in addition to economic, political, cultural, social, and technological dimensions, there is the ecological dimension of globalization. Given the significant environmental degradation that has resulted from staggering worldwide population growth and increased consumption of natural resources, the ecological dimension of globalization has taken on increasing importance. Environmental impacts are increasingly felt globally because the ecology of various countries of the world is intertwined. For example, greenhouse gas emissions in one country affect the entire planet (Yearley, 2007). In addition, deforestation affects the oxygen levels for the entire planet and contributes to difficulty obtaining water around the world.

Each dimension of globalization—economic, political, cultural, social, technological, and ecological—contributes to globalization's overall impact. It is important to understand each dimension while also recognizing that these components are interrelated.

Key Debates about Globalization

Given the varying conceptualizations of globalization that exist, a number of debates have arisen with regard to its impact. Key debates have emerged in both scholarly and popular contexts regarding three areas: (a) the formation of a world culture, (b) the inevitability of globalization, and (c) the role of nation-states in governing their own domestic affairs. These debates cut across a variety of disciplines, including global studies, sociology, political science, and education. In this section, I focus on the general parameters of the debates; in Chap. 3, I discuss the theoretical bases of these parameters. In Chap. 4, I discuss the world culture debate more fully with a specific emphasis on education.

One key debate concerns whether there is a uniform world culture that is developing throughout the world. Questions such as the following frame this debate: Is the world becoming a 'single place' (Robinson & White, 2007)? Will there be a unified global space in which we all live, despite the different locales from which we emanate? Are we moving to a situation in which one world culture dominates around the world, and, if so, should we be concerned about this? Globalization enthusiasts regard the possibility of a single space with a world culture as a positive development due to the increased interactions that it would allow as well as the potential for technological advances or the spread of the influence of the free market. Some would view the possibility of a 'single space' as a form of utopia in which all people within humanity would be interconnected. Others would highlight the ability of governments and corporate entities to reach a vast market around the world rather than localized pockets of interest, especially given recent technological innovations. In this view, the possible exchanges of products, ideas, and people are limitless because geographic borders no longer provide constraints.

From an alternative point of view, one of the most common concerns about globalization is that it is increasingly producing a homogenized culture that is synonymous with the values and culture associated with the USA and other Global North countries, a process sometimes referred to as Americanization (see, e.g., Cowen, 2004). The prevalence of US products and clothing, from Coca-Cola to Levis, in the farthest corners of the world is a concrete manifestation of the influence of globalization. Concerns have also been raised about the dominance of news and other media from the Global North and the pursuit of individualism and consumerism that is associated with an evolving world culture. In addition, the dominant use of English in today's world harkens back to colonialism and solidifies the power of the Global North (Spring, 2015; Steger, 2013). All of these developments are indicative of growing cultural homogenization in certain respects.

The degree to which homogenization is occurring, however, is being questioned. Several education scholars suggest that some level of uniformity may be happening at the macro level but that culture-specific dimensions also are present (see, e.g., Schriewer & Martinez, 2004; Steiner-Khamsi, 2004). An alternative to points of view that highlight the preponderance of a world culture is the notion of a 'hybrid' form of culture that marries both global trends with local customs (Rizvi & Lingard, 2010). For some, global culture and local culture need not be mutually exclusive; rather, they may be seen as two sides of the same coin. In this sense, globalization is not necessarily an either/or situation in which local cultures stay local or global culture dominates local cultures. Rather, the possibilities for a hybrid form of culture provide an interesting alternative to what might otherwise be a normative world culture based on precepts that emanate from the Global North.

A second hotly debated issue is the apparent inevitability of globalization. The concern is whether the changes that have occurred in the worldwide economic, social, political, and cultural order are irreversible or may be challenged and reshaped. A dominant concept among popular domains and the news media, in particular, is the TINA ('there is no alternative') approach. This notion, popularized by former British prime minister Margaret Thatcher in the 1980s, is closely tied to neoliberalism. The inevitability debate involves three main types of positionalities: hyperglobalists, skeptics, and transformationalists (Held, McGrew, Goldblatt, & Perraton, 1999). Others, from a variety of academic disciplines, have contributed to this debate, supplementing it with other terms and ideas.

Positionalities on the Inevitability of Globalization

Hyperglobalists contend that the profound changes that have taken place within our social, political, economic, and cultural domains cannot be reversed or altered. Most hyperglobalists align with the TINA approach and support neoliberalism, while others criticize neoliberal globalization, yet cannot envision that other possibilities might transpire.

Skeptics are not convinced that globalization exists and argue that it is a social construction of reality. They view notions of global culture, global norms, and global capitalism as myths.

Transformationalists recognize that globalization has real effects, which are unevenly distributed. They are critical of neoliberal globalization and envision alternatives to the status quo.

Hyperglobalists often align with the TINA approach and see globalization as a tangible process that has significantly altered our social, political, economic, and cultural worlds in ways that can never be changed. For hyperglobalists, the nation-state is rapidly losing its relevance, particularly given connected market forces. Hyperglobalists, whose views have been labeled as 'globaphilia', often tout the benefits of neoliberalism. The influential work of *New York Times* author and economist Thomas Freidman provides well-known examples of this train of thought. In *The Lexus and the Olive Tree* (1999) and *The World Is Flat* (2005), Freidman presents globalization as inevitable and inextricably tied to neoliberal economic ideals. He also uses the familiar neoliberal refrain of globalization as the great equalizer. Although most hyperglobalists align with the TINA view that is closely associated with neoliberalism and see great overall benefits to societies around the world in the march toward globalization, critically oriented hyperglobalists strongly critique globalization due to the inequalities it creates and the 'consumerist ideology' it spreads (Held et al., 1999). These authors focus on the exploitation and dominance of the neoliberal TINA approach.

Skeptics, in contrast, consider globalization to be a social construction of reality. In other words, globalization is not a 'thing' per se but, rather, has come to take on a life of its own because it has been named. They view global capitalism as a myth and suggest that fragmentation and regionalization are more prominent than is globalization, while the power of nation-states deepens, not wanes. Skeptics also view global culture and the development of global norms as myths, and some argue that the globalization structures that exist are simply designed to mask neoliberalism and the benefits that dominant countries in the Global North receive. Another term that has been associated with globalization skeptics is 'globaloney', which emphasizes the myths of globalization. This perspective has also been referred to as 'globophobia' for the distaste with which skeptics view globalization. Skeptics' rejection of globalization is not so much due to their decrying its outcomes but, rather, because they are not convinced that globalization exists.

Differing from the ideal types (or extremes) of hyperglobalists and skeptics are 'transformationalists' (Held et al., 1999). Transformationalists recognize that globalization has concrete manifestations, in the form of economic interdependence and social and cultural integration, yet they do not suggest that there is a single cause for globalization (e.g., market forces) or that the outcomes of globalization are predetermined.

Transformationalists are decidedly less certain about the trajectory of globalization and consider its spread to be uneven. Rizvi and Lingard (2010), Anthony McGrew (2007), Sparke (2013), and Steger (2013) all fall into this category, as they emphasize the myth that globalization is inevitable and cannot be changed, while simultaneously recognizing its profound impact.

In addition, transformationalists are critical of the shape that neoliberal globalization has taken and argue that this economic regime is neither natural nor a given (Sparke, 2013). In this vein, Rizvi and Lingard remind us that neoliberalism is only one of the ways in which globalization might be interpreted. Other critical scholars who take the transformationalist perspective argue that globalization is not a problem in and of itself but, rather, that the forms that it has taken, with the dominance of neoliberalism, are cause for concern. These authors suggest that a different kind of globalization is needed rather than a rejection of globalization outright (Ritzer, 2007). The transformationalist perspective thus offers a compromise of sorts, in which the impact of globalization is recognized it is not accepted 'as is'.

A third key debate over globalization centers on the role of the nation-state, specifically how globalization has an impact on the practices, policies, and sovereignty of the nation-state. Marcelo Suárez-Orozco and Desiree Qin-Hillard (2004) suggest that globalization tends to 'deterritorialize important economic, social, and cultural practices from their traditional boundaries in nation-states' (p. 14). In other words, globalization is happening at a global level rather than the local or nation-state level. Although nation-states are still territories in their own right, practices that were once entirely within their domains (i.e., social, economic, and cultural) are now governed at the global level, or deterritorialized,[12] to a certain degree. A number of global governance institutions now exist, both for political and financial regulations (e.g., the United Nations, the International Monetary Fund).[13] An international legal framework has also emerged with international laws and tribunals. Given the influence of market globalism with its neoliberal economic principles that call for a limited government role, some argue that the nation-state is losing much of its influence (e.g., Ohmae, 1996, 1999; Spring, 2015; Stiglitz, 2002; Strange, 1996).

Although some hyperglobalist commentators might decry the 'end of the nation-state', Sparke (2013) considers this view to be premature and connected to TINA rhetoric that accompanies globalization's being used as an ideology. This rhetoric is designed to emphasize the inevitability of economic interdependence and encourage national governments to limit their interventions and adopt the free-market system. As noted, this ideological spin, as tied to market globalism, remains dominant. At the same time, Steger (2013) posits that, even though market globalism challenges the power of nation-states, governments nonetheless must be actively involved in propagating market globalism. Rizvi and Lingard (2010) also point out the complicity of the nation-state in the global capitalist economic system. Clearly, the nation-states' role is changing in the face of globalization, although what form it is taking or will take remains a subject of debate.

Like market-oriented hyperglobalists, critical hyperglobalists might consider the move to a one-size-fits-all set of neoliberal reforms to be a death knell for the nation-state, while other critical scholars would see alternatives. Those who employ a transformationalist approach might suggest that the state is still vital, but with limitations. These commentators would likely recognize the concrete impacts of globalization while separating it from the dominant ideology of market globalism. They would also be able to imagine other possibilities. For example, Rizvi and Lingard (2010) suggest that while the role of nation-states is changing and power is shared globally in some respects, 'We are not so much experiencing the demise of the system of nation-states as witnessing its transformation' (p. 31). They explain that the authority of nation-states is continually questioned and point out that they need to take on new functions of policy coordination and delivery in the global era. A number of other scholars highlight the continued role of the nation-state in domestic affairs (see, e.g., Béland, 2010; Weiss, 2010).

Further, Rizvi and Lingard (2010) argue that the dominant form of market globalism that has an impact on the processes of globalization and the role of nation-states can be challenged and reshaped. Likewise, Sparke (2013) asserts that there is nothing inevitable about globalization as it stands now and that the dominance of neoliberal globalization could be shifted so that governance could be 'remade'. Today, nation-states are interconnected in intricate ways that were not present 100 years ago. At the same time, nation-states are still key actors on the global stage. They also still govern significant aspects of their local domains, including the military, judicial, and legislative as well as policing. It is important to note, however, that the ability of poorer nation-states in the Global South, which are most often former colonies, to forge their own paths is often circumvented by their geopolitical positions. Whatever their influence and the ways they have changed, nation-states are clearly not operating on a level playing field.

Costs, Benefits, and Dilemmas of Globalization

Given what we know about globalization so far, it is clear that it has both costs and benefits, which lead to debates about the nature and impact of globalization. Historically, globalization has had a greater number of costs than benefits. In the first stages of globalization during the rise of colonialism, the significant costs were the millions of humans who were killed, enslaved, or otherwise marginalized (Coatsworth, 2004). Colonial powers from the Global North were able to raise their countries' economic productivity at the expense of the countries that they colonized in the Global South. As history has progressed, countries that were formerly colonized continue to be marginalized, and there is a tendency for a small minority within countries (both in the Global North and the Global South) to receive the benefits of globalization such as an improved economic outlook. Globalization, specifically economic globalization, has therefore led to rising inequality and a decline in standard of living for the majority of the world's population.

Over the longer term, standards of living may be improved through economic integration into the world-system, although these benefits vary by country and come at the greatest cost to those who must endure the changes as they are occurring. Financial crises also have significant effects outside a nation-state's borders, displaying the impact of the global integration of the world economic system. Globalization's dark side affects many areas outside of the economic realm as well. For example, environmental concerns are no longer focused on local or national domains; they are now global in nature because processes such as global warming as well as air and water pollution are caused by, and have an impact on, countries around the globe. The spread of diseases is also not contained within national borders, given the increasingly greater movement of people. This movement and the ease with which people cross borders also lead to trafficking of humans, drugs, and guns as global problems (Tilly, 2004).

Globalization also has its benefits. People from various cultures are able to interact in ways that were not possible hundreds of years ago due to both technological innovations, such as the Internet and social media, and the increasing ease of international travel. Scientists are increasingly able to collaborate, and doctors may operate on patients in other areas of the world remotely, potentially providing much-needed healthcare in poorer areas. Governments around the world may also be able to work together more efficiently due to the existence of global governance organizations and communications technology, which may facilitate diplomacy rather than military actions. As an example, efforts toward global human rights have taken shape due to these global governance organizations.

Importantly, both problems and solutions are global in today's world. For example, health epidemics (e.g., Ebola) quickly become global due to the easy exchange of people across borders through technological means, such as airplanes. At the same time, a multinational group of doctors may share expertise to limit the spread and impact of a given health epidemic. The key dilemma of globalization is that along with the good comes the bad. To a certain degree, we need globalization and find it useful in our everyday lives. However, to continue to reap the benefits of globalization, many scholars, social justice activists, and individuals would like to find a way to limit the negative impacts of globalization. Related concerns involve the uneven nature of globalization's impacts, the role of the nation-state, and the possibility of further marginalizing countries in the Global South.

Conclusion

Whether we consider globalization to be positive, negative, or both, it is clearly a set of processes, an ideology, and a social imaginary that have had, and continue to have, a great impact on our society, both within our local contexts and within the broader world. Its history and origins will continue to be debated, as will the impact of the nation-state and the role of world culture. What is clear is that we live in a profoundly different world than that which existed at the end of WWII; it has changed in ways that have an impact on all of the economic, political, cultural, social, technological, and ecological dimensions of globalization. Given the saliency of globalization in today's world, it is crucial for everyone involved in any social sphere, including education, to understand how it is connected to our everyday practices. The next two chapters focus on deepening the reader's understanding of globalization prior to shifting the focus to globalization and education specifically. In Chap. 2, I detail the worldwide developments that have occurred from WWII onward that shape the context of contemporary globalization in which current educational policies are created. Chapter 3 provides a detailed discussion of the theories and constructs that have been used to understand globalization more fully.

Notes

1. The term 'globalization' first appeared in the *Oxford English Dictionary* in 1962. However, it was not until 1985 that Theodore Levitt first used the term in an academic sense, referring specifically to developments in the global economic sphere.
2. The German monk Martin Luther launched a major upheaval that led to the Protestant Revolution. At the time that he wrote his '95 Theses' and nailed them to a church door in Wittenburg, Germany, there was increasing dissatisfaction with the Roman Catholic Church in Europe due to corruption and the practice of selling pardons (called indulgences) for sins. The movement eventually led to the establishment of a separate Protestant religion.
3. See Chap. 3 for more details on the modernist perspective.
4. Importantly, Western countries have typically been juxtaposed against Eastern or other 'less developed' areas, such as Africa and Latin America. Whereas most of the country terminology discussed in this section refers primarily to economic distinctions, the term 'Western' also applies to cultural determinants. In this way, Westernization has been considered a process through which dominant forces from powerful countries, most notably the USA, have spread throughout the world. An example of this is the influence of film and media from the USA.
5. These terms arose during the Cold War, which ensued after WWII, when the capitalism of the USA and Europe was in competition with the communism of Russia. At that time, communist countries, such as the former Soviet Union, were considered part of the 'Second World'. Countries in the 'Third World' were not aligned either with the USA and its allies or with the Soviet Union. The term 'Third World' later became used as an economic and subtractive term to describe less developed countries that differed from the industrialized First World.
6. See Chap. 2 for a full overview of global governance organizations, including financial institutions such as the WB.
7. Chapter 2 details the rise of the aid and development regime after WWII and how claims of neocolonialism have been leveled against it.
8. Sparke (2013) uses 'Globalization' with a capital 'G' to denote the ideology of globalization rather than the tangible aspects of it.
9. See the explanation of different approaches to globalization later in this chapter.

10. See Chap. 2 for a more detailed discussion on resistance to globalization.
11. See Chap. 2 for a detailed overview of the different types of global governance organizations, including international monetary organizations.
12. See Chap. 3 for a definition of this term.
13. All of the global governance institutions are described in detail in Chap. 2.

CHAPTER 2

Why Study Globalization? Developments, Actors, Resistance

The contemporary era of globalization has been marked by increasing interconnections among nation-states and accompanied by numerous intense changes. Developments associated with increasing globalization have had an impact on virtually all aspects of society and define our world today. This chapter begins with an overview of the key developments that have been critical to the heightened nature of contemporary globalization since WWII: (a) technological changes, (b) economic globalization and the retreat of the welfare state, (c) the shift from Fordism to post-Fordism, (d) the emergence of the global knowledge economy, (e) changing patterns in international mobility and transnational migration, and (f) shifting cultural patterns.

With these developments in mind, I then cover the emergence of the aid and development regime as well as global governance organizations, including (a) intergovernmental organizations (IGOs), (b) regional organizations, (c) bilateral organizations, (d) international monetary organizations (IMOs), and (e) international non-governmental organizations (INGOs). I also consider additional actors that participate in the policy-making and policy implementation processes, including (a) transnational corporations (TNCs); (b) nation-states; (c) communities, policy implementers, and individuals; and (d) think tanks, special interest groups, and lobbyists. I also discuss the neoliberal-focused Washington Consensus (WC) that prevailed until the end of the 1990s and the Post-Washington

© The Editor(s) (if applicable) and The Author(s) 2016

L.M. Portnoi, *Policy Borrowing and Reform in Education*,
DOI 10.1057/978-1-137-53024-0_2

Consensus (PWC) that followed, which have governed the aid and development regime for several decades. The final section of the chapter covers the various forms of resistance that have arisen to counter the dominance of neoliberalism and market globalism.

Worldwide Developments in the Contemporary Era of Globalization

The post-WWII era has ushered in a series of widespread changes that have heightened the pace and impact of globalization. Central to the acceleration of contemporary globalization are (a) technological developments that are (b) coupled with new forms of economic globalization and (c) an emerging post-Fordist global division of labor, alongside (d) increasing immigration and (e) changing cultural patterns. Each one of these changes influences the way we live and work in the era of contemporary globalization. When taken together, they have a significant collective impact on all areas, including education.

Technological Developments

The pace of change in the area of technological innovation has accelerated in the postindustrial[1] period following WWII. Changes in information and communications technology (ICT) have proven to be particularly profound within this realm, leading to the notion of an 'ICT Revolution'. Since WWII, the world has experienced significant changes in technology in key areas, such as computing, data processing, and telecommunications. The ability to exchange ideas and conduct business in 'real time' is a significant change, as are the efficiency and convenience afforded by increasingly complex computers and cellular devices. The manner in which business, governmental work, and everyday life are conducted has changed dramatically due to the technological advances of the past half-century.

Changes in the ICT domain have been especially profound in recent years. Sanou (as cited in International Telecommunications Union [ITU], 2015), stated, 'Technological progress, infrastructure deployment, and falling prices have brought unexpected growth in ICT access and connectivity to billions of people around the world' (p. 1). It is difficult to imagine a world in which computers, cellular phones, and social media are not present. Yet, access to technology remains uneven. Although there are 7 billion cellular phone users worldwide, and 3.2 billion people have access to the Internet, there continues to be a global 'digital divide' wherein people from countries in the Global South are less likely to have access to these technologies than are their Global North counterparts. Indeed, 80 % of households in Global North countries have access to the Internet, whereas only 34 %of households have access in countries in the Global South (ITU, 2015). The digital divide is also prevalent within countries across the world, while it is especially prominent in the Global South, where ITU noted that less than two-thirds of these countries' populations access the Internet at all, whether from home or from other locations.

Other important innovations in the technological realm in this age of contemporary globalization include those in the areas of medicine, transportation (especially aviation), and the military. These advancements often make processes more efficient and make it possible to collaborate across borders. Many of the developments connected to the technological dimension of globalization have altered our notions of space and time, which Harvey, (1990a, b) refers to as "time-space" compression (see Chap. 3). Localities are no longer the center of the spaces in which we operate, and we can connect across borders quickly and easily through the use of technology, either over the Internet or by taking a plane ride. Inherent in the notion of time-space compression is the fact that everything is now happening much faster than it was prior to the advent of these technologies. Importantly, technological developments are both a driver of globalization and a result thereof; the relationship between the two is highly reciprocal.

Economic Globalization and the Retreat of the Welfare State

Contemporary globalization is also evidenced in the economic realm, which continues to become increasingly interconnected. A new economic world order was forged at the close of WWII through agreements that took place in 1944 at the United Nations Monetary and Financial Conference in Bretton Woods, New Hampshire (or Bretton Woods Conference). The conference involved representatives from more than 40 Allied countries. A key focus of this conference was postwar reconstruction, and it resulted in the development of two key international monetary organizations (IMOs)—the World Bank (WB), first called the International Bank for Reconstruction and Development, and the International Monetary Fund (IMF)—which are described in more detail in the section on global governance. Importantly, the Bretton Woods agreement was created at a time of war following a global depression, accompanied by high unemployment and financial instability. One of the most significant outcomes of the Bretton Woods Conference was an agreement regarding the importance of the free market economy and expansion of international trade. The agreement thus signaled a new era in which countries would no longer be able to nationally regulate their economies; instead, a global economic system was created in which binding rules would govern nation-states' economic activities. As such, the Bretton Woods Conference was highly significant in facilitating the acceleration of economic globalization.

During the post-WWII era, nation-states maintained control of their capital flows within their countries to a large degree, while building their capital through taxation. In the early postwar period, 'welfare' states flourished in the Global North (Steger, 2013). Welfare states, which focus on distribution of wealth to promote and protect the well-being of all citizens, had begun to emerge after the Great Depression and became increasingly standard in the Global North during the reconstruction period after WWII. At this time, Keynesian[2] economics, a form of capitalism in which nation-states significantly intervene in the free market system, was ascendant. Nation-states employed free market capitalism governed by the worldwide economic system while simultaneously providing significant social services to their citizens (e.g., funding for the poor and pensions for the elderly). The welfare state system began to collapse by the early 1970s,[3] however, due to global financial crises and instability marked by inflation, lower economic growth, and high unemployment (Sparke, 2013).

The economic crisis of the 1970s and resulting Great Recession caused political regimes in many geopolitically powerful countries around the world to turn to fiscally conservative measures, signaling the advent of neoliberalism and the retreat of the 'social welfare and ameliorative functions of the state' (Rizvi & Lingard, 2010, p. 29). From the 1980s onward, neoliberalism became the economic system that dominated the worldwide economy, leading to greater interdependencies of markets across countries. The liberalization of trade and integration of the free market system have significantly altered the way production and commodities are organized and have led to the growth and influence of TNCs, which are discussed as actors below. During this contemporary period of globalization, as societies moved from the Fordist to Post-Fordist era, production shifted from an emphasis on manufactured goods to services.

From Fordism to Post-Fordism

At the conclusion of WWII, the worldwide economy was focused on the production of manufactured products in line with the capitalist paradigm. As a remnant of colonial times, significant amounts of natural resources were extracted from the Global South and were used to create products in factories in the Global North. During this postwar time period, a system known as 'Fordism' took shape, which drew from organizational principles applied at the Ford automobile plant in Detroit, Michigan. These principles emphasized standardization, efficiency, and mass production. For the economy to function well in this environment, mass production had to be tied to mass consumption; in turn, employees needed to be paid sufficiently to have the ability to consume products (Sparke, 2013). Changes associated with globalization in the late 1960s and early 1970s led to the erosion of the Fordist system. The world (mainly the Global North) was moving into a postindustrial society in which science and knowledge became central (Bell, 1973). By the 1970s, technological and communication improvements began to signal a new era in which services were emphasized over goods. In addition, countries no longer relied on consumption from within their own borders in the increasingly globalized environment (Sparke, 2013).

The 'post-Fordist' mode of production that evolved in this new economic landscape is focused on services and has flexibility at its center. It also reflects the changing division of labor worldwide, as goods and services continue to move to countries that have the most inexpensive labor and production costs, often without protections for workers (see the discussion of TNCs). This new environment is also characterized by increasing inequality within countries, along with growing gaps between countries in the Global North and the Global South (Firebaugh & Goesling, 2007; Korzeniewicz & Moran, 2007; Stromquist & Monkman, 2014). Competition—between countries, regions within countries, and even workers—is a key component of the post-Fordist environment in a world dominated by neoliberalism. Given its emphasis on flexibility, the post-Fordist mode of production requires a new set of skills, including the ability to access and process information, which has created a hierarchy of workers based on their involvement in activities related to this new mode of production. The era of post-Fordism is closely tied to the importance of knowledge and the workers who possess it.

The Emergence of the Global Knowledge Economy

Given technological and scientific developments and the shift from Fordist to post-Fordist production, knowledge and information have emerged as central in the contemporary period of globalization. In the 'knowledge economy', a term coined by management consultant and author Peter Drucker in his 1969 book *The Age of Discontinuity*, knowledge has become recognized as another commodity that may be bought and sold. As such, the global knowledge economy involves the 'production, exchange, and circulation of research, knowledge, and information' (Marginson, 2013, p. 30). Technological and scientific innovation, which require less human labor and increase efficiency, are closely tied to the growing importance of information and knowledge in the knowledge economy (Gürüz, 2008). The concept of the knowledge economy is also connected to Castells' (1996, 1997, 1998) notions of the 'Information Age' and 'Network Society', which are discussed in more detail in Chap. 3.

All of these constructs highlight the importance of information and knowledge in postindustrial societies in the era of contemporary globalization. As modes of production have shifted to post-Fordism, the role of specialized, technical knowledge has increased in importance while the emphasis on physical labor and natural resources has declined. 'Knowledge workers', whom Drucker (1959) had first singled out in *The Landmarks of Tomorrow*, are central to the global knowledge economy, and the accumulation of knowledge corresponds to the accumulation of wealth in this realm. The economic value lies in the knowledge itself or in items produced using knowledge (Shields, 2013), which contributes to the hierarchy of workers noted above. In *The World Is Flat*, *New York Times* columnist Thomas Friedman (2005) distinguishes between knowledge producers, knowledge users, and passive/non-users. Critical commentators would suggest that those who are on the passive end of the spectrum (often manual laborers) are increasingly marginalized in the knowledge economy. Another key feature of the global knowledge economy is that it is not linked to a specific place as with former modes and types of production. Knowledge can be freely exchanged and, due to technological innovations, can easily and rapidly move across borders (Giddens, 2000; Harvey, 1990b).

International Mobility and Transnational Migration

With advances in technology, especially in the area of transportation, international mobility has become another central feature of the contemporary age of globalization. Some of this mobility is temporary, as when people travel to other countries for conferences, vacations, or study-abroad opportunities. However, a great number of the changes in international mobility patterns have to do with longer-term migration, which has altered the demographics of many countries around the world. Much of the migration that occurs in today's globalized world involves movement to the Global North, where immigrant populations have grown while indigenous populations have declined (Suárez-Orozco & Sattin, 2007). There is also considerable movement of people between countries in the Global North and between countries in the Global South. International mobility is affected by other developments within globalization. For example, many immigrants seek better economic opportunities in other countries, and talented workers are often able to choose the countries in which they live. This is particularly true for knowledge workers who tend to be in demand for their skills in the post-Fordist society, which is dominated by the global knowledge economy.

The movement of people across borders may be beneficial for individuals and for the countries that receive them, although some immigrants work in challenging circumstances in which they are paid low wages and live in substandard accommodations. Emigration of talented workers also proves to be problematic for many counties in the Global South, which experience 'brain drain' when their most talented individuals, often those who studied abroad, choose to live and work outside their home countries. Although current discussions on transnational migration often involve the term 'brain circulation' because international mobility is complex and multidirectional, it is nevertheless challenging for countries that are working on becoming globally competitive to lose their most talented citizens to other nations. To counter this trend, some countries have established programs to repatriate their citizens who are working abroad. China, for example, has launched a program designed to entice 'turtles', or scholars who live abroad, to return by offering them prestigious positions and research funding (Li, 2010; Spring, 2008). International mobility and the circulation of people across borders are not only relevant to the changing demographics of the labor force, they also give rise to new sensibilities and cultural practices that are not (entirely) national in origin.

Shifting Cultural Patterns

Due to migration, coupled with the ease of the flow of ideas and cultural practices across borders, cultural patterns around the world are changing. As discussed in Chap. 1, the cultural dimension of globalization is significant because we no longer operate within a closed environment. We are exposed to cultural determinants from other countries every day, including foods, languages, and religious practices. This exposure ties into Manfred Steger's (2013) 'global imaginary', or a growing awareness of our interconnections with other societies. Even if we are not consciously aware of the global connections to the everyday objects and practices around us, it is clear that the countries of the world are intertwined in many ways. For some, the awareness of global interconnections is stronger due to international mobility and direct (and sometimes intentional) exposure to other cultures.

Although many citizens may continue to identify with their home countries and local cultures, global interactions and migration have meant that people's social identities have become more complex, allowing for multiple loyalties (Rizvi & Lingard, 2010). Immigrants may retain their original citizenship while becoming citizens of the countries in which they now live. They often move between their former and current countries of residence on a regular basis. As noted in Chap. 1, this exchange of cultural practices results in hybridity. Hybridity occurs both within people's identities and within cultural practices. For example, Hindu immigrants from India who live in North America or Europe may have Christmas trees in December and celebrate secular aspects of the holiday while retaining their Hindu faith. Hybridity also may be seen in cultural expressions, such as in fusion foods and music that mixes styles and/or languages. Manifestations of hybridity may occur naturally and without significant challenges for some immigrants, although others, particularly those from the Global South who are quickly transported into the world of the Global North, may experience angst in reconciling their hybrid identities (Bhaba, 1994).

Despite changing cultural patterns, many commentators argue that local cultures are still alive and well, and Robertson (1992) argues that cultural changes within globalization still take place within local contexts to a large degree. Moreover, actors within a local context have agency to act upon and reshape the new cultural patterns that they encounter. Alongside the changes that have taken place in the heightened era of globalization, an aid and development regime has emerged in the contemporary era.

Launching the Aid and Development Regime

The end of WWII signaled the beginning of a new mode of international relations, which Shields (2013) calls the 'development era'. After years of war, and given increasing political awareness within the colonies, a wave of independence movements began to take shape and change the political landscape throughout the Global South. There was also a sense of moral responsibility on the part of prior colonial powers to ameliorate the effects of colonialism in newly independent countries, often referred to as the 'white man's burden' (Samoff, 2013). The swift removal of colonial powers caused its own set of problems, however, as many colonies were not prepared to govern independently after years of domination by countries from the Global North. Therefore, in his 1949 inaugural address, US president Harry Truman suggested a way to assist former colonies, which he referred to as the 'developing' world, that allowed them to simultaneously pursue democracy, economic growth, industrialization, and scientific advancement (Shields, 2013; Tikly, 2004). In accordance with modernist views of linear progress (see Chap. 3), Truman and other prominent worldwide leaders deemed these fundamental features to be necessary for newly independent countries to become developed, and an aid and development regime based on these principles was created.

The Aid and Development Regime

Launched in the post-WWII era of reconstruction, the aid and development regime was intended to ameliorate the negative effects of colonialism. It was founded on the modern notion of progress in which countries in the Global South would be 'brought up' to the level of development of countries in the Global North. Central to the aid and development regime's work is the notion that development brings about economic growth and progress. Global governance organizations, including IGOs, regional organizations, bilateral organizations, IMOs, and (increasingly) INGOs, serve as the core of the aid and development regime.

Truman's address coincided with the establishment of the Bretton Woods institutions (the IMF and the WB) as well as a number of other global governance bodies (see below), all of which serve as the core of the aid and development regime, leading to the institutionalization of international influence (Samoff, 2013). By 1950, aid and development had come to involve systematically intervening and restructuring other countries to purportedly improve their economic prospects and standards of living (Shields, 2013). At the heart of the aid and development regime's work is the modern notion that all countries should become developed in the same way, following common principles, highlighting and exacerbating the binary distinction between 'developed' countries, which have achieved a certain status based on progress achieved, and 'developing' countries, which still have a long way to go based on these measures.

Development indicators that are chosen to measure countries' progress and their associated labels are value-laden and reflect the goals of those who create them (Phillips & Schweisfurth, 2014). For example, as a reputable IMO, the WB has created the highly used indicators discussed in Chap. 1 (low, low-middle, high-middle, and high income), reflecting the bank's focus on economics. Given the growing influence of the WB and other IMOs, economics quickly became the central area of focus within the development realm and governed the neoliberal WC that prevailed in the aid and development regime throughout the 1990s (see the full section on this topic).

To a large degree, development has come to be seen as equivalent to economic growth. However, critics have expressed concern that unbridled economic development, along with further industrialization and urbanization, has led to unintended consequences, such as environmental degradation and greater inequalities within and between countries (Escobar, 2011; Phillips & Schweisfurth, 2014). Although the dominance of economic development remains today, the aid and development regime has broadened its scope to focus on social policies, such as poverty alleviation during the PWC. As previously noted, the UNDP created the HDI to address this broader range of factors. Nevertheless, the IMOs that provide loans to countries in the Global South continue to view economic indicators as, to a large degree, central. Thus, the aid and development regime remains focused on economic indicators and a relatively linear path toward progress that involves economic development as central to all other forms of development.

Global Governance Organizations

Alongside the sweeping changes that have taken place throughout many aspects of society during the contemporary period of globalization, the era of global governance has emerged. Launched at a time of instability and challenging economic circumstances at the close of WWII, these global governance institutions are positioned at the center of the aid and development regime. After WWII, several different types of institutions were created to govern worldwide concerns and provide aid, including IGOs, regional organizations, bilateral organizations, IMOs, and INGOs. Global governance organizations are not the only players involved in policy development and implementation in a globalized world, however. I outline other entities that take part in these processes in a subsequent section, including TNCs; nation-states; communities and individuals; and think tanks, special interest groups, and lobbyists. This expanded array of actors, which includes organizational and corporate interests, comprise a new 'architecture of global governance' that contributes to economic and social policies around the world (Ball, 2012). Although many local actors, such as communities and individuals, have relatively limited access to the policymaking process, they are often involved in implementing and (re) shaping policy.

Intergovernmental Organizations

IGOs tend to be formed on the basis of formal treaties or agreements. The first IGO was the United Nations (UN), formerly known as the League of Nations. Founded in 1945, the UN was designed to improve economic and social development throughout the world, especially within former colonies. Its principles tied health and social problems to economic factors and harmonized international efforts to address these issues for the first time. Between 1960 and 1970, the UN centered its efforts on the 'Development Decade' to foster economic development and growth in the Global South. During this period, the UN consolidated various programs for international development under the rubric of a new agency in 1965—UNDP. UNDP's focus is on economic growth, although education and healthcare are important components of the overall drive toward growth.

Two additional agencies were created under the UN umbrella after WWII—the United Nations International Children's Emergency Fund

(UNICEF) and the United Nations Educational, Scientific and Cultural Organization (UNESCO). All of these organizations continue to provide global governance, policy guidance, and monetary support throughout the world, with a focus on the Global South. Despite their importance, many would argue that the scope of the UN organizations' influence has diminished over the past 30 years due to the increasing policy guidance role that IMOs play (Samoff, 2013; Shields, 2013; Spring, 2015), as detailed below. Nevertheless, IGOs such as the UN are responsible for a number of important declarations, such as the Universal Declaration of Human Rights (1948), the Declaration on the Rights of Indigenous People (2008), and the World Declaration on Higher Education for the Twenty-First Century (1998).

Although the UN and its suite of institutions make up the predominant form of IGOs, several other such organizations exist. Another key entity in this domain is the Organisation for Economic Co-operation and Development (OECD). The OECD was founded in 1961, with an explicit focus on economic growth and increasing the standard of living of its member countries. The original number of member countries was 20, and membership now includes 34 wealthy nations from the Global North. The OECD was originally established as a mechanism for exchanging ideas among member countries, although it increasingly has become a vessel for advocating for neoliberalism, much like the IMOs and other entities that are part of the aid and development regime.

The OECD remains centered on economic growth in its member countries and on the development of the worldwide economy, although it has increasingly focused on the social sphere and operates in over 100 non-member countries. In this way, the OECD has become increasingly involved in setting policy agendas, including those focused on education (Rizvi & Lingard, 2010). The North Atlantic Treaty Organization (NATO) is another prominent IGO. It derives from the 1949 North Atlantic Treaty signed by Belgium, Canada, Denmark, France, Iceland, Italy, Luxembourg, the Netherlands, Norway, Portugal, the UK, and the USA as a form of shared military protection against the threat of the Soviet Union after WWII. At that time, the USA and its allies were concerned about the spread of communism and were also eager to help war-torn countries in Europe to rebuild. NATO calls for joint military action if one or more of the member countries should be attacked. Over the years, 16 additional members, mostly from Europe and including some of the former Soviet states, have joined this military alliance.

Regional Organizations

Regional organizations are a particular form of IGOs. Given their importance and for the purpose of clarity, I have separated out this type of organization for discussion in this chapter. Like other IGOs, regional organizations are generally created through formal agreements for shared purposes, such as economic development or political cooperation. Perhaps the most well-known regional organization is the European Union (EU), which was established in 1992 with the Maastricht Treaty. Other organizations preceded the establishment of the EU. In the wake of WWII, in 1951, Belgium, France, Italy, Luxembourg, the Netherlands, and West Germany formed the European Coal and Steel Community (ECSC) to create a free-trade environment for coal, steel, and iron ore. In 1957, the ECSC countries formed the European Economic Community (EEC) to further enhance economic cooperation and establish a common market. The EEC was later renamed the European Community and included a wider range of member countries.

The Single European Act of 1987 was another key development prior to the Maastricht Treaty and formation of the European Union. The act involved greater coordination related to foreign policy and contained economic and social dimensions. The key motivation behind the establishment of the EU (and its predecessor organizations) was to enhance the stability and cooperation between the member states, which currently number approximately 30. The EU has established a single currency (the Euro) that most member states use as well as shared trade laws that govern goods and products from member states, which may be exchanged freely within the EU. The EU also has common citizenship for its member countries and shared social policies related to education, health, the environment, and other areas.

Numerous other regional organizations have been created for similar purposes, including the African Union (formerly the Organization of African Unity), the Economic Community of Western African States, and the Association of South East Asian Nations. Additional regional organizations are versions of IMOs—for example, the African Development Bank, the Development Bank of Latin America, and the Islamic Development Bank—which all purportedly strive to provide resources, reduce poverty, and improve social progress in their member countries.

Bilateral Organizations

Bilateral organizations, also known as aid agencies, are closely tied with the international aid and development regime that emerged in the post-WWII era. These agencies were created to provide resources and technical assistance, both to European countries ravaged by war and to former colonies. At their inception, some of the agencies were devoted to assisting their former colonies (e.g., of France and the UK), and such relationships continue today. Indeed, most of the current work of bilateral agencies focuses on countries in the Global South. Although these organizations often involve multiple countries' being the recipients of aid, they are called 'bilateral' because they transfer aid from one country to another. The originating country's government is responsible for funding the aid provided.

The first bilateral agency was the United States Agency for International Development (USAID), created in 1961. The UK's Ministry of Overseas Development (now called the Department for International Development, or DFID) followed in 1964. Numerous other countries in the Global North, including Australia, Canada, France, Germany, Japan, Norway, and Sweden, also have established bilateral organizations to provide aid and reduce poverty in the Global South. The EU is also a key player in this regard, although it does not fall into the original two-country definition of 'bilateral'. Most bilateral organizations provide aid in the form of grants rather than loans, although there may be strings attached, such as using particular products or prescribing particular policies. For example, some USAID education projects require the use of certain textbooks produced in the USA.

International Monetary Organizations

IMOs have become central to the development paradigm. Although they were not originally created to provide technical assistance, their operations have increasingly moved into that domain. Two of the most significant IMOs—the WB and the IMF—were created at the Bretton Woods Conference, as noted earlier. The WB's central purpose at that time was to fund reconstruction in Europe after WWII. By 1960, the WB began to take a role in international development, with the introduction of its International Development Association, focused on the poorest countries in the world. Initially, the WB stressed key areas that were likely to produce a return on investment, such as developing infrastructure. Over the years, the WB has become a key player in the development regime, offering not only financial assistance but also technical advisement in many policy areas, including education (see Chap. 4 for further discussion). The WB's focus is connected to the development of human capital, and the bank perceives education as a sound investment for economic growth (see Chap. 4 for a further discussion of this point).

Over time, the WB has become the largest external source of funding for countries in the Global South (Spring, 2015). The IMF is another key IMO, which was originally created to administer the new international monetary system after WWII. Since its inception, the IMF has taken on an oversight role in managing the economic system of the world. In essence, the WB and the IMF are global banks that provide loans to poor countries, mainly in the Global South. However, these loans are not of the traditional variety; they come not only with repayment requirements and interest, but also with conditions. These conditions have become uniform and are explained in the section on the Washington and Post-Washington Consensus.

Another significant player in policymaking and policy implementation is the World Trade Organization (WTO), which stemmed from discussions that began at the Bretton Woods Conference. Although it was not created until 1995, its origins lie in Bretton Woods and the 1948 General Agreement on Tariffs and Trade (GATT). The WTO has over 150 members and more than 30 'observer' members. Two important offshoots of the WTO include the General Agreement on Trades and Services (GATS) and Agreement on Trade-Related Intellectual Property Rights (TRIPS). GATS is an agreement between member countries with regard to how services will be produced, marketed, distributed, and sold across their borders. It affects not only the trade of products, but also of services, such as cross-border higher education (discussed in Chap. 4). TRIPS focuses on protecting individual, university, and corporate intellectual property.

IMOs based in and comprised of geopolitically powerful nations from the Global North, although not traditional governance associations, have played a significant role in developing global policy, particularly with regard to economics. As Steger (2013) contends, 'These three institutions [the WB, IMF, and WTO] are in the privileged position of making and enforcing the rules of a global economy that is sustained by significant power differentials between the global North and South' (pp. 55–56). In the 1970s, the WB, the IMF, and the WTO became the chief instigators and enforcers of the neoliberal economic regime. Their impact, bolstered through the WC, has been particularly profound in the Global South, where Structural Adjustment Programs (SAPs) were required as a condition of funding (see below). At the same time, IMOs have increasingly become involved in other policy domains, including health and education. In addition to loans, they provide guidance and set global norms and standards in this regard.

International Non-Governmental Organizations

INGOs provide humanitarian aid and technical assistance. A wide range of INGOs exist, and their international scope distinguishes them from domestic non-governmental organizations (NGOs). Most INGOs are independent, not-for-profit endeavors. Well-known examples of INGOs include the Red Cross, Save the Children, Amnesty International, Oxfam, and Doctors Without Borders. Collectively, INGOs provide aid and technical assistance in the Global South related to a wide range of issues, including HIV/AIDS, girls' education, and human rights, while some also provide disaster relief in emergency situations. INGOs differ from IGOs or bilateral organizations because they are not expressly connected to either international or national government entities, although they may receive funding from governments, IGOs, or IMOs and often work collaboratively with these entities (Thomas, 2007).

Although these organizations are not directly connected to the official global governance institutions that serve as the core of the aid and development regime, they often act in concert with these organizations, and many INGOs are criticized for dictating what solutions countries need or even for providing them with culturally inappropriate solutions. Questions are also raised regularly with regard to the portion of funds donated that go to assist those in need and the overall accountability of these organizations. Nonetheless, these INGOs provide significant aid worldwide each year, and many have accountability measures in place or practice responsible aid practices by seeking local input on what is needed in a given country. In addition, philanthropic organizations may be considered INGOs in some cases, particularly if they operate on a global scale, such as the Bill and Melinda Gates Foundation, the Open Society, and the Ford Foundation.

Other Policy Actors

Transnational Corporations

In addition to the more formal structures of global governance, another important force in the policy environment is TNCs.[4] Although TNCs are not considered to be arbiters of global governance in an official sense, they are nonetheless central to the way nation-states operate within a global economic system. To this end, TNCs serve an important global governance function. TNCs operate across multiple countries, although their power base resides in the Global North countries where they are headquartered, which are limited mainly to North America, Europe, Japan, and South Korea (Steger, 2013). Familiar TNCs include Chevron, Nike, Philip Morris, Toyota, and Walmart. Although some countries from the Global South have TNCs, those in the Global North dominate. Given their size and number (over 40,000), TNCs have significant power and control the majority of worldwide capital flow for investments as well as access to international markets. Nation-states no longer fully govern working conditions and environments in a post-Fordist economy dominated by TNCs (Rizvi & Lingard, 2010). TNCs are also key to the spread of neoliberalism. These influential corporations tend to operate in countries where labor is inexpensive, and concerns have arisen with regard to labor practices and exploitation of both people and the environment in these poorer countries.

Because TNCs operate in multiple countries, they can shift production rapidly if conditions within a given country prove to be unfavorable or regulations stymie their objectives. In many countries, however, TNCs are welcomed because they contribute significantly to the national economy, and governments typically offer tax reductions to attract and retain TNCs in their countries. In many cases, governments allow TNCs to operate in special export processing zones (EPZs), or free-trade areas, which allow them to function with limited or relaxed regulations (e.g., for labor, customs, and export). Many EPZs are located in poorer countries (e.g., Bangladesh, Belize, Kenya, Mexico, Pakistan), and social justice advocates often criticize the TNCs that operate in these zones due to the exploitation and poor working conditions in many of their factories (often called 'sweatshops'). TNCs that operate in EPZs have a particular impact on women, who make up the bulk of the employees in these areas. The

International Labour Organization, a UN agency founded after WWII, has set international labor standards and investigates claims against TNCs and other companies that operate in its member nations.

Nation-States

Although the role of nation-states is evolving with globalization, they remain key players in today's globalized world. Despite the influence of global governance organizations and other entities that regulate economic, political, and social domains across countries, nation-states remain sovereign. The origin of nation-state sovereignty and self-determination dates back to the Peace of Westphalia treaties[5] of 1648, which established the Westphalian principle that nation-states should not intervene in the matters of other nation-states (Sparke, 2013; Steger, 2013). Nevertheless, nation-states are now increasingly governed by international laws, conventions, and norms (e.g., for human rights, free trade), yet they maintain control over many arenas within their countries' boundaries, including education, healthcare, policing, citizenship, and language policies. Moreover, nation-states are now expected to regulate the domains of their citizens' lives that were once private, such as reproductive health and planning, which enhances the authority of the state to a certain degree (Boli & Petrova, 2007). In addition, global capitalism 'requires strong, reliable nation-states, which do not pose great risks to global economic activity' (Rizvi & Lingard, 2010, p. 29). Nation-states provide the security, structures, and stability required for capitalism to flourish within their countries and across the world. At the same time, nation-states have the ability to resist global mandates and mediate global trends in their local contexts, a point that has relevance throughout this book.

Communities, Policy Implementers, and Individuals

Nation-states are not the only localized actors within globalization. Local communities are also key components of globalization, particularly with regard to how global policies or agendas may be interpreted in the local context. In many parts of the world, local communities set agendas for important areas, such as education, and have an important role to play with regard to the manner in which policies and international mandates are implemented in practice (see Chap. 5 for more information on local implementation). At the same time, communities may set their own course, which may be influenced by global trends, but yet reflect the needs of the local context through vernacular globalization. As will become evident below, communities also have the power to resist various aspects of globalization.

Another set of local stakeholders comprises the policy implementers who directly interact with the policies on a daily basis. As explained in Chap. 5, those tasked with implementing policy often have a significant impact on the way it is carried out in practice. In the realm of education, for example, policy implementers might be administrators, teachers, and other educators, students, and parents. Even if these actors are not consulted during the policy development phase, they will be directly or indirectly involved in policy implementation.

Other individuals also play a key role in globalization, and their influence may be global or local in nature. Some individuals, such as influential business and government leaders, including TNC presidents, national presidents or prime ministers, and leaders of global governance organizations, actively participate in globalization as part of the neoliberal regime. In addition, policy entrepreneurs, who are generally academics from the Global North who operate as consultants, market global policies to various countries (Cairney, 2011). Many of these individuals have an impact on global policy agendas. Operating from an opposing perspective, social justice–oriented individuals participate in actively resisting globalization, especially the dominant form, neoliberal globalization, that prevails today (see the section below for a fuller discussion of resistance). These individuals often take part in demonstrations about fair trade and unfair labor practices at TNCs that operate in EPZs, or refuse to buy certain products as a protest (also known as 'boycotting'). Some of the efforts that individuals make in resisting globalization may be waged at the global level, as in the case of international protests, while others are local or personal in nature. Whether they are supporters or detractors of neoliberal globalization, these individuals serve to influence policymaking and policy implementation.

Think Tanks, Special Interest Groups, and Lobbyists

In most countries, three additional actors take part in the policymaking and implementation process: think tanks, special interest groups, and lobbyists. Think tanks, or private policy planning groups, are common in countries throughout the world, especially in the Global North. These organizations, which may be either for-profit or non-profit, are involved in research and advocacy on specialized issues. Think tanks generally have a relatively elite membership, consisting of high-level researchers, influential government figures, corporate leaders, and media representatives. They conduct research related to common issues of interest and try to build consensus on policy recommendations, which are distributed to the media and government (Dye, 2012). Prominent examples include the Brookings Institution in the USA, the Friedrich-Ebert-Stiftung in Germany, Civitas: The Institute for the Study of Civil Society in England, and the Tokyo Foundation in Japan. Think tanks from the Global South include the Center of Research and Development in Mexico, the Centre for Civil Society in India, and the Amadeus Institute in Morocco.

Think tanks are often connected to special interest groups. Special interest groups coalesce around shared interests and objectives with regard to the policy imperatives they would like to see on the government's agenda. They may operate on any level of government, and their primary objective is to educate both policymakers and the public about the issues that matter to them, often through websites, public campaigns, commissioned studies, and issue briefs. Special interest groups exert their influence through direct lobbying (e.g., meeting with politicians, presenting research results, testifying at government hearings), contributions to political parties, and interpersonal contacts and networking. Both think tanks and special interest groups operate on the logic of collective action, which suggests that individuals will band together because they will be more likely to achieve their personal objectives with the power of a group (Kraft & Furlong, 2014). Lobbyists, whose main job is to influence government actions, often work for think tanks or special interest groups. They typically spearhead campaigns related to specific issues and meet with government individuals directly.

The Washington Consensus and Post-Washington Consensus

Many of the organizational and nation-state actors involved in setting policy agendas believe that neoliberalism should guide economic and social policy worldwide. During the rise of neoliberalism in the 1970s and 1980s, the WB and the IMF provided loans to countries in the Global South, and their unpaid debt became a source of concern for the banks.

At the same time, these financial institutions were focused on deregulating markets worldwide and solidifying neoliberal economic practices. The term 'Washington Consensus' was coined by John Williamson, who was a financial advisor at the IMF during this time period. The 'Washington' part of this term reflects the Washington-based financial organizations that promoted the reform package for developing countries as well as the fact that the US Treasury was central. The Washington Consensus, which became a standard for many of the players in the aid and development regime, called for a strict set of neoliberal practices as part of SAPs that were required for countries to obtain further financial assistance. The main goal of SAPs was to ensure that indebted countries would be able to pay back their loans, rather than social development or reduction of future loan dependency (Sparke, 2013). Central to SAPs and the WC were the following principles or conditions: fiscal discipline, cutting of public spending, tax reform, financial liberalization (market reform), competitive exchange rates, trade liberalization, procurement of foreign direct investment,[6] privatization of state services, deregulation of the economy, and protection of property rights (Steger, 2013). Relevant to education, SAPs also prescribed that 'user fees' be added for many social services that countries had typically provided to their public for free.

IMOs used SAPs and the loans that came with them to force countries into accepting this set of principles. Progress on economic indicators was gauged by the use of rates of return (ROR) analysis, which, in turn, fueled further funding when development and assistance was deemed to provide potential future returns. SAPs offered a one-size-fits-all approach that involved the same central principles no matter the country in which they were imposed (Babb, 2010). Generally, SAPs were set up by IMOs from the Global North and dictated to countries in the Global South, leading some to suggest that they constituted a new form of colonialism, or neocolonialism[7] (Steger, 2013). In fact, Samoff (2013) posits that IMOs became the enforcers of global dictates in the post-WWII era rather than the colonialists.

For IMOs such as the WB, loans and technical advisement became increasingly intertwined (Jones, 2004). The WB's combination of technical assistance and funding is problematic because IMOs are the entities that decide what knowledge is valued and should be used in countries in the Global South (Samoff, 2013). Indeed, the knowledge function of the WB may be further complicating its function as a bank, as it now calls itself a 'knowledge bank' (Jones, 2004; Klees, Samoff, & Stromquist, 2012).

Using this mix of loans and technical advisement, SAPs served to embed neoliberal principles within the development regime and led to the focus on free markets to solve economic and other problems, at the expense of national government oversight. Interestingly, however, SAPs required national governments to be complicit in bringing their countries into the global capitalist regime (Rizvi & Lingard, 2010; Samoff, 2013). Although the WB and the IMF were the initial architects of SAPs and the WC, the broader development regime, including other types of organizations (e.g., bilateral organizations, the OECD), embraced the principles of this consensus for many years as well. Essentially, WC policies became the taken-for-granted manner of business for all types of development agencies that operated in a number of sectors worldwide. The impact of the aid and development regime on education, fueled by the WC, will be discussed in Chap. 4.

The Washington and Post-Washington Consensus

Coinciding with the creation of the aid and development regime in the aftermath of WWII, the WC emerged as a standard to guide the regime's efforts. Neoliberalism was central to the WC, and it focused on the economic return on investment. A key feature of the WC was prescribing SAPs as a set of conditions for aid and loan recipients. SAPs, which failed to a large extent, involved cutting public spending, liberalizing trade, and privatizing state services. At the beginning of the 2000s, the PWC emerged with a shift toward considering both economic and non-economic factors in development under the umbrella of 'poverty alleviation'. The neoliberal emphasis remains, however.

Despite apparent consensus about their benefits, SAPs failed to produce the desired results. Because significant infrastructure challenges and poverty existed in the countries that SAPs targeted, failing to provide social services led to increased poverty in the Global South and to insufficient stimulation of financial markets. Indeed, the WC has been criticized for leading numerous countries into financial crises. Not surprisingly, many indebted countries have not been able to pay back their debts acquired during the postcolonial period. Moreover, many countries are now spending large portions of their national budgets on servicing debt obtained during the height of the SAP period, leading to calls for debt reduction and forgiveness.

Led by the IMOs, the aid and development regime began to recognize in the late 1990s that SAPs were not working as intended and suggested a new form of regulation, called the PWC. Even the architect of the WC, Williamson (2000), admitted some of the limitations of the original rubric and the need for change. The PWC has ushered in a new era in the development regime as a whole. With the PWC, there has been a move away from the sole focus of the neoliberal tenets of the WC to an emphasis on poverty alleviation and improving the economy through free-market economics combined with social programs. To a certain extent, development agencies also began to recognize that contextualized solutions were needed.

Poverty alleviation seems to be a more palatable emphasis and is a goal that nearly all would agree is beneficial (Samoff, 2013). This shift in focus became evident in the WB and the IMF's move to use Poverty Reduction Strategy Papers as a basis for loan and development strategies within a given country. These papers are designed to create plans to reduce poverty and promote growth and are developed in collaboration with the country involved (IMF, 2015b). At the same time, it is not clear how much the input of the countries that receive aid is taken into account. To a certain degree, the PWC has continued WC practices because neoliberal principles are still central (Rizvi & Lingard, 2010); indeed, the WB is motivated by an 'efficient investment in human capital' rather than in human rights (Mundy & Manion, 2014, p. 46).

There has, however, been some limited acknowledgement that debt relief is necessary in the PWC era. One such proposal is known as the 'Gleneagles' accord due to the golf course in Scotland where the meeting took place. It allowed 18 countries to stop making payments and would eventually reduce their debt to zero. However, the write-off that the WB used to cover the debt effectively further limited aid to these countries, thus placing them in a compromised and unstable position (Sparke, 2013). As with similar endeavors, the Gleneagles acknowledgment of the need for debt relief had an impact on a small number of countries, leaving the others, the bulk of the postcolonial countries in the Global South, still mired in debt. Another initiative, a collaboration between the IMF and the WB, involves a process for assisting heavily indebted poor countries that is designed to accelerate progress toward global targets, such as the Millennium Development Goals (IMF, 2015a) (see Chap. 4).

Although there has been some movement on debt relief, providing loans with conditions is still central to the aid and development regime. Indeed, it has become the standard for both postcolonial countries and global governance organizations to assume that external support is needed (Samoff, 2013). Over time, the result is that decisions have become increasingly influenced by external agencies and funders who provide support rather than by local governments. Nevertheless, as discussed in the section on resistance to globalization, there is room for agency and national imperatives, especially in the implementation arena.

Despite the continued emphasis on development for economic purposes in the aid and development regime, two new areas of development have emerged as part of the broader human development paradigm[8]: development as human rights and development as freedom (Phillips & Schweisfurth, 2014). The human rights focus has been embraced by many of the global governance organizations, and the UN Declaration of Human Rights (1948) plays a key role in human rights efforts, although it was not fully recognized in the development sphere until the PWC era. Basic rights set out in the declaration include the right to life, liberty, and security; the right not to be subjected to slavery, servitude, or torture; the right to be equally protected before the law; the right to choose a religion; and the right to free and compulsory education. The human rights agenda questions the efficiency of ROR analysis and offers other standard ways to measure progress, such as the HDI, introduced in Chap. 1 (Bajaj, 2014).

Development also may be related to freedom. Indian professor of economics and philosophy Amartya Sen (1999a) demonstrates how economic development is possible only if humans are free from oppression. Sen proposed a capabilities approach[9] that emphasizes basic rights that are important to development as well as to economic prosperity, such as language rights and freedom against various forms of discrimination. The work of Brazilian educator Paulo Freire (1970, 1973, 1998) also has been influential to the notion of development as freedom. Freire argues that the modern system of education involves a 'banking' system in which teachers deposit information into students, who recite it uncritically. He advocates for a liberating form of education that allows students to develop a critical consciousness regarding the world in which they live, causing them to seek to transform it. Freire's impact was not limited to the realm of education, however, and his work was particularly influential in countries in the

Global South that were experiencing regime changes in the postcolonial era.[10] These alternative ways of viewing development provide fresh perspectives that the development and aid regime has taken into account to a certain degree in the PWC era with its greater emphasis on human and social development. These emphases are also reflected in the development of specific initiatives in education, such as the Education for All agenda, as discussed in Chap. 4.

Whatever the failings of the development regime in the PWC era, there has been a clear shift from focusing on economic growth as an end point in and of itself to using it as a means to reduce poverty and improve other social domains, such as healthcare, education, and human rights (Shields, 2013). As such, development has involved a broader range of activities in the PWC time period, which is a positive step. Nevertheless, questions remain regarding the potential for neocolonialism, particularly given the specific solutions for reforms that are offered to countries in the Global South as a condition of obtaining loans. Moreover, there is still an emphasis on bringing countries in the Global South 'up' to Global North levels, while the bar continually moves because the Global North's economic indicators improve over time. Operating under the PWC, the aid and development regime has also continued to ignore the circumstances under which countries in the Global South came to be poorer, namely, through domination and colonialism by the Global North. The domination of the WC and the PWC has not gone uncontested however, and numerous resistance movements have arisen to counter these notions as well as to counter the economic focus of contemporary globalization.

Resistance to Globalization

Despite the profound influence of global governance organizations, especially IMOs, in the contemporary era of globalization, resistance to globalization has been significant. As indicated in Chap. 1, resistance to globalization is not necessarily a rejection of globalization entirely. Sparke (2013) argues that Friedman and other hyperglobalist commentators too easily dismiss resistance movements as anti-globalization and, therefore, unrealistic. Although anarchist organizations, right-wing nationalist movements,[11] and some individuals seek to obliterate globalization entirely, most resistance to globalization is critical in nature and is centered on reforming it and alleviating its negative effects. Critical forms of resistance often focus on the dominant form of globalization that is propounded throughout the world (market globalism) and, thus, to a great extent, emphasize the negative effects of economic forms of globalization, including heightened social inequalities, enhanced marginalization of the poor, and increased consumerism that fuels individual self-interest.

Scholars and activists have sought to contest the notion (or myth) that neoliberalism leads to greater equalities, and they have often rejected the commonly held view that neoliberalism and capitalism are the only option and path toward development (Rodrik, 2011; Sen, 2005; Shiva, 2005; Stromquist & Monkman, 2014). Additional areas of concern are the cultural, political, and environmental aspects of globalization, and critics often focus on negative impacts, such as global environmental degradation, erosion of participatory forms of democracy, and increasing conflicts and violence that take place on a global scale. Resistance has been waged at various levels, including the global, regional, nation-state, and local levels.

In the global domain, social justice organizations and individuals, operating from Steger's (2013) justice globalism perspective, have been involved in a global social justice movement since the 1990s. The movement has variously been labeled 'globalization from below', 'people's globalization', and 'grassroots globalization' (Sparke, 2013). The network involved in this movement includes both international and domestic NGOs and individuals not affiliated with a specific group. According to Steger, this global movement for social justice sees itself as a global civil society centered on the belief that 'another world is possible' (p. 118). The movement's focus is not only on inequalities that exist between the Global North and Global South, but also on the environment, women's rights, fair trade and workers' rights, indigenous people's rights, and numerous other concerns.

Although this global social justice movement is composed of a compilation of organizations and individuals focused on a wide range of injustices, they have joined together around a rejection of market globalism and its neoliberal tenets as a dominant ideology. Even those organizations that are focused on local issues (e.g., indigenous rights) acknowledge the need for collaboration with other alter-globalization[12] entities in the world (Sparke, 2013). The global social justice movement and the organizations and individuals within it share the view that globalization from above should be countered and that there should be a 'Global New Deal' in which wealth and power would be redistributed to counter the negative effects of neoliberal globalization on marginalized, poorer countries and individuals (Steger, 2013).

Global social justice movements coordinated to resist neoliberal globalization took place throughout the 1990s and 2000s, and similar protests continue today. In November 1999, the WTO held its annual meeting in Seattle, Washington. Approximately 50,000 people from hundreds of different local and international groups and organizations protested the WTO's policies related to neoliberalism in what is known as the 'Battle for Seattle'. Protestors, mostly peaceful, blocked traffic and delayed the proceedings. Inside the meeting, talks stalled when representatives from the Global South chose not to sign on to resolutions regarding international labor and environmental standards that came from the Global North. Other protests have followed over the years, including one that shut down the April 2000 meeting of the IMF and the WB in Washington, DC, and another that interrupted the IMF and the WB meeting in September 2000 in Prague. In July 2001, 100,000 protestors gathered to protest the G8[13] summit in Genoa, Italy, and protests are held every year at the World Economic Forum (WEF) meeting in Davos, Switzerland.[14]

Most recently, the Occupy movement, which started in New York City as *Occupy Wall Street* and spread across the USA and to many other countries in the world, has served as another opportunity to protest neoliberal globalization. The Occupy movement focuses on global inequalities and how the elite 1 % in the world dominate the remaining 99 %. Importantly, the Occupy movement and many other protests and efforts to counter neoliberal globalization use communications technology and social media (e.g., text messaging, Facebook, Twitter) to coordinate events and build support (Sparke, 2013). The use of communications and media technology that are available due to globalization is significant and reflects protestors' efforts to alter the current course of globalization rather than to stop it entirely. Indeed, these movements provide a space for alter-globalization efforts to emerge (Kahn & Kellner, 2007; Sparke, 2013; Steger, 2013).

The 2000s also ushered in the emergence of multiple international organizations that stand in opposition to the impact and policies of neoliberal global governance organizations. One prominent example is the World Social Forum (WSF), which is essentially a counter organization to the market-globalist WEF (Steger, 2013) and often meets during the same time period as the WEF. The WSF Charter of Principles includes providing an open meeting space for groups that oppose neoliberalism and that are seeking alternatives to the current dominant form of globalization. It is, however, loosely organized and does not have clear leaders. Another group is the People-Centered Development Forum, which argues that neoliberal globalization as it stands is inevitable only because we have allowed it to be this way; like other groups, the forum acknowledges that economic forms of globalization are not inevitable (Sparke, 2013). Other groups that are fighting against the influence of neoliberal globalization include the Third World Network and International Forum on Globalization, Popular Resistance, and the Peoples' Global Action Network.

In the regional domain, several organizations and movements have evolved over the years. For example, the green parties in Europe are part of the protest of neoliberal globalization (Steger, 2013). The 2001 Porte Alegre Declaration, which was signed by activist groups in Iberia and Latin America, is another such example. This declaration focused on rejecting deregulation policies that the signatories argued served to derail the sovereignty of nation-states and alter local cultural values and practices. Despite the impact of this declaration, many of the nation-states involved found it difficult to resist pressure from aid and development agencies to accept deregulation, especially because they were in need of further aid (Rizvi & Lingard, 2010). To a certain extent, the Arab Spring of 2010 and 2011 might be considered a resistance movement that counters neoliberal forms of globalization. Although the Arab Spring was essentially a pro-democracy movement and contestation of repression, it also was brought on by economic circumstances that are connected to neoliberal globalization. Even though resistance efforts have not always proven to be lasting, collectively, they serve to counter dominant forms of globalization.

Resistance also has been seen at the nation-state and local levels. As an example of national resistance, in the early 1990s, Zambia rejected all food aid from INGOs and bilateral organizations that included genetically modified organisms (GMOs). The country was concerned about how GMOs would affect local food sources and opted not to subject its citizenry to the possible ramifications of accepting food aid that contained GMOs. Several countries in Latin America have been particularly vocal about rejecting some or all of the conditions of the WC and PWC. For example, Argentina and Bolivia waged uprisings against neoliberalism in 2002. University students across Latin America also have been vocal about their opposition to neoliberal globalization and its ramifications. For instance, students held a strike at the National Autonomous University of Mexico in 1999 against tuition increases amid pressure from IMOs for the government to reduce public expenditures on higher education. The protest involved more than an anti-globalization event, and the protestors leveled criticism against imperialism and privatization that they associated with changes due to globalization (Rhoads, 2003).

At the local level, India's Chipko movement and the Zapatista uprising in Mexico provide two poignant examples of resistance by the Global South. The Chipko movement was centered on environmental destruction from deforestation; the local population relied on the forests for their livelihoods. In 1973, a protest took place in the village of Mandal, in which local women encircled trees that the government had provided a company a license to fell. The protest was successful, and the tree cutting company retreated. Similar protests continued to spread throughout India, with much success, and served as a basis for international movements against deforestation connected to globalization. The Chipko movement also emphasized the need for peaceful protests and the importance of women in efforts to resist globalization. This latter point is salient because women have often been the most negatively affected by neoliberalism and SAPs (Steger, 2013).

On January 1, 1994, when the North American Free Trade Agreement (NAFTA)[15] went into effect, the Zapatistas, led by the Zapatista Army of National Liberation, mounted a resistance campaign. The movement involved indigenous rebels who seized four major cities in Chiapas and demanded to reestablish control over local national resources that TNCs had monopolized in the region. Although this movement was waged at the local level against the Mexican government and its involvement in NAFTA, the Zapatistas gained an international following via the Internet. Thousands of international activists protested with the Zapatistas in Chiapas in later years, and the uprising was critical to advancing other counter-globalization efforts, such as the Battle for Seattle (Johnston & Laxer, 2003). The Zapatistas emphasized the localized nature of their issue, while recognizing that resistance to neoliberalism needs to be global in nature, and advanced a comprehensive agenda to counter the negative impacts of neoliberal globalization (Steger, 2013). Through local movements, these countries and other local entities have succeeded in expressing their agency and in resisting the imposition of dictates made by the Global North and its associated governance organizations.

Conclusion

The contemporary period of globalization has ushered in a number of significant worldwide developments, including advances in communications and technology, international mobility, economic changes and the spread of neoliberalism and Western capitalism, the decline of the welfare state, a new international hierarchy of labor connected to Post-Fordism, the advent of the knowledge economy, and changing cultural patterns. In the post-WWII era, the aid and development regime has evolved, along with the emergence of global governance institutions, as a result of the WC and the PWC. At the same time, dominant global governance institutions and TNCs are not the only actors, and nation-states, communities, individuals, and others also actively participate in the policymaking and implementation processes. Local actors also exercise agency to resist the dominant, neoliberal form of globalization. Further, advances in communications and technology have helped disparate organizations and individuals collaborate and unite for shared action. As educators, our awareness of the impact of globalization and the interconnections between global and local actors in policy processes is important for understanding not only global educational reforms but also local endeavors.

Notes

1. Daniel Bell (1973) coined the term 'post-industrial society' to refer to the system that was becoming dominant in the Global North and was increasingly focused on information. The post-industrial society involved (a) increasing the emphasis on scientific industries and innovations, (b) moving from an economy focused on manufacturing goods to one that provides services, and (c) establishing a new group of technical elites. These notions align with Castells' (1996) 'Network Society' and the global knowledge economy, which are discussed in Chap. 3.
2. Keynesian economics derives its name from John Maynard Keynes (1936), a British economist who wrote the influential book *The General Theory of Employment, Interest and Money* during the Great Depression.
3. Although welfare states are no longer common, modern-day welfare states do exist, for example, in the Nordic countries of Denmark, Finland, Iceland, Norway, and Sweden. These countries continue to combine high taxation and provision of social services to all, including healthcare, childcare, and pensions.
4. Another type of corporation that is closely tied to TNCs is the multinational corporation (MNC). The terms TNC and MNC are often used interchangeably; however, MNCs differ in that they do not operate commodity chains across borders or offshore their production without outsourcing (Sparke, 2013).

5. These treaties, which were preceded by monarchies and empires, ended the Thirty Years' War of the Holy Roman Empire and the Eighty Years' War between Spain and the Netherlands Republic. The treaties are named after the German state of Westphalia, in which the talks took place.
6. Foreign direct investment is investment that comes from outside sources (e.g., TNCs).
7. See Chap. 3 for a discussion of neocolonialism as a theoretical construct.
8. This paradigm has four main considerations: equity, sustainability, empowerment, and productivity (see Phillips & Schweisfurth, 2014).
9. Sen earned a Nobel Prize in Economics in 1998 for his development of this approach.
10. For example, *Pedagogy of the Oppressed* was a key text for the anti-apartheid struggle in South Africa.
11. These movements, such as the British National Party, practice xenophobia and seek to preserve their cultural and religious traditions. These groups may be organized around racial/ethnic lines (e.g., White supremacy) or religion and often seek to limit immigration while maintaining existing social hierarchies.
12. As noted in Chap. 1, the term 'alter-globalization' is common in current discourse, as opposed to 'anti-globalization', which suggests a complete rejection of globalization. Alternative forms of globalization are now commonly suggested to counter 'predatory globalization' (globalization from above) rather than anti-globalization, per se (Falk, 1999).
13. Originally established as the Group of 6 in 1985 (including France, Germany, Italy, Japan, the UK, and the USA), the G8 has historically focused on economic policy, particularly reforms and measures associated with neoliberalism (Sparke, 2013). Canada became a member (and the group was known as the G7), as did Russia, bringing the total countries to 8 (G8). Russia subsequently lost its membership due to its military actions in the Ukraine, and the group is now known as the G7 again.
14. The World Economic Forum brings together elite business leaders and government officials each year at a resort in the Alps. Political scientist Samuel Huntington (1996) referred to the elites who frequent this meeting as sharing a 'Davos culture' that governs their exchanges and makes them feel comfortable with interacting with others from this group. This notion has been utilized frequently since that time to characterize and critique the elite group of people who control a large part of the world's economy.
15. NAFTA is a free-trade agreement between Canada, Mexico, and the USA designed to reduce barriers to trade and investment between the countries. NAFTA eliminates export tariffs, reduces other trade barriers, and secures intellectual property rights.

CHAPTER 3

Theorizing Globalization

Studying theories and constructs related to globalization allows us to delve further into its complex set of associated processes and developments. This chapter provides an in-depth presentation of a wide range of theories and constructs that have been used to study globalization, most of which originate outside the educational realm.[1] Theories and constructs specific to education and its intersection with globalization also are included, and I provide brief explanations of how theories and constructs that originate from other domains have been used to analyze education and globalization, where applicable. Although some of the theories cited here predate the field of global studies and may not be what some would refer to as 'globalization theories' per se, globalization scholars or policymakers from the aid and development regime frequently employ these theories to understand contemporary globalization and develop reforms, including those in the educational arena.

There is no established way to categorize or organize the theories and constructs related to globalization; various authors who cover this spectrum of theories do so in different ways. Many of the theories included in this chapter originated in one discipline, while scholars from other disciplines later adopted (and often adapted) them. For example, poststructuralism arose from the traditions of philosophy and literary criticism and is now used in sociology, political science, and education.

© The Editor(s) (if applicable) and The Author(s) 2016

L.M. Portnoi, *Policy Borrowing and Reform in Education*,
DOI 10.1057/978-1-137-53024-0_3

Importantly, theories and constructs are not neutral, and scholars' theoretical perspectives determine the ways they define the processes associated with globalization (Robinson, 2007). This chapter emphasizes competing and complementary theories and constructs as well as how differing approaches to globalization have led to a variety of perspectives in the literature.

This chapter begins with an overview of the foundational theoretical domains on which many theories and constructs are built. First, I make the distinction between modern and postmodern analysis at the high theoretical level. I then briefly describe two salient areas of modern analysis: Marxism and structural-functionalism. I do so not to privilege modern analyses but, rather, as a way to set a foundation for the reader because many of the critical and postmodern theories arose as critiques to, or extensions of, structural-functionalism and Marxism. I then briefly explain conflict theory and the constellation of critical theories that became popular in scholarly circles from the 1970s onward before delineating the theories that have been used in studying globalization, highlighting their connections to education, where applicable. In the final section, I provide an overview of additional theoretical constructs that are central to the study of globalization.

Foundational Theoretical Domains

Before discussing specific theories and constructs related to globalization, I need to point out a significant distinction between two high-level theoretical domains that have set the parameters for many specific theories and constructs: modernism and postmodernism. Importantly, distinctions between modern and postmodern approaches apply to all social and cultural theories, not only to those related to globalization. Modernism has been the dominant paradigm throughout most of the history of Western thought, from the medieval period through the late 1970s and 1980s, when postmodernism rose as a competing paradigm. Modernism is a particular way of viewing the possibilities and direction of human life. It is rooted in Enlightenment[2] thinking and focuses on rational thought, scientific observation, and objective versions of reality. Modernism also presumes stages of progress and posits that humans will gain increased freedom and success as they move through these stages.

Modernism and Postmodernism

Modernism and postmodernism represent two competing overarching theoretical domains, under which theories related to globalization may be positioned. Modernism has been dominant throughout history, while postmodernism arose as a counter to modernism in the 1970s and 1980s. In modernism, theorists presume that a series of linear stages represent the progression of human progress (individually or as nation-states). Modernists privilege rational thought, scientific observation, and objective reality. In contrast, postmodernists argue that multiple versions of reality exist; they also reject the notion of stages of progress. Postmodern theories generally maintain a critical orientation and focus on alternative views of reality and emphasizing marginalized voices.

Postmodernism arose as a response to modernism in the 1970s, and many contemporary social and cultural theories operate from a postmodern perspective. Postmodernism rejects the modernist view that reality is objective and can be measured rationally; for postmodernism, reality is socially constructed and dynamic. It also dismisses the premise that humans go through stages of progress. Postmodernism is closely intertwined with poststructuralism (see below) and is intentionally difficult to describe, as it has no set rules or standard assumptions. Postmodernism encourages alternative views of reality, emphasizes voices from the marginal (also known as subaltern) perspective, and is generally associated with critical approaches to understanding social and cultural phenomena, including globalization.

Now that I have presented this overview of the parameters of modern and postmodern analyses, I turn to a discussion of two modern perspectives that have proven to be foundational to many of the theories of globalization discussed in this chapter: Marxism and structural-functionalism.[3] Marxism, which takes the name of its chief creator, Karl Marx,[4] is, at its core, an economic theory of capitalism, the structure of society, and class struggle. Operating in the mid-nineteenth century, Marx was writing at a critical juncture in human history in which capitalism was beginning to take root. Marx argued that history is the product and process of human labor and that human beings create themselves through labor.

In Marxism, the structure of capitalism is viewed as having a division of labor that falls into two distinctive classes: the bourgeoisie (or capitalists), who own and control the means of production and extract labor from workers, and the proletariat (or workers). Marxism suggests that working for others' profit causes the proletariat to become 'alienated' from their labor. In this way, capitalism dehumanizes people. At the same time, resistance is a key component of Marxism; Marx saw class struggle as leading to a revolution that would overthrow capitalism and replace it with communism. By the end of World War II (WWII), Marxism had become a central theory in sociology (Seidman, 2008), and it remains an influential basis for other areas of theory, such as conflict theory and the general constellation of critical theories, some of which are Marxist and others of which are neo-Marxist or post-Marxist, as described below.

During the mid-twentieth century, roughly coinciding with the development of new global governance organizations, structural-functionalism (also called functionalism) competed with Marxism as a predominant theoretical lens and came to dominate social and cultural analyses in many disciplines. It remained a significant theoretical approach for several decades and has since become less influential, while conflict and other critical theories have risen in prominence. Key theorists, such as Talcott Parsons and Robert Merton, created structural-functionalism, in which society is viewed as a functioning social system, as an alternative to Marxism (Kubow & Fossum, 2007). Drawing from the biological metaphor of the human body, Parsons and other structural-functionalists argued that each part of the social system is necessary for it to function. Social order would be possible through both social coordination and cultural consensus. In this model, social coordination involved a fit between the motivations and needs of individuals and the requirement for people to play various roles in the social system. To maintain its equilibrium and avoid convict, the system also required a minimal level of shared understandings and values through cultural consensus.

Structural-functionalism was built on modern notions of progress, which, for this theory, involved moving toward a higher degree of individual freedom, democracy, and social integration. Although not a humanist perspective, due to its acceptance of inequalities as natural for the system's functionality, structural-functionalism was optimistic in a certain sense because it allowed for the possibility for societies to work together to develop shared norms and values (Kubow & Fossum, 2007). It is noteworthy that structural-functionalism was prominent in the field of education due to Parsons' (1959) influential analysis of the school as a social system that performs a key role in socialization to societal roles and shared values. Structural-functionalists would view education systems as a means for sorting people into their respective 'biological' functions, while overlooking the inequalities regarding which racial and socio-economic groups take on which roles in society. Although structural-functionalism has fallen out of favor in scholarly circles, it is still reflected in education—for example, in the prevailing belief in a meritocratic system in which success is viewed as due to individual effort and in which the inequities of social structures are discounted.

Before moving into an explication of theories and constructs of globalization, I must note two other key developments: the establishment of conflict theory and the rise of a constellation of critical theories rooted in Marxist or neo-Marxist analyses. Conflict theory draws from Marxism and arose as a counter movement to structural-functionalism. With its attempts to create equilibrium at the expense of equality and its reputation as a politically conservative theory, structural-functionalism was critiqued as limiting. Conflict theory emerged as an alternative, although Ritzer (2007) suggests that it was not particularly influential in and of itself because it was simplistically the opposite of structural-functionalism. Conflict theorists essentially agreed with structural-functionalists regarding the way the social system was organized, but they critiqued, rather than accepted, the system as it was. According to conflict theory, order is maintained through coercion and domination. Conflict theorists also critiqued inequalities as existing not due to social consensus but, rather, because the small group in power controls others through domination. Although conflict theory did not enjoy a long-lasting run, it was a useful bridge to a resurgence in the use of Marxian theory (Ritzer, 2007).

Marxism saw a revival in the form of a constellation of critical theories, which were based on Marxism and its antecedent, Critical Theory, and rose in prominence from the 1970s onward. Critical Theory (capitalized) refers to a theoretical paradigm that stems from a group of theorists, including Theodor Adorno, Max Horkheimer, Herbert Marcuse, and Max Weil, who formed the Frankfurt School in 1922 at the University of Frankfurt in Germany. The main thrust of the Frankfurt School theorists' work was to criticize capitalism and its discontents. This group is often considered to be neo-Marxist because, while they drew on Marxism, they added elements from areas outside of economics, such as Freudian psychology. As a broader range of theories, critical theory (not capitalized) refers to a conglomeration of theories, some of which have modernist tendencies (neo-Marxist), while others have postmodernist tendencies (post-Marxist). In the realm of critical theory are critical pedagogy, critical feminism, poststructuralism, and numerous other critical orientations.

With this overview of foundational theoretical domains in view, I now present theories and constructs connected to globalization. In the discussion, I note instances in which these theories have been used in educational analyses, where applicable.

Human Capital Theory

Closely associated with modernization theory, described below, human capital theory (also known as human capital development theory) has been a key driver of the aid and development regime. Human capital theory derives from the study of economics, although it has been appropriated for analyses in many other areas, including education. Economists Jacob Mincer (1958), Theodore Schultz (1963), and Gary Becker (1964) developed the theory to describe the aspects of a person's life that can be considered economically productive. After WWII, the industrialized nations of the Global North sought a way to tap into the ability of human traits to produce economic development and progress to assist countries in the Global South in becoming more 'developed', based on the tenets of modernism. Human capital formation served that purpose because it focuses on developing people to be functional in, and contribute to, an economically advanced society. Human capital theory was, central to the foundation of the aid and development regime that arose after WWII and contributed to the Washington Consensus (WC) and Structural Adjustment Programs, whose negative effects are still felt in many countries of the Global South today.

The development of human capital theory connects to the post-Fordist requirements of the global knowledge economy, in which knowledge is considered to be a commodity alongside more traditional products and commodities. The outcome of investing in human capital leads to the development of 'skills, knowledge, and motivations for economic productivity' (Phillips & Schweisfurth, 2014, p. 86). Tapping into human potential, therefore, became a key component of development, and this theory has (implicitly or explicitly) guided the aid and development regime for many years. Critics have raised concerns, however, regarding this emphasis on the economic gain that can be extracted from human beings. In human capital theory, people are viewed as having the ability to add to their capital; it is not an inherent trait. Indeed, developing human capital is seen as an investment in the creation of wealth (Brown & Lauder, 1997).

Given its potential as an investment in human capital, education has been seen as particularly essential for development (Samoff, 2013). In economic terms, the notion that there is a high return on investment (ROI) for aid and other funding targeted toward education became prevalent. Therefore, human capital theory has been connected to educational analyses for many years. Indeed, many of the economists who developed the theory wrote about education as well. Scholars such as Becker and Schultz have demonstrated how additional years of education provide economic advantages, not only to the person who receives the education but also to a country's economic development. Critical scholars problematize these analyses, however, and question the causal link that economists who employ human capital theory make between education and development for economic competitiveness.

Modernization Theory

Like human capital theory, modernization theory falls in line with the broad modern lens described earlier. It also aligns with the WC views that underlie the aid and development regime that arose in the post-WWII era. Modernization theory was developed during the same time period, when colonial independence movements were taking place and global governance organizations were being established in the era of contemporary globalization. Through modernization theory, progress is viewed as linear, and there is a prescribed pattern of development that countries should follow. Various sectors of development are also viewed as intertwined. For example, one of the early scholars of modernization theory, Seymour Martin Lipsett (1959, 1960) connected social and political progress (based on democratic ideals) to the depth of countries' industrialization and economic development.

Modernization theory privileges a Western view of development and suggests that, for countries to improve socially, they must emulate the development patterns of countries from the Global North. In his influential work *The Stages of Economic Growth*, Walt Rostow (1960) prescribed five stages of development based largely on the trajectory of European countries: (a) a stage of traditional societies' characterized by subsistence agriculture, low technological innovation, and monarchies or dictatorships; (b) a stage of preparing for 'takeoff', when countries are ready to industrialize and become 'advanced' economies because they are beginning to shift from agricultural to industrial societies, experience more technological innovations, and trade becomes more common; (c) a period of economic takeoff, in which countries achieve technological innovation and economic progress and integrate with the global market; (d) the drive toward maturity when countries realize lasting economic growth that involves the application of technologies; and (e) an age of high mass consumption in which countries' populations experience high industrialization and greater degrees of wealth. According to modernization theory, education and other social institutions are key to development because they provide avenues for Western values associated with the Global North (e.g., individualism, democracy) to be fostered throughout countries all over the world (Kubow & Fossum, 2007).

This linear view of modernization, with its one-size-fits-all approach, provided the foundation for the WC, which, as discussed in Chap. 2, proved to be problematic because it did not account for local variations or the particularities of the postcolonial experience in the Global South that differed from that of European countries. Nevertheless, the use of modernization theory led to the notion that aid and loans were necessary to reach higher stages of development. Modernization theory had originally been proposed as a progressive view in which equality plays a significant role; however, modernization did not lead to equality for the countries that had 'arrived' at the final stage of development or among countries on the worldwide stage (Stromquist & Monkman, 2014). The view of modernization as a means for countries in the Global South to emulate countries in the Global North also has been criticized for portraying countries in the Global South as deficient and neglecting to recognize the contributions that these countries may have been able to make even while following a different path. In addition, modernization theory assumes that the problems evident in the Global South are due to internal issues rather than to external forces, such as colonialism (Samoff, 2013).

Dependency Theory and World-System Theory

Dependency theory and world-system theory are similar, and the terms are often used interchangeably. Both theories are critical in nature and focus on the unequal relationships between different types of countries throughout the world. Both dependency theory and world-system theory arose as critiques of modernization theory's emphasis on one form of development for all nation-states and its failure to recognize the importance of global governance organizations as units of analysis. Both theories challenge the rise of capitalism and neoliberal ideals as well as the assumption that equality will result from the free market system. Dependency theory, which originates from Latin American economists and scholars,[5] including Raúl Prebisch (1950), Theotonio dos Santos (1970), and Fernando Henrique Cardoso (1972), focuses on the exploitation of poorer countries in a growing unequal distribution of power between the Global North and Global South. World-system theory, developed by US sociologist Immanuel Wallerstein (1974, 2010), expands and builds upon dependency theory. Although there are nuanced differences between the two theories—for example, dependency theory focuses to a larger extent on exploitation—I concentrate on what the two approaches have in common when describing these theories in this section.

In contrast to world culture theory, which has a benign, perhaps utopian, outlook on the diffusion of world culture (see below), dependency and world-system theories view the role of the international aid and development regime as prescribing a dominant set of values of the Global North, particularly the elite. These theories stem from a critical perspective that questions the inevitability of globalization and, instead, views it as geopolitical power positioning. Wallerstein (1974) argued, for example, that the modern world-system and its unequal division of labor are not a given; rather, they result from the dominant world-system in place at this time, which emphasizes capitalism and global economic integration. Importantly, these theories are based on the notion that globalization is not new but has existed for hundreds of years.

According to world-system and dependency theories, the world is organized into three types of countries: core, periphery, and semi-periphery.[6] A small group of core countries from the Global North dominate; they have high per capita incomes, high economic integration into the world-system, high capital accumulation, and a strong military. Core countries are centered on high-skilled, post-Fordist types of labor and production. Countries on the periphery, mainly those in the postcolonial Global South, constitute the largest group and are dependent on the core to a large degree because the core dictates the 'rules of the game'. Peripheral countries have lower per capita income, low capital accumulation, and a weaker military, and their production is focused on low-skill activities, often those that involve the exportation of raw materials.

Semi-periphery countries typically come from the periphery originally (although they could be core countries that are being 'downgraded') and have industrialized to an extent that places them in between core and periphery countries. Nation-states on the semi-periphery seek to align themselves with the core and typically take all measures necessary to maintain progress away from their periphery status, including opening their markets and signing on to conventions or other political mandates supported by the Global North. Although the category of BRICS countries (Brazil, Russia, India, China, and South Africa, as described in Chap. 1) was not used when dependency theory and world-system theory were created, these countries are the type that would fall within the semi-periphery. Key to the three-tiered world-system is the premise that the competition it engenders leads to the reproduction of this hierarchical system (Robinson, 2007).

In dependency theory, in particular, the core is viewed as exploitative of the periphery, which extracts certain resources for distribution to the core. In world-system theory, a greater number of players are involved due to the addition of the semi-periphery as a category and the inequalities that exist within countries. Despite these nuanced differences, both analyses mimic Marxism at the global level, with the core countries representing the bourgeoisie and the periphery countries serving as the proletariat (Kubow & Fossum, 2007; Shields, 2013). Because countries from the Global North dominate not only in the world-system but also within global governance organizations, they are key to dictating mandates from the core. Therefore, these global governance organizations are part of the process of prescribing a hegemonic set of values for the rest of the world. Critical theorist Antonio Gramsci (1971) suggested that hegemony is a constellation of beliefs and assumptions that become taken for granted and assert dominance in a social system without using force. Instead, implicit consent is given by those who participate in the process of the ruling class or group's asserting dominance over subordinate classes—in this case, of core over periphery countries. The current world economic system of capitalism, including the values of neoliberalism, represents the hegemonic discourse. World-system theory suggests that nation-states are complicit in this process because they align with these hegemonic values to maintain or, perhaps, to change their status in the world.

Dependency and world-system analyses have been used to understand education, particularly with regard to explaining the 'global' model of schooling that has developed (see Chap. 4). These analyses have also been used to explain that evolving educational systems around the world are set up not to provide education for the world's populace but, rather, to ensure the unequal world-system in which the core countries dominate. Through education, world-system theorists would argue, the young people of the world learn the fundamental values of capitalism and to accept as 'normal' the hierarchical nature of the global division of labor. In essence, education is a key part of the process of the core's maintaining power over the periphery. Although dependency theory and world-system theory are neo-Marxist in nature, and notions of struggle are evident in their analyses, theorists from this domain do not provide clear alternatives to the prevailing world-system that they critique. Dependency and world-system analyses, nevertheless, have provided a clear way to understand the dominance of the core over the periphery, and, thus, have been influential.

World Culture Theory

World culture theory, also known as world polity or neoinstitutional theory, posits that there is increasingly one world culture to which all nation-states and their populaces subscribe. This world culture is built upon Western ideals and cultural values, including democratic governance, individual rights, and rational thought. According to world culture theorists such as Frank Lechner and John Boli (2010), the global governance institutions that emerged after WWII are central to the diffusion of a world culture because member states and countries that receive aid are typically encouraged to accept universal norms and must often sign on to conventions that align with the values of their peers of their peers (e.g., indigenous or human rights). This tendency to create similar structures and policies based on worldwide standards and norms is called isomorphism.

World culture theory espouses the 'convergence' narrative that is popular with hyperglobalists who subscribe to the TINA (there is no alternative) approach. At the same time, world culture theorists argue that cultural changes are central to developments inherent in globalization, rather than just the economic dimension. Despite growing convergence, world culture theorists would contend that there is no one central actor that is orchestrating the development of a global culture. World culture theory posits that, although global governance organizations are highly involved, nation-states remain the central units of analysis, or the key 'rational actors' in the global sphere because they are heavily involved in the global governance organizations that establish norms (Meyer, Boli, Thomas, & Ramirez, 1997). Further, in world culture theory, global governance organizations are considered to be benign benefactors that represent nation-states through the consensus of member countries rather than the global elite (Shields, 2013).

World culture theory developed from the work of a group of sociologists from Stanford University, including John Boli, George Thomas, Francisco Ramirez, and John Meyer. These scholars and others have theorized about world culture and education, specifically. Thus, world culture theory is a commonly cited perspective for understanding how globalization has an impact in the educational sphere. The provision of formal schooling in countries throughout the world would be categorized as an early manifestation of world culture, while current trends in schooling, such as standardization, accountability, and testing as well as massification and global competition in higher education, might be cited as demonstrating further evidence of this increasingly global culture today (see Chap. 4). Education is also particularly important to world culture theory because educational institutions serve as one of the primary mechanisms for the diffusion of the world culture, especially the notion that education is a right that all citizens should have in a democracy (Shields, 2013; Spring, 2015).

Given that world culture is posited as developing through the consensus of nation-states, it is often perceived as reflecting 'best practices' in education. Certain scholars, particularly those who operate from a critical perspective, would critique this view, citing the power differentials that exist with regard to what types of countries have been central to the diffusion of a common system of education—namely, those in the Global North that play a key role in international organizations and politics. Other critical scholars, especially those who operate from the culturalist approach, question the convergence perspective altogether, suggesting that the notion is more imagined than real. The convergence-culturalist debate is the focus of a section in Chap. 4.

World Culture Theory and the Culturalist Approach

World culture theory and the culturalist approach offer differing ways to understand the impact of globalization. These competing perspectives are central to the study of education and globalization specifically. World culture theory is a normative approach that assumes convergence, or isomorphism, in the similar structures and policies that are emerging in various sectors throughout the world, including those in the domains of schooling and higher education. For world cultural theorists, the 'best' models and practices rise to the top and are diffused around the world. Culturalists are decidedly more critical of the impact globalization has had on education. They recognize that an increasingly global model of education is emerging, though they reject the notion that there is a consensus on the 'best' practices. For culturalists, local contexts are significant and serve to mediate global trends.

The Culturalist Approach

Another form of analysis of the impact of globalization, the 'culturalist' approach, emerged from the realm of education specifically (Spring, 2008, 2015). In line with the general parameters of the critical tradition, the culturalist approach to globalization questions the assumptions inherent in world culture theory, particularly the notion that education models around the world are becoming uniform and that there is a consensus regarding what the 'best practices' are or should be. Both the world culture and culturalist domains view culture as central, although in very different ways. From a culturalist perspective, it is important to recognize that globalization has a direct impact on education, although culturalists would discount the notion that there is a common global model of education on which an international community of experts has agreed (Steiner-Khamsi, 2012). Researchers in this domain demonstrate how there may be a certain level of 'policy talk' around uniform models in education, while the on-the-ground realities may be quite different. They also show how global governance institutions may provide conflicting advice that does not always follow the neoliberal paradigm that these institutions tend to espouse (Spring, 2015). In other words, culturalists reject the convergence hypothesis and argue that borrowing educational policies does not constitute a wholesale adoption of them, especially not in practice.

Moreover, the culturalist approach objects to the deterministic outlook of world-system theory that appears to be overly pessimistic with regard to the way in which the world has been divided into a tiered, competitive system. Whereas world-system theorists would argue that the core/periphery system in place is not inevitable but, rather, is particularly intransigent, culturalists would take the analysis a step further to emphasize the possibility of local resistance to and mediation of global trends. For culturalists, local culture is still central to the development of policies and reforms. When global trends are implemented in local contexts, they are adapted to the conditions and needs present in many cases. Another aspect of the culturalist position is the acknowledgment that a variety of types of knowledge and educational models exist (Spring, 2015), as I describe in more detail in Chap. 4. Much of the scholarship in the domain of policy borrowing and lending stems from a culturalist approach and is the focus of Chap. 6.

Theories That Emphasize Global Capitalism

A constellation of theories and constructs emphasizes global capitalism. At the heart of theories related to global capitalism is a critique of its structure. As such, texts in this domain are critical in nature. Differing from world-system theory (and the culturalist approach), theories related to global capitalism tend to view the onset of globalization as relatively new and as coinciding with the development of a worldwide system of capitalism in which financial markets and economies across the world are increasingly interconnected (Robinson, 2007). Key to global capitalism theories are Leslie Sklair's (2005, 2010) notions of transnational practices (TNPs) and the transnational capitalist class (TCC) that are part of his 'global system theory'.

According to Sklair (2005), TNPs are practices that are carried out across borders that are not initiated by actors from nation-states (e.g., governments, national institutions); nation-state actors may be involved in TNPs but are not their drivers. TNPs function in three spheres: economic, political, and cultural-ideological. In alignment with the transnationalists, who bridge the hyperglobalist and skeptic points of view (see Chap. 1), Sklair argues that the current global system is dominated by capitalism, although this does not have to be the case. In other words, it is not inevitable and can be changed. He also suggests that, even if it is becoming increasingly challenging to do so, it is possible to function outside of the global capitalist system. Sklair contends that TNCs and the TCC are the 'building blocks' of global system theory.

People who belong to the TCC tend to work across borders as part of their everyday lives and have a 'globalizing', rather than a locally bounded, perspective. Sklair (2005) argues that, although there are four factions of the TCC that form the global elite—corporate (TNC operators and their affiliates), state (bureaucrats and politicians who work globally), technical (skilled professionals who interact across borders), and consumerist (merchants and media)—there is a collective TCC that makes decisions that protect the interests of the class. The TCC also shares common lifestyles and tastes, for example, as consumers of luxury goods. The notion of the TCC is, thus, similar to Samuel Huntington's (1996) notion of Davos sophisticates who attend events such as the World Economic Forum. Sklair contends that, despite the impact of TNPs and the TCC that guides them, the TINA narrative is too fatalistic. Thus, Sklair suggests ways to transcend capitalist globalization, including socialist globalization, in which human rights replace the consumerist ideology.

Sociologist William Robinson (2001, 2004, 2010) provides a similar perspective. His theory of global capitalism has three main components: transnational production, a transnational state (TNS), and transnational capitalists. As a theorist of global capitalism aligned with the view that globalization is relatively recent, Robinson argues that there was an 'epochal shift' as the world transitioned from nationally based economies to one global or transnational economy. In this new stage of world capitalism, production becomes transnational through the process of globalization. Robinson argues that there is a TNS that operates as a form of global governance. Differing from Sklair (2005) and others who emphasize the rise of global governance organizations as a function of globalization, however, Robinson acknowledges the interplay of the global and local. He argues that it is not only the TNS that comprises the overarching structure but also nation-states. The latter's interests are globalized, and they are players in the process of capitalist globalization. This structure is set up to reproduce the circumstances that have allowed global capitalism to dominate. A third key component of Robinson's theory of global capitalism is the transnational capitalists, who are similar to Sklair's TCC. They are the class of people who manage and operate within the globalized circuits of the transnational production process. According to Robinson, capitalist globalization has resulted in a new form of class relations that exacerbates inequalities both within countries and between countries in the Global North and Global South.

Globalization as Empire

Closely connected to theories of global capitalism is Michael Hardt and Antonio Negri's (2000, 2004) notion of Empire. Hardt and Negri, whose analysis extends beyond the economic domain, contend that global capitalism is a central driving force of globalization. According to Hardt and Negri, Empire (with a capital 'e') is a new economic, cultural, and political order in the age of globalization that differs fundamentally from the prior imperialist agenda that dominated colonialism and coincided with the spread of capitalism. In this sense, Hardt and Negri share with the theorists of global capitalism the view of the current era as new or markedly different from the past. Although Empire is broader than global capitalism theories that focus on the economic realm, it has been criticized for not fully considering the cultural dimensions of globalization. Empire involves a new type of sovereignty, 'a single logic of rule', in which nation-states, TNCs, and global governance institutions share power (Hardt & Negri, 2000). In this system, there is no one central power or controlling force.

In contrast to Sklair (2005) and Robinson (2001, 2004), Hardt and Negri (2000, 2004) do not envision a TCC that is integral to the process. Instead, the central power is 'faceless' and therefore not identifiable (Robinson, 2007). According to Hardt and Negri, this shift in power sharing is a byproduct of the changes that occur as we move from a modern society in which nation-states were key, hierarchical relationships prevailed, and Fordism dominated production to a post-Fordist, postmodern society in which numerous kinds of entities are part of the power dynamic. Hardt and Negri, however, are not deterministic and suggest, in neo-Marxist fashion, the possibility of counter-Empire and resistance through the 'multitude', a collective of revolutionary thinkers that is made possible by the lack of boundaries in Empire.[7] Hardt and Negri contend that Empire is 'digging its own grave' due to the vast multitude that will rise up against it (Sparke, 2013).

Networks and Flows in Globalization Theory

Several authors, most notably Arjun Appadurai (1996) and Manuel Castells (1996, 1997, 1998), write about globalization from a perspective of flows or networks. In contrast to global capitalism and Empire analyses, Appadurai's investigation focuses on the cultural dimension of globalization to a large degree, and he delineates the tension between cultural homogenization and cultural heterogenization. He acknowledges that there is a certain amount of homogenization that occurs as people across the world are exposed to elements of global culture (e.g., music, fashion). At the same time, Appadurai states that, due to the heterogeneity that remains, new forms of hybrid cultures are evolving that 'indigenize' elements of other cultures or global culture by integrating them into their own. This process is related to the construct of 'vernacular globalization' (see below).

Appadurai's (1996) analysis centers on five 'landscapes' that individuals confront and reshape in their local contexts, which are interrelated and in a constant state of flux. 'Ethnoscapes' involve the flow of people across borders (e.g., for immigration, commerce, travel, study abroad), resulting in fluid societies and communities that are continually exchanging cultures. 'Financescapes' concern the constantly changing economy that is not easily manipulated, while 'technoscapes' involve advances in technology that change the frequency, speed, and modality of our interactions that now occur across boundaries that were previously closed. Appadurai stated that these three landscapes, while operating separately, are closely linked because they constrain and have an impact on the movements of the others. Two additional landscapes are 'mediascapes' and 'ideoscapes'. Mediascapes comprise the distribution of media images through television, radio, and the Internet as well as the images themselves, which, together, shape our understanding of the world. Ideoscapes are derived from nation-states (particularly Enlightenment ideals, such as freedom, democracy, and representation) and the counter-movements against them.

Related to Appadurai's (1996) landscapes is the notion of networks that is central in Castells' (1996, 1997, 1998) works. Although Castells acknowledges the importance of global capitalism, his focus is on technological change as a foundation of globalization. Whereas global capitalism theorists focus on global capital as a central force, and Hardt and Negri (2000, 2004) highlight the new organizational structure of Empire, Castells views technology as the most important factor in globalization because it has enabled us to move from an industrial society to a 'Network Society'. For Castells, the rise of the 'Network Society' is the result of two main factors: (a) new information technology, such as the Internet, leading to 'informationalism' as a new mode of development; and (b) the evolution of a 'new economy' based on 'information capitalism'. The new economy is characterized by its basis in knowledge or information, its global nature, and its productivity organized around global networks. It is a Network Society that is flexible and can act in real time, related to post-Fordist modes of production. Castells argues that, given the importance of the technological changes and networks as a new form of organizational structure based on an economy driven by information, arguments about the role of TNCs as the driving force within a globalized world are no longer valid. In this sense, Castells tends to present globalization as occurring without agency. When used in the educational realm, for example, theories such as Castells' often assume that education is imposed on countries without their consent, involvement, or resistance (Spring, 2015).

Differing from theories of global capitalism and Empire, in the realm of the Network Society, the cultural dimension of globalization is more significant than the economic one. According to Castells, a new culture is evolving in which the space of flows and 'timeless time' are central and related to the theories of time and space discussed below. In contrast to the space of places that characterized the industrial period, the space of flows is more abstract and is centered on the networks that have developed during a period he calls the Information Age. In addition, interaction can be asynchronous due to advances in technology. As noted, this new culture is also characterized by timeless time, a situation in which time is compressed and in which the order of occurrences changes due to technological advances, which arises from the space of flows.

Theories That Emphasize Changes in Time, Space, and Place

Similar to Appadurai (1996) and Castells (1996, 1997, 1998), several other theorists have focused on the changes connected to globalization that alter notions of time, space, and place. Central to changes related to time and space is the notion of a 'global village', which Marshall McLuhan (1962) predicted would be a result of moving to a highly technological human society in which communication is instantaneous and often devoid of its local context. Writing before the Internet was invented, McLuhan suggested that this emerging global village would upset long-standing power structures and change social interactions. From a more contemporary perspective, Anthony Giddens (1990) uses the phrase 'time-space distanciation' to refer to the commonly held notion about globalization that there has been a profound change in the way people interact due to technological changes that allow for deterritorialized[8] interactions.

Similarly, David Harvey (1990b), a geographer, characterizes the postmodern condition as one of 'time-space compression' due to the increasing ease of air travel and electronic communication that accompany the spread of capitalism. He argues that the economic integration that comes with globalization breaks down both space and time as well as speeds everything up. Robinson (2007) points out that, although Giddens and Harvey provide similar concepts, Giddens presents the changes that are occurring in benign terms, while Harvey critiques the structures of global capitalism. In this sense, Giddens might be considered to be a hyperglobalist, while Harvey would be classified as a critical scholar and transformationalist.

Time and space compression is connected to changes in spatial organization. The sociologist Saskia Sassen's (1991, 2012) analysis of space relates to notions about the profound changes that have taken place through technology and the global economic system. She argues that nation-states have weakened to a large degree due to the changes that accompany globalization and proposes that networks of 'global cities' and 'global city regions' have become important key players in the processes of globalization. Because economic developments are now integrated and spatially dispersed with regard to the outsourcing of labor, the complexity of the market, and the need to provide global products and services, global cities no longer operate on a national level but, rather, on a global level. Sassen argues that New York, London, and Tokyo are the premiere global cities that are leading the way to the formation of transnational urban spaces due, in large part, to the combination of global integration and dispersal of people.

For Sassen (1991, 2012), global cities and global city regions are key structures that organize the global capitalist economy because they are at the center of global financial capital and offer 'producer services' that involve both public and corporate consumption. As such, global cities have four main functions: (a) to serve as 'command post' structures for the global economic system, (b) to provide spaces where producer services take place, (c) to serve as headquarters and sites of innovation for producer services, and (d) to act as markets for products or services in their domains. All of these theories related to time, space, and place share an emphasis on technological and spatial changes. They remain relatively limited in providing a rubric for overarching analyses, however, because they focus only on specific aspects of globalization rather than analyzing its complexities more fully.

Transnationality and Transnationalism

Scholars of transnationality and transnationalism share Sassen's (1991, 2012) assumption that the role of the nation-state is diminished due to globalization. According to Robinson (2007), transnationality and transnationalism are closely related. Transnationality refers to the new communities and social identities that form in place of those that have been historically connected to the nation-state, while transnationalism 'denotes a range of social, cultural and political practices and states brought about by the sheer increase in social connectivity across borders' (Robinson, 2007, p. 136). The origins of the constructs of transnationality and transnationalism are found in immigration studies and constitute an acknowledgment that migration is no longer a one-way, lasting process. Many immigrants maintain ties to their home countries, often visit their countries of origin, and may even move between the two (or more) spaces. The technological advances tied to globalization have had a positive impact on the ability of people to more easily move across borders, either physically or virtually, which relates to notions about changing spaces. Aihwa Ong (1999) argues that transnational migrants, rather than becoming deterritorialized and 'stateless', maintain a strong connection between the global and the local context.

In recent years, analysis of transnationalism has evolved into an interdisciplinary area of study (Huang, 2009). Although different disciplines (e.g., anthropology, political science, sociology) have specific ways of understanding transnationalism, a common feature is that actions and processes occur across borders at a level that transcends the nation-state. As with much of the analysis related to globalization, transnationalism remains a contested concept about which there are many different points of view, in part, because the term 'transnational' has often been used by critical scholars to connote a negative influence of supranational entities on nation-states (as with TNCs or the TCC).

Global Governance

Like many theories related to globalization, global governance stems from one academic domain (international relations) and has now been appropriated by numerous others. Influenced by the study of transnationalism, authors began to question the dominance of nation-states as the unit of analysis in international relations scholarship in the 1970s and suggested a distinction between the activity of governments and that of global governance organizations. This distinction led to an emphasis on the study of 'regimes', which are understood to be the rules that govern how nation-states should interact on the global stage. Eventually, the field moved to an analysis of the role of IGOs and other non-state actors, such as TNCs, in global governance. The construct of global governance then began to be incorporated into other disciplines, and the notion of a plurality of actors within governance took shape. In global governance theory, one actor (global governance organizations) does not need to replace the other (nation-states), as both can coexist (Dale & Robertson, 2007). However, lines can easily become blurred between the desires and mandates of global governance institutions and nation-state actors (Iriye, 2002). It is in this complex space that key interactions between agents take place.

David Held (1995, 2004, 2010), a key theorist in the area of global governance, posits that democratic practices should spread throughout the global sphere. Held argues for the need for regulation at the global level, which he refers to as a 'cosmopolitan democracy', to ensure representation and participation from all nations. In keeping with Held's notions of representation, Mary Kaldor (2003), another prominent scholar of global governance, developed the notion of the 'global civil society'. She argues that global civil society, which serves as an extension of national civil society into the global environment, has the power to be either repressive or hopeful. In the current context, the influence of global governance organizations, which predominantly represent the interests of the Global North, can be repressive, whereas the possibility of social movements that emerge from a global civil society (e.g., the Occupy movement) can be liberating. In short, global governance and the global civil society allow for the possibility of people to shape their own societies. Although theorists in this area remain hopeful about the possibilities for democratic governance worldwide, notions of global governance are often criticized as being idealistic because attaining agreement on global civil society and achieving a cosmopolitan democracy are challenging.

Several scholars have brought theories of global governance into the educational realm. Even though education has historically been a local and national affair, comparative international education scholars Roger Dale and Susan Robertson (2007) argue that the rising impact of global governance organizations in realm of education provides an interesting opportunity for reflection. In the context of contemporary globalization, the dominance of neoliberalism has led to the market's harboring a greater degree of power than nation-states have in the provision of public services, such as education. Education is an area that has come to be dominated by global governance institutions to a large extent, especially in countries in the Global South where aid and loans often prescribe the types of educational reforms that countries must undertake. At the same time, as with general global governance theories, education is viewed as offering hope and possibilities because it may spread human rights and other justice-oriented elements.

Various scholars who focus on policymaking debate the impact of global governance institutions in education. As I discuss in more detail in Chap. 4, world culture theorists argue that global governance organizations diffuse a world culture of schooling, while culturalists critique this point of view and argue that global trends are always mediated by local forces. For example, Connie McNeely (1995) argues from a neoinstitutional approach that global governance organizations have come to prescribe education policies, even if agreement among the international community with regard to global norms is symbolic rather than realistic. Alternatively, Karen Mundy (1998) takes a critical approach and argues, like Held (1995, 2004, 2010) and Kaldor (2003), that global governance has the possibility of bringing a more just world order, particularly within education.

Poststructuralism

Poststructuralism is part of the broad paradigm of postmodernism that I described at the beginning of this chapter; it is also part of the overall critical theoretical enterprise. It emerged as a reaction against structuralism, which is closely related to structural-functionalism. Structuralism is derived from linguistics,[9] with a focus on textual analysis, and was later incorporated into anthropology, sociology, and even Marxism. At the center of structural analysis is what theorists pose as a stable system in which meaning is made within cultures. Essentially, structuralism provides a way to understand the structure of human culture. As a modern theory, structuralism focuses on how structures determine human behavior. Both postmodernism and poststructuralism provide critiques of such modern discourses, particularly assumptions about one-size-fits-all, linear evolutionary approaches that stem from Western points of view. These two perspectives are challenging to define expressly because theorists in these areas reject the absolute truths that typically define theoretical domains.

In essence, postmodernism and poststructuralism recognize and privilege diverse viewpoints, alternative forms of knowledge, and multiple forms of reality. Theorists who operate from these perspectives critique power structures and question the supremacy of scientific knowledge that is constructed through a Western perspective. Poststructuralism originates from a group of scholars, many of whom were former structuralists, who embraced critical theory and began to question structuralism in the 1960s, leading to the 'post' in poststructuralism. Many of the scholars associated with the emergence of poststructuralism espouse the French philosophical and literary criticism traditions and include Jacques Derrida (1966, 1967), Michel Foucault (1975), Julia Kristeva (1982), Jaques Lacan (1977), and Roland Barthes (1967a, 1967b). Because structuralism emerged within the discipline of linguistics, poststructuralism focuses on textual analysis to a large degree.

Poststructuralism, which is intentionally difficult to outline, stands in opposition to structuralism. In general, texts are thought to have multiple purposes and multiple potential impacts, depending on the positionality and traits of the reader (e.g., gender, race, ethnicity, sexual orientation). The reader, rather than the author, becomes the key focus through a process termed 'decentering'. For poststructuralists, knowledge, rather than economics, as in many Marxist critiques, is central to analyses (Shields, 2013). A key component of poststructuralism is deconstruction (Derrida, 1967). Deconstruction brings into question the binaries (opposites) that are emphasized in structuralism, such as the binary of 'developed' and 'developing' countries, which are built on the notion that there is a hierarchy between the objects labeled, with one as the dominant and the other as the subjugated. Poststructuralists would deconstruct the meaning of this binary terminology but would not suggest alternative terms, causing frustration for other critical scholars who would like to see clear alternatives outlined. Specifying alternatives, however, would be antithetical to the nature of poststructuralism.

Postcolonial Theory

Like poststructuralism, postcolonial theory arose as a response to the modernist discourse that has been dominant since the medieval era. As a postmodern theory, postcolonialism shares with poststructuralism the challenge of defining itself, especially because the field is disparate and the theorists themselves contest its boundaries. Postcolonialism developed from the realm of literary criticism and has now been incorporated into a wide variety of fields. Literary theoretician Edward Said, a key founding theorist of postcolonialism, brings an international dimension to poststructural analysis (Shields, 2013). Said's seminal text, *Orientalism* (1978), demonstrates how the world is divided into two types of people: Westerners and Orientals. In his book, Said criticizes scholarship from the West written about Africa, Asia, and the Middle East as self-serving and designed to portray exotic 'others' in postcolonial countries as fundamentally different from (and lesser than) Westerners or Orientals. According to Said, Westerners from the Global North have preconceived and condescending notions of Orientals, based on 'othering' them due to their belief in Orientals' inferiority. Said connects the subtractive notions that Westerners hold about Orientals to the legacy of imperialism and the ways in which dominant countries from the Global North continue to subjugate those from the Global South.

In addition to critiquing literature from the West, postcolonial scholarship in the literary criticism domain analyzes the complex identities of people from postcolonial environments. Bhaba (1994) developed the construct of 'hybridity' to explain how postcolonial people often integrate dominant global norms espoused by the Global North into their identities alongside the values and norms that stem from their countries of origin in the Global South. Bhaba presents hybridity as an angst-invoking state of being between two spaces. Despite being in a state of angst, Bhaba argues that hybrid postcolonial individuals have agency and may uproot dominant discourses. Bhaba's work and that of other postcolonial scholars demonstrate how people from the Global South resist dominant views of them and reclaim their identities to tell their own stories.

Although postcolonial theory has its roots in the field of literary criticism, it has become a broader perspective that is used to analyze the impact of colonialism and imperialism on nation-states and societies in a globalized world. In a general sense, postcolonialism focuses on the subjugation of people, cultures, and countries from the Global South. This subjugation initially occurred via imperialism and colonialism and continues today through the neocolonial relationships that remain dominant throughout the world (see below). Postcolonial theory also addresses resistance of countries and peoples from the Global South and emphasizes the possibility that these agents may reshape the dominant discourse through asserting alternatives. Postcolonialism refers more broadly to social movements and responses from the Global South that challenge domination from the Global North, as is seen in the work of Paolo Freire or Franz Fanon that highlights resistance to neocolonialism (Andreotti, 2006).

Postcolonial theorists also raise questions about how the aid and development regime has imposed normative views regarding the standard way development should occur. In analyzing education, in particular, postcolonial scholars critique the dominant structure (the Western formal schooling model) that has become the standard of the continued cultural imperialism of the Global North (Spring, 2015). Joel Spring sees postcolonial perspectives as standing in opposition to world culture theory, which holds that the global model that has evolved has become prominent because it is the best. Postcolonial theory instead suggests that components of this global model have spread through the neocolonial aid and development regime that stems from the Global North. Viewed through the postcolonial lens, the Global North's emphasis on Western schooling implies that Western forms of knowledge are superior.

Additional Constructs Related to Globalization

In addition to the theoretical domains presented earlier, other analytical constructs have been developed to more fully explain globalization, including deterritorialization, McDonaldization, neocolonialism, glocalization, and vernacular globalization.

Deterritorialization

Nation-states have traditionally been the sites of social, economic, and political interaction within societies. In today's globalized world, however, developments within nation-states are no longer entirely tied to local circumstances, especially due to technological advances and the ease with which people move across borders (both physically and virtually). Scholars use the construct of deterritorialization to refer to developments that occur around the world without the constraints of geographical location. In addition, deterritorialization highlights the cultural, political, and economic interconnections that abound in the everyday experiences of the world's populace (Steger, 2013). Hyperglobalists, who argue that there is no alternative to the march toward globalization, might consider deterritorialization as signaling the demise of the nation-state and local cultures. Other scholars would argue that cultural distinctions remain prominent and nation-states and other localities continue to thrive (Tomlinson, 2007). Rather than taking an either/or approach, another view of deterritorialization would connect to the notion of hybridity. In this view, people integrate aspects of global culture into their local cultures without losing what was local; instead, these aspects are an 'added dimension' (Tomlinson, 2007).

McDonaldization

The sociologist and critical scholar George Ritzer (1993) coined the term 'McDonaldization' to characterize the rational model used by the McDonald's fast-food chain. This model calls for (a) efficiency (in particular, keeping time to a minimum), (b) calculability (quantity over quality), (c) predictability (standardization in both products and the work environment), and (d) control (using uniform processes that substitute technology for humans when possible). Ritzer argues that, despite the model's basis in apparent rationality, McDonaldization is an irrational model that leads to dehumanization and, ultimately, to inconsistencies because products and people do not necessarily follow the model and do not do so all the time. Ritzer states that, even though this model may be irrational, these same values have moved out of the business or economic realm into the evolving global culture. The widespread use of McDonaldization leads to cultural homogenization. In contrast to world culture theorists, however, Ritzer does not connect McDonaldization to 'best practices'; rather, he problematizes it.

Due to the dominance of the USA in many international spheres, especially in the cultural sphere (e.g., in terms of music, food, clothing), the term 'Americanization' has often been used to express a notion similar to McDonaldization. Americanization raises concerns about the negative impacts of cultural imperialism that accompany globalization. The concepts of McDonaldization and Americanization have been employed in the educational context to critique the Western schooling model.

Neocolonialism

Developed from postcolonial analysis, the construct of neocolonialism (also known as neoimperialism) refers to the pressure that countries from the Global North and the associated global governance organizations place upon countries in the Global South. Neocolonialism mimics the differential power relationship of the colonial era. With neocolonialism, however, influence is no longer asserted through the military means as during colonial times but, rather, through less direct avenues, such as the mandates of the aid and development regime and international conventions and treaties. Some critics even suggest that neocolonialism is simply a new version of the same process. In many cases, countries in the Global South have no choice but to accept assistance from their former colonizers; this assistance serves to keep postcolonial countries dependent on the former colonial powers of the Global North.

Harvey (2003) refers to this new form of colonialism as 'capitalist imperialism' and notes that it involves both capitalist expansion and political control. Whereas national governments were clearly the instigators in the colonial era, the free market is seen as the chief driver of neocolonialism, although local governments are involved in implementing neoliberal economic practices and in agreeing to aid and development constraints (Roy, 2001). Even within postcolonial environments, elites often dictate whose interests should be served at the expense of the masses.

An example of how neocolonialism takes shape in education is seen in the structures of education of many postcolonial societies, which were founded on the practices of colonial powers and maintain the Westernized perspective due to the influence of the normative aid and development regime. Given neocolonial influences, national governments in the Global South often ascribe to the world culture hypothesis (whether they truly believe it or comply for the purposes of political expediency) and continue to subject their populaces to education that may not be relevant for their contexts.

Glocalization

'Glocalization' is a term that originated in Japanese business circles and was brought into the scholarly literature by British sociologist Roland Robertson (1995). The construct, which combines the terms 'globalization' and 'localization', has typically been used to analyze globalization in economic terms. Glocalization connotes an overall global approach to financial markets combined with a targeted local approach that incorporates the local context and culture. For example, a global car manufacturer might sell smaller vehicles in certain parts of the world or use different model names to appeal to people in specific countries, while international potato chip manufacturers may offer different flavors for various international markets. The construct of glocalization contradicts the notion of a world culture or homogenization because local tastes and variations remain salient. The term also has been appropriated for non-economic forces to include any incorporation of local values into global developments and trends. In this sense, the global can be seen as influencing the local and vice versa in a relationship of reciprocity that results in hybridity.

Vernacular Globalization

The concept of vernacular globalization is related to glocalization and hybridity. Vernacular globalization implies that not all global forces are monolithic and that agency and resistance always mediate dominant global trends. As such, vernacular globalization allows for the possibility of local agents such as governments, organizations, communities, or individuals to mediate global trends (Appadurai, 1996; Lingard, 2000; Rizvi & Lingard, 2010). Vernacular globalization posits that, despite the influence of global forces, developments and trends are always occurring within local contexts that have particular histories and cultures. This theory rejects the notion that globalization is simply about Westernization and developing a world culture. Instead, vernacular globalization allows for the possibility that both homogenization and heterogenization can occur simultaneously. In this sense, vernacular globalization is related to the cultural aspects of globalization and to hybridity. The construct of vernacular globalization rejects the TINA approach of hyperglobalists and the world culture theory hypothesis. When considering education, for example, vernacular globalization allows us to understand how global trends (e.g., standardization, accountability, global competition) are reshaped and lead to a variety of outcomes that are not reproductions of the original policies that they represent. As such, vernacular globalization provides evidence of countries in the Global South 'speaking back' to those in the Global North and charting their own courses (Lingard, 2000).

Conclusion

Familiarizing ourselves with globalization theories and constructs provides a foundation for better understanding how globalization operates more generally and how it makes an impact on education and educational reform, specifically. The broad theoretical domains of modernism and postmodernism, which stem from multidisciplinary analyses, provide a framework that undergirds the constellation of theories and constructs related to globalization. Using these broad lenses, scholars and commentators develop specific theories and constructs related to globalization that privilege particular aspects over others (e.g., cultural, social, or technological dimensions), which leads not only to contrast between theories but also to complementarity among the various lenses. These theories and constructs reflect different approaches to viewing the world; some are normative in nature, while others have a critical emphasis. This variety of perspectives is evident across the literature on globalization, including scholarship directly related to education. Understanding the theoretical foundations of globalization allows us to critically consider developments in educational policy in the era of contemporary globalization. For example, as I discuss in Chap. 4, even though the movement for 'Education for All' appears on the surface to be a humanistic endeavor, closer analysis reveals the neoliberal and human capital influences of this reform. With this overview of the theoretical terrain from Chap. 3, as well as the background on the broad parameters of globalization provided in Chaps. 1 and 2, we now move on to an explicit focus on education for the remainder of the book.

Notes

1. The set of theories and constructs covered in this chapter is comprehensive but not exhaustive. The chapter covers primarily the rich set of theories that have arisen in the social sciences, including anthropology, political science, economics, and sociology.
2. The Enlightenment, also known as the Age of Reason, is a philosophical movement that took place between the mid-1600s and the early 1800s, mainly in Europe. It coincided with the 'scientific revolution', in which every aspect of human life began to be studied and understood as absolutes. Well-known Enlightenment thinkers include Francis Bacon, René Descartes, Isaac Newton, Immanuel Kant, and Mary Wollstonecraft.
3. The contributions of these theories as foundational for contemporary cultural and social analyses are significant, and entire chapters could be devoted to each theory. I have opted to focus on theories of globalization in this chapter, which makes my overview of structural-functionalism and Marxism necessarily brief. See George Ritzer (2007) and Patricia Kubow and Paul Fossum (2007) for more detailed discussions of each of these areas.
4. Marx wrote many of his works with collaborator Friedrich Engels.
5. In the early 1950s, economists in the United Nations Economic Commission for Latin America began to advance the point of view that postcolonial countries in the Global South were not going to move from a less developed to a more developed status, as modernization theory would suggest, due to their colonial legacy. Therefore, they argued that new structures were needed for these countries to modernize. This work formed the basis for dependency theory as an alternative to modernization theory.

6. The semi-periphery was added as a third country type when world-system theory expanded on dependency theory.
7. See Hardt and Negri's (2004) work that elaborates on the multitude.
8. See the final section of this chapter, on theoretical constructs related to globalization, for more information on deterritorialization.
9. French linguist Ferdinand de Saussure is a central figure in the emergence of structuralism, as is French anthropologist Claude Lévi-Strauss.

CHAPTER 4

Globalization and Education

Given the scope and pervasiveness of globalization in nearly every sector of society, worldwide developments and trends related to globalization have a significant impact on education across local contexts around the world. In this chapter, I first delineate global educational trends within the domains of schooling and higher education,[1] many of which are related to manifestations of globalization discussed in Chaps. 1 and 2, particularly the impact of neoliberalism. Although some trends related to schooling and higher education overlap (e.g., privatization), I cover these two levels of education separately for greater clarity. Next, I consider the historical and current impact of the aid and development regime and its global governance institutions on the educational sector, particularly in countries in the Global South. Although global governance institutions are increasingly paying attention to social development indicators in the PWC era, the aid and development regime's focus on education as a driver of economic growth and development remains central.

Given global trends in schooling and higher education, as well as worldwide movements such as Education for All (EFA), I conclude the discussion with a consideration of whether there is convergence in educational models worldwide. Although it is important to understand the global trends that have an impact on the educational realm, it is equally important to recognize that local entities still govern education and many other aspects of their societies (Lingard, 2000; Spring, 2015). Global trends

© The Editor(s) (if applicable) and The Author(s) 2016

L.M. Portnoi, *Policy Borrowing and Reform in Education*,
DOI 10.1057/978-1-137-53024-0_4

are not monolithic, and nation-states or local communities interpret and (re)shape global policies and agendas through vernacular globalization.

Global Trends in Schooling

Numerous global trends have been observed in schooling around the world: (a) marketization and shifting values; (b) corporatization, (c) decentralization, privatization, and choice; (d) accountability and standardized testing; and (e) the Information and Communications Technology (ICT) Revolution. These trends are highly interconnected and stem from the processes of globalization—more specifically, from the influence of neoliberal globalization, with its emphasis on schooling as an economic investment.

Marketization and Shifting Values

One of the most significant developments in the realm of schooling is the increasingly widespread view of education as an extension of the market, accompanied by the values associated with this perspective. The purpose and aims of education have been debated since the inception of mass schooling in the 1800s and have not necessarily been shared around the world. David Labaree (2003) delineates three competing views of education: democratic equality, social mobility, and social efficiency. The democratic equality view assumes that the purpose of education is to develop a democratic citizenry that is engaged in society; therefore, every person must be fully educated as a means to participate in civic activities. The social mobility view, which privileges the notion that education will lead to opportunities for individuals to improve their social status and acquire a range of private consumer goods, is competitive and market-driven. The social efficiency view holds that education plays a functional role in preparing individuals for the world of work so that they may be economically productive.[2] This productivity is individual but also provides a return on investment for nation-states and the economy in general.

These competing views have enjoyed alternating prominence within various historical periods. For example, during the reconstruction era after WWII, the democratic view was ascendant. The social mobility view corresponds to embracing capitalism and opening markets, as many nations have done from the 1970s onward. More recently, the salience of globalization and neoliberalism has led to the rise of an enhanced version of the social efficiency view becoming the standard for education around the globe (Rizvi & Lingard, 2010). Joel Spring (2015) calls this enhanced social efficiency view the 'economization of education' model, in which the market, competition, and human capital theory take center stage and drive educational provision and reform. The economization of education model is rooted in the Global North (or 'Western') model and is becoming globally pervasive (Nordveidt, 2009).

A move from the democratic perspective to this new social efficiency/ economization of education model turns education into a marketable commodity rather than a public good. In this sense, education's purpose becomes economic growth. Education becomes increasingly intertwined with notions of workforce development for the global knowledge economy. Whereas versions of democratic education often involve concerns such as human rights, environmentalism, civic engagement, and learning for the sake of learning, the new social efficiency view of education emphasizes the development of knowledge, skills, and competencies for the post-Fordist economy. Therefore, the new social efficiency model assumes that schools must develop individuals who are innovative, flexible, and adaptable given the demands of the twenty-first century, characterized by post-Fordist production. At the same time, schooling aligns with a factory model to a certain degree, given the rigid structures and stepwise progress of moving through grades (Cheng, 2007). Because the social efficiency emphasis moves away from the notion of equality toward preparing people for jobs, fields that are not directly connected to the market decline in importance (Stromquist & Monkman, 2014). The emphasis is on 'basic' subjects, such as reading, mathematics, and science, rather than on social sciences and humanities, to achieve the measurable production of human capital (Luke, 2011).

The shift toward the economization of education model is both implicit and explicit (Noddings, 2003). The economization of education is propagated by global governance institutions, especially IMOs and TNCs, and has become embedded implicitly in national education systems through reforms that are market-oriented. It is also explicitly incorporated into many educational systems because there is a tendency for nation-states to adopt education policies that will contribute to global competitiveness (Carnoy, 2014). Contributing to this new social efficiency/economization of education model are influential education economists from the WB and the IMF, who typically conduct research and make assessments about education in purely economic terms. For example, the WB (2011) contends that the emphasis should no longer be on the amount of time devoted to schooling but, rather, on what is learned in terms of measurable output for the global economy.

Efficiency and accountability are central in the new social efficiency/ economization of education model and lead to standardized testing to measure educational outputs (see below). This model has seemingly changed the purpose, structure, and provision of schooling around the world and has refocused schooling on economic outputs. Despite the rise of the new social efficiency or economization of education model, social values such as democracy and equality have not necessarily been abandoned altogether; rather, they have been relegated to a marginalized position (Rizvi & Lingard, 2010). In addition, although the social efficiency model is dominant right now, it is not the only way for education to be organized, and alternative models of education exist (see the final section of this chapter).

Corporatization

Global networks of TNCs (including publishers and providers of educational technology), global governance organizations, for-profit educational providers, philanthropic foundations, and regional trade groups contribute to the 'global corporatization of education' (Spring, 2015). Corporatization takes the marketization of schooling a step further and involves concrete manifestations of industry within education. Through corporatization, corporate values—including accountability, measurement, and privatization—contained in the 'new public management' regime that took shape in the corporate world in the 1990s are introduced into schooling (Rizvi & Lingard, 2010). New public management mirrors neoliberalism to a large extent and is reflected in the social efficiency model of schooling as well as the standardized testing movement described below. Corporatization is aligned with the economization of education model and serves to control students' knowledge, skills, and competencies to support the global workplace and global economy (Spring, 2015). Corporate elements also seek to harmonize school planning and practice with business methods (Ball, 2012). For example, countries that receive educational aid are generally required to use business templates to report back to donors.

Although corporatization is often characterized as an imposition of corporate values onto education, collaboration between the public and private sectors is becoming increasingly common and is sought out by education providers in countries throughout the world. Governments and education leaders are increasingly becoming involved in educational efforts that are directly tied to industry and that may involve funding, thus blurring the lines between public and private educational provision. Importantly, however, governments and educational leaders may align themselves with industry and corporate influences because they require loans to support their educational systems, and it is generally understood that the way to obtain aid is to embrace corporatization and the economization of education model. Notions of corporatization are now widespread within the development community. It is not just TNCs and IMOs that are involved in education–industry partnerships that engender corporatization. Other types of global governance institutions too are increasingly involved in education–industry partnerships, including INGOs, such as UNESCO.

Decentralization, Privatization, and Choice

The implementation of decentralization policies coincided with the retreat of the welfare state in the post-WWII era (Arnove, Franz, & Torres, 2013). Decentralization is one of the chief tenets of neoliberalism and has had an impact on the structure of educational systems around the world. In many cases, the provision of education, which was historically centralized, has shifted to state or provincial authorities, either by choice or by imposition. Countries that participated in acronym SAPs[3] were forced to decentralize all public services, including education, as a condition of their loans. The implementation of decentralization has not been uniform, however, and, in certain instances, it has amounted to decreased central spending on education, while some control has been maintained over the curriculum, and the practice of education or governance is shared (Samoff & Carrol, 2013). Nevertheless, the decline in central government funding for education that has accompanied decentralization in most countries has led to privatization.

Privatization occurs in several forms. One key form involves public–private cooperation. Although the majority of schools in most countries remain public and government-run, user fees were established in many countries in the Global South due to the conditions of SAPs. Aid and development organizations as well as private investors may be involved in funding education. This combination of public (government) and private sources of funding for education is essentially a partial form of privatization. Another central manifestation of privatization that is full rather than partial is the establishment of private schools, which have proliferated despite the fact that their quality is often poorer than that of public schools throughout most of the Global South. Although these private schools offer greater access overall because they add to the number of schools available, especially in the Global South, where schools are more limited, they maintain divisions with regard to which individuals within a society receive a quality education because they are typically attended by the poorest children (Arnove et al., 2013). Despite evidence in the literature about the low quality of private schools throughout much of the Global South, global governance organizations and corporate interests continue to highlight the value of private schooling and assert that private school management is more efficient (Carnoy, 2014; Rizvi & Lingard, 2010). In this sense, privatization functions as an ideology because private schools are not an evidence-based effective alternative, yet neoliberals continue to promote them (Rizvi & Lingard, 2010).

The discourse about privatization also concerns choice. Given the emphasis in the new social efficiency/economization of education model, it follows that students and parents should have the opportunity to make choices about their schooling in the open market. One of the most common ways to facilitate this choice is through a 'voucher' system, in which students and families use vouchers to attend their schools of choice. Martin Carnoy (1998), argues that vouchers serve more of a political purpose of expediency than a functional one, especially in the face of limited government funding for education. In reality, school choice typically means that those who are socially mobile have the opportunity to attend better schools. For this reason, vouchers provide a way for governments to present a facade of responsibility for democratizing education while not providing resources to level the playing field between schools.

Accountability and Standardized Testing

Given the dominance of the social efficiency view of education as well as the corporatization of schooling, educational systems and schools are increasingly expected to be accountable to society, national governments, and, in many cases in the Global South, to the aid and development regime. Accountability focuses on measuring schools' return on investment for their governments (Lingard, Martino, Rezai-Rashti, & Sellar, 2015). Quantification is central to efficiency and accountability, and regular data collection provides the opportunity to track the quantity and the quality of education. Both David Kamens (2013) and Joel Spring (2015) consider the audit culture that international testing engenders, and Spring labels this continual monitoring process an 'audit state'. Standardized testing has become the method of choice for establishing quantifiable data on schooling outcomes at both the national and international levels, and national testing mechanisms are in place in many countries around the world. Some countries have standardized tests at each grade level or at various intervals, while most assess students at the conclusion of secondary school and/or entry into higher education.

Although international testing has been prevalent since the 1950s, it has increased in importance with the advent of the knowledge economy (Shields, 2013). The movement toward testing is driven by the need for countries to become globally competitive in this economy. Carnoy (2014) notes that a network of global governance institutions, including the OECD, the WB, INGOs, and bilateral organizations, push for testing for accountability and efficiency, implying that best educational practices can be measured. Standardized tests are connected to the social efficiency worldview as well as world culture theory (see below), and governments and policymakers often assume that countries that perform poorly should emulate the best practices of the educational systems of high performers. International standardized tests are also used to establish the effectiveness of loans supplied to countries in the Global South for improving their education systems. In some cases, poor testing results cause countries to take immediate action to address the apparent deficiencies that the tests reveal. More often, however, test results are used to provide the rationale for continuing practices already in place or to support changes that are under way (Grek, 2009; Shields, 2013).

Three international standardized tests are central to the accountability movement: Trends in International Mathematics and Science Study (TIMSS), Progress in International Reading Literacy Study (PIRLS), and Programme for International Student Assessment (PISA). TIMSS and PIRLS are both administered through the International Association of the Evaluation of Educational Achievement (IEA). Prior to the establishment of TIMSS and PIRLS, earlier versions of IEA's achievement tests that focused on mathematics, science, reading comprehension, and geography had been used since the 1960s.

By the mid-1990s, the importance of science and mathematics had been established as central to global competitiveness in the post-Fordist knowledge economy, and TIMSS became a central source of international comparison. Over 60 countries participate in the TIMSS assessment of science and mathematics (Institute of Education Sciences, 2015). The test is administered every four years, which means that it will generally be taken twice in students' schooling careers, in the fourth and ninth grades. TIMSS purports to measure not only student performance but also aspects of teaching and the curriculum. Notably, the test can be used to compare the government's planned curriculum with student outcomes on the test (Shields, 2013). TIMSS Advanced, which focuses on advanced mathematics and physics learning in the final year of secondary school, has been given to a small number of countries in the 1995, 2008, and 2015 administrations of TIMSS (TIMSS and PIRLS International Study Center, 2015). PIRLS has been assessing reading comprehension and is given in five-year cycles to students in the fourth, fifth, or sixth grade since 2001.

PISA is an alternative testing regime instituted by the OECD and first administered in 2000. PISA combines the three areas highlighted in TIMSS and PIRLS: science, mathematics, and reading literacy. PISA tests are administered to 15-year-olds every three years and rotate between these three areas of focus. The testing emphasis is on functional skills that students have learned in these areas throughout their schooling (OECD, 2015). According to the OECD, over 70 'economies' (rather than 'countries' which highlights the influence of economic competition) participate in the test, including economies from both the Global North and Global South. Although the OECD governs this increasingly influential assessment of students from countries throughout the world, the OECD's membership is primarily representative of the Global North (see Chap. 2).

The ICT Revolution

The ICT Revolution, introduced in Chap. 2, is a fundamental development related to globalization that has an impact on nearly every sector of society. Education has experienced three major impacts related to the ICT Revolution (Carnoy, 2014). First, computers have made their way into classrooms in many countries of the world. Some of these computers are shared and owned by schools, while others are personal computers owned by students. Teachers also increasingly use computers and ICT to complete their daily work. The diffusion of computers and ICT has not been as widespread as expected (Carnoy, 2014), however, and there is a digital divide with regard to access to technology, as I explain in Chap. 2.

Second, technology is used to bridge this digital divide, to a large degree, by facilitating instruction via the Internet or television, which are often used to ensure that teachers reach rural locations virtually if not physically. In this sense, the spread of ICT has assisted with facilitating access to education (Shields, 2013). Third, global governance institutions push the use of technology to support their accountability and testing mechanisms. ICT also facilitates the reporting of test results. Indeed, results from standardized tests, such as TIMSS and PISA, for all countries involved are readily available online. In a general sense, global governance institutions also push technology as a means for individuals and societies to become more economically productive. Technology is thus intertwined with the developments of globalization, more generally, and the move toward the social efficiency/economization of education model, in particular. Nevertheless, evidence about the efficacy of ICT for the areas in which it is being used is mixed (Carnoy, 2014), and there is a need to continually reevaluate its use.

The Impact of (Neoliberal) Globalization on Education

Trends in the realm of both schooling and higher education display the impact of globalization, particularly neoliberal globalization. Education is increasingly viewed as an extension of the market, and competition has become common, both within and between countries. This competitive environment has manifested in international assessments in the schooling domain and in global university rankings within higher education. Education is also increasingly privatized, with most governments divesting funding in education. At the same time, corporate and other outside interests (e.g., global governance organizations) have an increasing involvement in the provision of education worldwide.

Global Trends in Higher Education

Many of the changes that have taken place in the higher education sector mirror those in schooling to a large degree. Because higher education is closely tied with knowledge production for the global knowledge economy, however, a specialized set of changes have taken place in this sector: (a) expansion, (b) shifting funding patterns and privatization, (c) corporatization and commodification, (d) internationalization, and (e) university rankings and global competition.

Expansion of Higher Education

The expansion of higher education, also referred to as 'massification', is directly linked to globalization, post-Fordist modes of production, and the accompanying importance of the knowledge economy. Expansion involves two central components. First, countries around the world have broadened their higher education sectors to accommodate a greater number of students through building infrastructure, hiring more staff, and offering a wider array of degree options. Second, the number of people who take part in higher education has risen dramatically in the past 100 years, especially since WWII. At the beginning of the 1900s, higher education enrollment was approximately 500,000 worldwide (1 % of the corresponding age group) and grew to 100 million, or 20 % of the corresponding age group, by 2000 (Schoffer & Meyer, 2005). Moreover, by 2030, the number of higher education students worldwide is expected to dramatically increase, to over 400 million (Calderon, 2012). The expansion of higher education, however, has been uneven across regions of the world and within countries. Countries in the Global North, especially in North America and Western Europe, have historically claimed the largest share of higher education enrollments, although East Asia and the Pacific are beginning to eclipse these countries in terms of sheer enrollment numbers, with China and India leading this enrollment growth (Calderon, 2012).

Growth is not only about enrollment numbers, however, as participation rates depend on population size. Thus, participation is often compared across countries using the gross enrollment ratio (GER), which takes into account the population size of the corresponding age group. A comparison of enrollment across geopolitical regions shows that GERs are highest in North America and Western Europe, while sub-Saharan Africa has the lowest GERs in the world, followed by South and West Asia. An analysis of several countries' 2013 GERs furthers our understanding of global differences: The USA has a GER of 89 %, while Costa Rica has a GER of 48 %, and Rwanda's is 7 % (UNESCO Institute for Statistics, 2015).

Countries that have high participation rates in basic and, especially, in secondary schooling are more likely to have higher GERs at the higher education level (Schofer & Meyer, 2005). In this way, the global inequities of the schooling system that reflect historical legacies, such as colonialism, transfer to, or are reproduced in, higher education. Discrepancies also exist worldwide and within countries in regard to the participation of women, people from racial and ethnic minorities, and those from the lower end of the income spectrum (Altbach, Reisberg, & Rumbley, 2009). Higher education institutions (HEIs) are also more likely to be located in populous urban regions, and therefore, access is generally more limited for those who live in rural areas. In many cases, countries, especially those in the Global South, are not able to keep up with demand for university enrollments, which has led, in part, to the privatization of higher education and the introduction of user fees (Stromquist & Monkman, 2014).

Shifting Funding Patterns and the Privatization of Higher Education

Many governments throughout the world, especially the wealthier nations of the Global North, provided free or subsidized higher education during the height of the welfare state after WWII, when the Fordist economy was still dominant. After the economic downturn of the 1980s, when neoliberalism began to take root, governments started to retract from higher education spending and support, slowing down their growth to a certain degree (Schugurensky, 2013). Fueled by the tenets of neoliberalism, the privatization of higher education provided a partial means to expand higher education to meet the demand for access in the post-Fordist global economy. Many of these user fees were imposed during the period of structural adjustment and led to resistance in countries across Latin America (Arnove et al., 2013; Rhoads, 2003). As with other social services in the neoliberal paradigm, user fees were added in many countries where higher education had previously been offered free of charge. The imposition of user fees aligns with the belief that higher education provides greater returns to the individual than to society (Shields, 2013). For some countries, user fees have provided a means to expand higher education with limited government funding.

At the same time, the introduction of user fees exacerbates the access issues discussed earlier. Higher education access is already limited in many countries, and user fees have added to the divide between those who can afford higher education and those who cannot (Stromquist & Monkman, 2014). In a recent case, Germany experimented with charging tuition fees from 2006 onward, amid student protests over access issues for people from less advantaged backgrounds. Germany eventually revoked that policy and reinstated tuition-free higher education at the end of 2014 (Freeman, 2014). Because most countries are not able to provide free higher education, a hybrid public–private model has become common. In this model, the government pays a modest percentage of the overall costs of higher education, while the rest is paid through user fees and private sources, such as philanthropic donations and industry sponsorships.

The privatization of higher education has also led to the growth of private universities, which are funded mainly through private sources (often via high tuition), although they may receive some governmental assistance in certain countries. The USA and Latin America have an established history of private higher education, while African and Middle Eastern countries tend to have more recently introduced private institutions. Private HEIs may be for-profit or not-for-profit, and they are generally not accountable to local and national governments in the same way as are public HEIs. In most countries, the demand for public higher education exceeds the available spots, and, thus, students turn to private higher education. Nearly every country has private HEIs, and private higher education has eclipsed public higher education in Japan, Indonesia, the Philippines, and South Korea (Altbach et al., 2009).

Not all private HEIs are created for the same purpose. Four different types of private HEIs exist: (a) elite and semi-elite, (b) identity, (c) demand-absorbing, and (d) for-profit (Altbach et al., 2009). Elite and semi-elite private institutions are top or above average in each country and are generally not-for-profits. While the USA is the only country in which private HEIs dominate the top tier of elite institutions, other countries have numerous institutions at the semi-elite level (Altbach et al., 2009). Identity institutions typically have a religious character and most operate as not-for-profits. Demand-absorbing private institutions have experienced the most growth in the era of globalization and massification. These institutions are not elite and often are not full-fledged universities; as such, they may be of lower quality. Ethnic minority and lower-income students are more likely to attend these demand-absorbing private institutions (Mir, 2013). For-profit institutions, which operate purely as businesses, also fall into the demand-absorbing category.

Corporatization and Commodification

HEIs are valued for two main purposes in the post-Fordist environment of the global knowledge economy: producing highly skilled forms of human capital and developing knowledge for commercial use (Shields, 2013). To fulfill these functions, higher education is becoming increasingly corporatized. The language of the 'new public management' that derives from the corporate world has found its way into higher education, with terms such as 'client' or 'consumer' increasingly common as labels for students. Moreover, as corporate interests become more prominent in higher education due to industry collaboration and/or funding, there is an increasing emphasis on vocational skills that are needed for the workplace, known as the vocationalization of higher education. This development aligns with global governance institutions (and, therefore, some national governments), placing emphasis on post-Fordist skills and competencies, and many students especially those who pay high user fees, seek out these skills for the workplace (Schugurensky, 2013). Another component of the influence of private philanthropic organizations and corporate interests in higher education is the loss of autonomy in the higher education sector. When HEIs seek to align their curricula with entities that provide substantial funding, they have less control over what is taught. If HEIs are developing academic programs based on industry needs and the instrumental purposes of job preparation, they are not able to focus on basic research and on learning for learning's sake to the degree that they may have previously.

Corporate influences in higher education also lead to its commodification, especially in an environment where the economic role of HEIs is expressly salient. As introduced in Chap. 2, the WTO's GATS made higher education a tradable commodity for the first time. Commodification is closely associated with internationalization, the subject of the next section. According to Jane Knight (2002), GATS governs four kinds of higher education that take place in the international sector: (a) cross-border higher education (e.g., distance learning), (b) consumption abroad (e.g., study-abroad and international exchanges), (c) commercial presence (e.g., branch campuses in foreign countries), and (d) the presence of natural persons (e.g., professors and scholars who work abroad). As with the influence of private agencies or companies, the commodification of higher education raises concerns about the role of HEIs. HEIs have historically held a great deal of autonomy and have not been directly subjected to market forces. With GATS and the movement to commodify higher education for the global knowledge economy, however, many HEIs are aligning themselves with the expectations of global governance institutions and corporate interests.

The increasing commodification of higher education has also led to the recent phenomenon of university branding in a globally competitive higher education environment. National governments and HEIs seek to create symbols and slogans that attract students as well as faculty and donors (Sidhu, 2006; Stensaker, 2007). Branding occurs in a variety of forms. In the age of the Internet, websites play a key role, as does the opportunity to spread the university name through online curricular activities, including massive open online courses, or MOOCs (Rhoads, Li, & Ilano, 2014). University branding is also evident in the increasingly widespread use of clothing and other products with HEI names and logos as a means to develop interest in and commitment to particular institutions.

Internationalization and Student Mobility

To a certain degree, higher education has always been an international affair because the exchange of ideas and scholars has ensued across borders since the first HEIs were established. Since WWII and the onset of contemporary globalization, internationalization efforts have increased markedly (Altbach & Knight, 2007). Knight (2004) explains that internationalization has two interdependent pillars: internationalization at home (curricular and extracurricular innovations) and internationalization abroad (activities in which people and programs move across borders). A key component of internationalization abroad is cross-border higher education (CBHE), also known as transnational or borderless higher education. There are six main types of CBHE: (a) branch/satellite campuses operated by sponsoring HEIs with faculty from the host country, (b) franchise campuses, in which local providers offer courses approved by a sponsoring institution, (c) twinning programs that involve students' spending a portion of their studies at home and receiving their degree after spending a certain time abroad, (d) joint-degree arrangements, in which students receive a degree from both HEIs, (e) articulation programs, in which students commence their studies at home and then transfer to the sponsoring institution with advanced standing, and (f) online distance education, in which an entire program is offered electronically (Portnoi & Bagley, 2011).

Internationalization has accelerated due to the dramatic increase in student mobility that is possible in the age of globalization. In 2012, over 4 million students traveled abroad for study, compared to 2 million in 2000 (UNESCO Institute for Statistics, 2015). Student mobility is uneven, however, as the largest number of outbound students is from Central Asia, with the smallest numbers from Latin America and the Caribbean and North America. At the same time, the USA is the top destination country for inbound students. Access to CBHE is also limited by factors such as social class, which again raises concerns about who has the opportunity to participate in higher education.

University Rankings and Global Competition

The emphasis on knowledge and knowledge production in the era of contemporary globalization has contributed to the important role of HEIs, particularly in this increasingly competitive environment (Bagley & Portnoi, 2014; Marginson, 2006; Portnoi, Bagley, & Rust, 2013). Global competition has an impact on all types of HEIs, although research-intensive universities are perhaps the most affected due to their key role as knowledge producers. Indeed, HEIs are in a 'reputation race' for stature and global prominence (Hazelkorn, 2014; van Vught, 2008), and, as a result, global university rankings have been implemented. Multiple ranking systems have been developed over the past ten years, although three rankings have had the most significant impact: Shanghai Jiao Tong University's *Academic Ranking of World Universities* (*ARWU*), the *Times Higher Education* (*THE*) *World University Rankings*, and the *Quacquarelli Symonds* (*QS*) *World University Rankings*.[4]

Global rankings use indicators that define excellence based on a narrow set of measures, such as research and scholarly output in English-language journals (Portnoi & Bagley, 2011). Critiques have therefore emerged regarding the validity and reliability of the rankings' methodology as well as their focus on English-language publications (see, e.g., Marginson, 2013; Ntsohe & Letseka, 2013; Spring, 2015). Nevertheless, rankings have become central to higher education decision making (Hazelkorn, 2008, 2014). Given that rankings focus on research and scholarly production to a large degree, elite research universities have become the model to which other institutions aspire. Simon Marginson (2006) labels such institutions 'Global Research Universities' (GRUs), while Kathryn Mohrman, Wanhua Ma, and David Baker (2008) use the term 'Emerging Global Model' (EGM) to describe elite institutions that are globally oriented, research centered, and increasingly partnered with industry.

Given the emphasis on competition in higher education, governments and their HEIs utilize six main strategies to transform HEIs into the most globally competitive institutions possible (Bagley & Portnoi, 2014; Portnoi & Bagley, 2011). Connected to rankings, the first strategy is creating 'world-class' universities that mirror GRU/EGM institutions to a large extent. Even though many governments have divested from higher education funding, some use targeted expenditures to develop a small number of world-class institutions (e.g., China[5]), while others have created entirely new institutions with the express purpose of building a world-class university[6] (Salmi, 2009). The second strategy, engaging in institutional mergers, is closely connected to the strategy of developing world-class universities because governments seek to restructure their higher education sectors to make their HEIs more globally competitive.

The third strategy is internationalizing universities along the lines discussed in the prior section, especially given the global nature of the elite institutions that top university rankings. The fourth strategy is offering cross-border higher education, and the fifth is assuring quality. Most countries have their own quality-assurance bodies in addition to regional networks, such as the Asian-Pacific Quality Network, the European Association for Quality Assurance in Higher Education, and the Arab Network for Quality Assurance in Higher Education. Despite the importance of quality in global competition, quality assurance related to CBHE remains uneven (Hugonnier, 2007). The sixth strategy is participating in regional alliances. The European Union's (EU) Bologna Process is the best-known example. In this collaboration, students may pursue degrees in any member country, and qualifications transfer within the EU. All of these efforts to improve the global competitiveness of higher education are aspects of the neoliberal emphasis on education (Robertson, Bonal, & Dale, 2012).

With this background on the broad global trends related to both schooling and higher education in view, I now shift the focus to a related area that affects the Global South most directly—education and development—which ties into the influence of global governance organizations in this realm.

Education and Development

As education shifted from an elite to a mass endeavor in many countries in the Global North in the nineteenth century, these countries began to view education as a right for their citizens but not for their colonial subjects.[7] The notion of EFA emerged as a factor in international relations only with the advent of the development era. As I explain in Chap. 2, the post-WWII era, in which globalization intensified, was marked by a significant shift in international relations. The world had recently experienced two major wars, and many colonized countries were gaining their independence. It was at this time that the aid and development regime emerged, in part to compensate for the damage done by colonialism. In Chap. 2, I introduced the evolution and tenets of the Washington Consensus (now the PWC) that began to guide development and relations between the Global North and the Global South, mainly in newly independent countries, during this time period. In this section, I turn to a discussion of how global governance institutions and the principles they propound have an impact on education specifically.

Before exploring the connection between education and development, I first discuss the general context in which education functions in many of the relatively poor countries of the Global South,[8] which the aid and development regime deems to be in need of assistance. In many cases, Global South countries experience high poverty rates, especially in rural areas. Their educational infrastructure and facilities for schooling (e.g., buildings, desks, sanitation facilities) may be relatively limited or inadequate, particularly in conflict zones or rural areas, where schools often exist in open-air environments. This limited educational infrastructure may be especially challenging during certain parts of the year, such as during cold or hot months. In addition, low resource expenditure for education often translates into an insufficient number of educators, and teachers are often paid poorly, with intermittent distribution of pay. This lack of adequate material and human resources carries over into the limited HEIs that exist.[9]

Health and cultural factors also have an impact on education in poorer countries, especially with regard to attendance. For example, common ailments in the Global South (e.g., typhoid, malaria) may keep students from attending school, while the HIV/AIDS epidemic significantly affects both teachers and students, who may be infected or have ill or deceased family members. These health issues contribute both to challenges in staffing schools and to student (non)attendance. Having to pay user fees to attend both public and private schools, plus the cost of books and uniforms, means that many families cannot send all of their children to school, and boys are often selected first for school attendance. Indeed, 60 % of primary-age children in the world who are not attending school are girls (Shields, 2013). However, both boys and girls may be needed to assist with supporting their families in household duties, which may limit children of both genders' ability to attend school. Violence and conflict are also major factors that affect the ability of children to attend school, as children in countries that are experiencing wars or civil uprisings may have their education interrupted, often for a lengthy period. Given this general context in which education takes place, the need for aid to support education in impoverished countries was established when the aid and development regime emerged.

The Connection between Education and Development

Within the aid and development regime, which has a host of global governance organizations at its core, education and development are considered to be closely intertwined. The connection between these two elements harkens back to modernization theory and human capital theory. Since the postwar and WC years, global governance institutions have perceived education as a key link to economic development, especially because countries ostensibly may use education to produce human capital to contribute to their economies. In this climate, the IMF and the WB have increasingly become the purveyors of technical assistance in education in the Global South, marginalizing institutions such as the UNESCO. Key IMOs such as the IMF and the WB often collaborate with intergovernmental or nongovernmental organizations to deliver global educational agendas, such as EFA, especially in the Global South. Girls and women have become a key area of emphasis in these efforts because global governance organizations suggest that mothers have an important role to play in improving the chances of their children receiving education, allowing them to be economically productive members of society.

Beginning with the post-WWII era, education became a key component of development. Proponents of both modernization theory and human capital theory, which have roots in the modernist discourse that was widespread during the middle of the twentieth century, contributed to the connection between education and development. As noted in Chap. 3, modernization theory holds that there is one path toward development: economic progress. Educational institutions are seen as key to development because they provide the means to cultivate human capital, which can be translated into economic capital. Importantly, the emphasis shifted away from national economies as central to development to a focus on individuals (Chabbott, 2009b). A key function of educational institutions following WWII was to impart the values associated with Western democracy (e.g., individualism, scientific progress), which was particularly important to the aid and development regime during the Cold War[10] period. Indeed, education became the chief avenue for inculcating modern values into the world's populace through the 'hidden curriculum'[11], particularly given the influence of modernization theorists within global governance institutions at the time that SAPs were put into place.

Although modernization theory and human capital theory have not necessarily had a lasting impact in terms of educational structures, tenets from these theories are present in the enduring WC notion that education is essential for development (Shields, 2013). Global governance institutions guided by the WC have played a crucial role in linking education with development and have had a significant impact on education worldwide, especially in the Global South, where SAPs were instituted (Ball, 2012; Steiner-Khamsi, 2012). The leaders of these institutions were operating under the assumption that improving education, especially in newly independent countries, automatically requires aid or other assistance (Samoff, 2013). Receiving aid often comes with the 'internalization within [aid recipients'] education systems of the notion that improvement and change require external support, advice, and often personnel' (Samoff & Carroll, 2013, p. 413), which has led to a cycle of dependency on loans from external sources that continues today.

Another legacy of the WC years is the influence of IMOs on education and development. As noted, neoliberalism had gained ascendancy in the 1980s. By the 1990s, IMOs, especially the WB, had become the chief purveyors of technical assistance and enforcers of mandates related to education, pushing out organizations such as the UNESCO, which were designed to focus on education (Samoff, 2013). In the early post-WWII era, when human capital theory was in common use, education was deemed a solid investment both for individuals and for society, particularly at the level of basic (or primary) education. Staffed by education economists, the WB and other IMOs focused on economic analyses of education, especially rates of return (ROR) analysis. ROR indicates that the more educated a person is, the higher the benefit to the individual rather than society. Therefore, the focus of development was on lower levels of education, in particular, to achieve the maximum gains for society (Mir, 2013; Phillips & Schweisfurth, 2014). Economist George Psacharopoulos (1973, 1985, 1994) produced influential analyses that demonstrated that the benefit of obtaining a basic education outweighed the cost, both for individuals and for society.[12] Due in large part to these factors, global governance agencies led by the WB have typically focused on basic education at the expense of secondary and higher education. In line with the human capital theory perspective, IMOs also assumed that, with increased education of countries' populaces, these countries would be more likely to be able to repay their loans (Shields, 2013).

As a related strategy, IMOs connected lifelong learning (LLL) to improving prospects for economic development. The original concept of LLL, which emphasized individualism, social equality, and social progress, was popular in democratic education movements in the 1960s and has been used for decades to refer to ongoing learning, particularly after individuals have completed formal schooling (Rizvi & Lingard, 2010). LLL has taken on new meaning in the era of globalization, particularly given IMOs' emphasis on its economic dimension. The new LLL is focused on economic impact in the global knowledge economy and involves the following principles: (a) updating and acquiring new skills, (b) formal and non-formal learning, (c) learning how to put information into practice, rather than simply mastering facts, (d) the benefits of intergenerational learning, (e) individuals' being responsible for their own education, (f) the existence of a variety of learning pathways from childhood through adulthood, and (g) skills and competencies related to the knowledge society (Spring, 2015). Given the changes in technology and the post-Fordist mode of production under which we live, along with the perceived value of knowledge in today's society, LLL has become key to maintaining currency and being a productive member of society. Although UNESCO provides an alternate vision of a humanistic approach to LLL that involves developing individuals for their own sake rather than for economic purposes, this narrower view of LLL as connected to the economic dimension of globalization has come about in large part due to the WB's influence in the realm of education and development.

Despite the WB's influence in the education sector, the WC began to wane when SAPs failed, as explained in Chap. 2. At that time, the WB, as the 'lead' development entity for education, needed to establish another program to regain legitimacy (Jones, 2004; Tarabini, 2010). Poverty alleviation became this new focus, which Mundy (2006) describes as the 'new development compact'. In this PWC compact, education and poverty reduction are intertwined, while the view of education as critical for development remains central. As the aid and development regime has moved away from SAPs to focus on poverty alleviation, education has become a vehicle for other forms of development that have an impact on the overall economic development and progress of countries in the Global South. In this view, economic growth is recognized as not being sufficient to alleviate poverty; rather, investing in education is a key means for doing so (Tarabini, 2010), as evidenced by the EFA movement (see the next section). Notably, however, the poverty reduction measures espoused by the WB and other IMOs tend to position poverty as a problem within the locus of individuals. Thus, basic education continues to be seen as a way to equip people with the means needed to be economically productive (Tarabini, 2010).

The PWC era has also ushered in a new phase in which collaboration and partnerships with local communities that receive aid are more common. More recent aid and development efforts also tend to focus on the use of sector-wide approaches rather than separate parts of development (e.g., education and health). These approaches allow greater receiving country 'ownership' of the aid and development process (Phillips & Schweisfurth, 2014). Nevertheless, according to Samoff (2013) and Tarabini (2010), much of this ownership is theoretical, and the new era of the PWC has not seen changes because very similar conditions are prescribed as part of poverty reduction strategies as they were with SAPs.

A key component of the new poverty alleviation strategy stems from research on the role of women and mothers in the welfare not only of their families but also of their communities and countries. Research has shown that educating females has great returns because they are likely to (a) have fewer children, (b) send their children to school, and (c) be educated about health issues so that their families may experience fewer health-related issues (LeVine, 2004; Moeller, 2014). Thus, there has been an emphasis on empowering and educating girls, in particular, as seen in the UN MDGs, which are discussed below. TNCs, such as Intel, Nike, and the Gap, also have become increasingly involved in efforts to educate girls,[13] although their involvement is for the instrumental purpose of educating girls for economic growth and job preparation rather than for social justice reasons (Moeller, 2014). Another change in the new poverty alleviation environment is greater support for higher education—a response, in part, to receiving countries' accusations that the aid and development regime intentionally focused on basic education and, thus, precluded people in poorer countries from obtaining advanced skills and research capacity that are important for the knowledge economy (Samoff, 2013). Basic education brings people only to a level right above the poverty line, while higher education can help sustain those who are above the poverty threshold level (Tilak, 2007).

To challenge these WC and PWC approaches, some scholars have studied the possibilities of 'successful' or 'sustainable' globalization, in which education plays a key role in a country successfully engaging with the global economy while simultaneously working toward achieving equality and social cohesion (see, e.g., Little & Green, 2009; Nordtveit, 2009). In this regard, UNESCO coordinated the 2004–2014 United Nations Decade of Education for Sustainable Development, and the MDGs have recently been recast as goals for sustainable development, as I describe below. Notions of 'successful' or 'sustainable' globalization focus on new ways of understanding sustainability that concern equal voices, representation, and social justice. Advocates of sustainable globalization seek to underscore that neoliberal globalization can have a negative impact on both the environment and social justice.

Post-Washington Consensus Aid and Development Initiatives

Several worldwide initiatives have developed from the PWC of the aid and development regime, which tie directly to education: EFA, the MDGs/Sustainable Development Goals (SDGs), and the Fast Track Initiative (FTI)/Global Partnership for Education (GPE). These initiatives have been part of the shift to focusing on poverty alleviation and moving toward a global understanding of education as a human right for all people, rather than purely as an investment that yields economic returns (Shields, 2013). Nevertheless, as I discuss below, these initiatives reflect the lingering influence of human capital theory.

Education for All

Although the UN Declaration of Human Rights established education as a basic human right in 1948, this notion did not take hold fully until after the turn toward poverty reduction in the PWC period. During this era, UN institutions reasserted their influence, to a certain extent, in setting the global educational agenda. Three UN agencies—UNICEF, UNDP, and UNESCO—and the WB organized the first World Conference on EFA, held in 1990 in Jomtien, Thailand. A key product of the conference was the World Declaration on Education for All (also known as the Jomtien Declaration), which called for all signatories to provide universal access to basic (primary) education within ten years. Universal primary education (UPE) was defined as the completion of six years of education, which translates, in most countries, into finishing primary school. The UN (2015b) reported that over 1500 delegates attended the conference, representing 155 different countries and more than 150 IGOs, INGOs, and IMOs. The original EFA agenda included several equity provisions based on the rights of girls as well as of indigenous and disabled people. Girls' education was singled out, to a large extent, due to the previously cited research that highlights the impact of educating females on the health and overall welfare of society. Consensus was achieved at Jomtien regarding the basic parameters of EFA, and bilateral organizations and IMOs committed their support (Phillips & Schweisfurth, 2014). Provisions were put into place to monitor progress toward achieving the Declaration's goals, with much of the implementation process left to the discretion of national governments (Shields, 2013).

A follow-up World Education Forum was held in Dakar, Senegal, in 2000. The same three UN agencies and the WB participated, along with the United Nations Population Fund. Approximately 1100 people attended the conference, including 100 Ministers of Education and representatives from various IGOs, INGOs, and IMOs (UNESCO, 2015b). The conference resulted in the Dakar Framework, which renewed the commitment of signatory countries; established a set of six goals, which all participating countries and donors agreed to follow; and extended the deadline to achieve universal primary access to 2015. The goals include

(a) expanding and improving early childhood care and education; (b) providing access to quality education for all, especially girls, ethnic minorities, and other disadvantaged children; (c) providing equitable access that meets the learning needs of all children and adults, including lifelong education; (d) improving adult (especially women's) literacy by 50 % and equitable access to basic education for adults; (e) achieving equitable access to quality education for girls and eliminating gender disparities; and (f) providing and ensuring quality education for all, especially with regard to basic skills, such as numeracy and literacy.

Importantly, the Dakar Framework broadened the EFA mandate beyond UPE to include lifelong education and basic literacy and numeracy skills for adults. EFA also expanded the understanding of education as crucial to broad efforts toward sustainable development (Mundy, 2006; Tarabini, 2010). Although these goals are laudable and represent an acknowledgement of education as a human right, the EFA movement still strongly resonates with the tenets of neoliberalism and human capital theory. Education is still seen as an investment in human capital, and donors or lenders must be able to receive a return on their investment. Further, EFA could be viewed as reproducing social inequalities because it focuses on basic education. Household income is the strongest indicator of school attendance, and those who do not attend miss the opportunity to improve their economic circumstances and continue on to higher education; thus, those who come from the lowest economic means are most likely to remain in that position (Phillips & Schweisfurth, 2014; Tarabini, 2010).

Although progress has been made with increasing access to education in many countries, the EFA movement was not successful in universalizing primary education by 2015. Each year, the UNICEF issues a Global Monitoring Report that details the progress and challenges of countries individually and globally.[14] In general, there have been gains in access and enrollment in basic education, particularly for girls. Specific countries have experienced varying degrees of success, depending on the original magnitude of the problem in the country, the country's infrastructure, and population trends. In some cases, enrollment has gone up in sheer numbers, although not in percentages because there are increasing numbers of children, given the country's current demographics (Shields, 2013). In addition, quality and retention remain key challenges (Phillips & Schweisfurth, 2014). Given that the goals of EFA have not been met, a new timeline of 2030 has been established.

Most recently, in May 2015, over 1600 participants from 160 countries and various global governance organizations gathered for the World Education Forum held in Incheon, South Korea (UNESCO, 2015a). This iteration of the conference saw the addition of two additional UN branches: UN Women and the United Nations High Commission for Refugees. The forum resulted in the Incheon Declaration 'Education 2030: Towards inclusive and equitable quality education and lifelong learning for all'. The delegates 'affirm[ed] that education is a public good, a fundamental human right and a basis for guaranteeing the realization of other rights' (UNESCO, 2015a, pp. 6–7). Reflecting the notion that education contributes to many areas of social development, the declaration further notes that education 'is essential for peace, tolerance, human fulfillment and sustainable development. We recognize education as key to achieving full employment and poverty eradication' (UNESCO, 2015a, p. 7). These sentiments are in keeping with Joel Spring's (2015) critiques of the economization of education. The revised EFA vision includes: (a) 12 years of high-quality, free (government-provided) primary and secondary education; (b) inclusion and equity for all to participate in education, especially people with disabilities; (c) gender equality through gender-sensitive policies and elimination of gender discrimination; (d) quality education for foundational skills (e.g., literacy, numeracy) as well as higher level skills, such as problem-solving, analytical, interpersonal, and social skills; (e) lifelong opportunities for all, especially girls and women (with information and communications technology playing a key role); and (f) greater attention to education in conflict regions. Although progress is slow, the focus on education as a basic human right remains central to EFA and, thus, to the global discourse about education.

Millennium Development Goals/Sustainable Development Goals

The United Nations' 2000 MDGs, which were slated to be achieved by 2015, provide a broad agenda of intersectoral development goals that recognize the intersection of sectors and reflect the ethos of the PWC. All 192 member countries of the UN were signatories to this declaration, which has eight goals: (a) eradicating extreme poverty and hunger; (b) achieving universal primary education; (c) promoting gender equality and empowering women; (d) reducing child mortality; (e) improving maternal health; (f) combating HIV/AIDS, malaria, and other diseases; (g) ensuring environmental sustainability; and (h) fostering a global partnership for development (UN, 2015d). Each goal has specific targets attached, but only one goal is associated directly with education: achieving universal primary education. Nevertheless, the goal of promoting gender equality contains specific language about eliminating gender disparities in education in its targets. Further, nearly all of the eight goals are related to education in some way; for example, eradicating hunger and poverty would likely improve educational gains, as would combating health epidemics. These goals also highlight the aid and development regime's notion of women as important to development. In the educational realm, the MDGs are focused only on primary education (at the expense of secondary or higher education) and limited to access (Maxwell, 2003; Tarabini, 2010). Although the influence of human capital theory is clearly present in these goals, it is moderated by the human rights perspective to a certain degree.

Like EFA, the MDGs were not achieved by 2015, and the UN has launched a new campaign, '2015: Time for Global Action'. The MDGs have been criticized not only because they were difficult to achieve in 15 years but also because they provide a limited view of development. This new initiative goes beyond the MDGs to focus on sustainable development in the broadest sense of the term, which connects directly to a similar emphasis in the EFA movement. The UN (2015a) states, '2015 presents a historic and unprecedented opportunity to bring the countries and citizens of the world together' to 'determine the global course of action to end poverty, promote prosperity and well being for all, protect the environment and address climate change' (para. 1). At the center of the new campaign are the SDGs, which replaced the MDGs and were established in September 2015 at the UN General Assembly in New York. The SDGs represent an attempt to forge a new, comprehensive path for development in the PWC era. There are 17 SDGs, ranging from 'no poverty' (the first goal) to 'affordable and clean energy' to 'peace, justice, and strong institutions' (UN, 2015c). 'Quality education' is the fourth SDG.

The Fast Track Initiative/Global Partnership for Education

Given the challenge of funding EFA in many countries in the Global South, the WB established the FTI in 2002 (now called the Global Partnership for Education [GPE]) to provide guaranteed funding to countries that meet specific eligibility criteria and comply with certain requirements. The FTI is a corollary of both EFA and the MDGs and emphasizes achieving universal primary education. Low-income countries with Heavily Indebted

Poor Country status are eligible to apply. To receive aid, countries are required to prioritize primary education, to have poverty reduction strategies in place, and to develop 'sound national education plans' that address how UPE will be achieved (WB, 2005). The FTI started as a collaboration between IMOs, IGOs, and bilateral agencies and, in its current form, includes INGOs to form the GPE. The FTI/GPE contains an element of country ownership that characterizes the PWC because countries are able to develop their own plans for achieving UPE. The GPE takes this collaborative element a step further by establishing Local Education Groups within each country to be involved in the policy development, implementation, and monitoring process.

Originally established with seven countries from the Global South, the GPE now works with over 60 countries, primarily in Africa and Latin America (GPE, 2015). The GPE maintains the original FTI focus on UPE, especially for the most marginalized members of society, including girls, people with disabilities, and those who live in conflict zones. Some would argue, however, that the FTI/GPE has served to aid countries that would likely have achieved EFA on their own while further marginalizing the countries most in need (Shields, 2013). Moreover, others suggest that the WB has used this initiative to reassert its dominance in the realm of education and development and to control the EFA agenda (Rose, 2003; Tarabini, 2010), while still others suggest that the FTI/GPE led to 'planned dependence' on aid (Samoff & Carrol, 2013).

Debating the Convergence Hypothesis in Education

Given global trends that have an impact on education across countries, the establishment of various educational declarations,[15] and the influence of global governance institutions on education, the debate about whether education systems around the world are converging into one global model continues. As I discussed in Chaps. 1 and 3, this debate involves proponents of world culture theory, on one side, and critically oriented scholars who raise questions regarding the accuracy of the normative convergence hypothesis, on the other. World culture theorists suggest that educational institutions serve as venues for dispersing global culture (see, e.g., Boli, Ramirez, & Meyer, 1985; Meyer, Boli, Thomas, & Ramirez, 1997) and that education provides the opportunity to impart specific cultural values that are important in contemporary society, such as democratic citizenship, individual rights, rational decision making, individual autonomy, universalism, and world citizenship (Boli & Thomas, 1997). In the realm of world culture theory, global governance institutions, particularly INGOs, are viewed as central to this diffusion of world cultural values (McNeely, 1995).

World culture theorists would argue that schooling is moving toward one global model of education that has evolved as 'best'. Since the early 1990s, researchers from the Stanford group (e.g., John Meyer, John Boli, Francisco Ramirez) have been arguing that education is increasingly becoming similar across countries. John Meyer, John Boli, George Thomas, and Francisco Ramirez (1997) suggest that both the organization and curriculum of schooling have become shared across the world. For example, nearly all countries have centrally organized formal schooling systems with professionally trained teachers. Further, Meyer, David Kamens, and Aaron Benavot (2005) state that an educational structure that involves graduated levels of education was intentionally developed and argue that policymakers actively seek to incorporate global school culture into their systems. Subject matter is also remarkably similar across countries, so that all children have the same basic foundation through their education (Meyer et al., 1997; Meyer et al., 2005), which is due to the 'credential society' and the need for credentials to be transferable across contexts in the global economy (Baker & LeTendre, 2005; Ramirez, 2003).

World culture theory scholars have argued that globalization and its associated processes continue to push us toward one global model of schooling based on best practices (see, e.g., Astiz, Wiseman, & Baker, 2002; Baker, 2014; McNeely, 1995; Meyer et al., 2005). This notion of convergence in education as evolving from best practices resonates with the hyperglobalist approach of Thomas Freidman (1999), who posits that countries will adopt the educational practices that are the most effective around the world. Although world culture theory is not outwardly aligned with neoliberalism, its premise aligns with the capitalist notion of free markets that ensure that the best ideas will rise to the top. World culture theorists typically see the common schooling model that is evolving as representing the best that the world has to offer, although some acknowledge that the global model of schooling is based on a Western perspective (see, e.g., Ramirez, 2003).

On the other side of the debate about convergence are various sets of critical scholars who critique the origins and functions of the emerging world culture of schooling or dismiss it altogether. Critics argue that the global model of schooling espoused by global governance organizations and the 'core' countries that dominate them is a form of neocolonialism (Arnove, 1980). Scholars from the critical domain also question the notion that the best educational practices have risen to the top, noting that the global model of schooling is based on the educational and economic environment in the Global North. This global model is also closely connected to actors such as the WB and the IMF, which are affiliated with neoliberal corporate interests that serve the Global North and represent these groups' interests and values (Spring, 2015). From this perspective, global trends and models align with the agenda of the powerful elite, and world educational culture provides the opportunity for these elites to impose their values.

In this environment, the question also arises as to who has the opportunity to decide what values should be shared because the model of world school culture is not simply about structure; it is also about values, such as individualism, which may not resonate with countries around the world. Roger Dale (2000) argues that the current model stems not from world culture and what are truly best practices but, rather, from a 'globally structured educational agenda' in which various powerful actors have decided what should matter in education. From a postcolonial perspective, the imposition of a world culture of schooling is a form of continued imperialism on the part of the Global North and the global governance institutions associated with this regime (Tikly, 2001). Postcolonial theorists would argue that a world culture of education leads to privileging certain forms of knowledge—those perceived as important and imposed by the Global North.

As noted in Chap. 3, critics of world culture theory would suggest that, even if a (contested) version of a global model of schooling is developing, this does not mean that this model is manifested in the same way in various local contexts or that it is not reshaped during the implementation phase. Critics of world culture theory who belong to what Spring (2015) calls the 'culturalist' group would argue that global trends are always mediated in the local environment. Therefore, as noted in Chap. 3, they suggest that convergence is occurring at a policy level but not necessarily in practice. For example, Dana Burde (2004) demonstrates that, while global governance institutions' policies are having an impact at the global level, many of their mandates are not carried out in practice in a local context. In other words, there is greater convergence in rhetoric than in action.

Burde (2004) posits that there is a game that is being played in which local players adapt the language of the aid and development regime in their proposals and interactions but then follow their own agendas on the ground. Although lenders and donors may be increasingly focused on monitoring, there remains a great deal of latitude for implementation (Anderson-Levitt, 2003; Samoff, 2013). There is also a great deal of opportunity for local actors (i.e., teachers and other educators) to resist and reshape global trends. Moreover, culturalists reject the foundation of world culture theory that suggests that global governance organizations are working toward one model of schooling (Steiner-Khamsi, 2004, 2012). In essence, this group of scholars is not convinced that there is a world culture or world model of schooling, and they provide empirical evidence[16] of instances in which policies are borrowed in theory, but not in practice, or when multiple models are used.

Critical scholars also suggest the possibility of multiple models of schooling. The present model, referred to as a global culture of schooling, which is being propounded through global governance bodies, is tied to the economic aspects of globalization and seeks to prepare youth to be integrated into the global economy. There is also, however, a progressive model of schooling that is student-centered and focuses on social justice (Anderson-Levitt, 2003). The progressive model of education is based, in large part, on the work of US education philosopher John Dewey (1907, 1916). Dewey sought to educate students in a way that would help them to be productive members of society in multiple realms, not just in an economic sense. He advocated for concrete, practice-based teaching methods, called 'learning by doing'. More recently, the work of Paolo Freire and other critical pedagogues have taken up the charge of fostering social justice and transformative change through education.

Both the dominant and the progressive models of schooling are based on Western values, and Spring (2015) outlines two models that are not based on such values. The first is the religious education world model, which is generally found in religious schools. Religious schools focus on values connected to spirituality rather than those connected to the economic domain (Spring, 2015). The second model is indigenous education, which may or may not be described as a model because it comes in a variety of forms, many of which are non-formal. Indigenous education is generally offered in indigenous languages and is under the control of indigenous groups. It emphasizes multiple ways of knowing and views the world in a holistic fashion (Spring, 2015).

Conclusion

Key developments related to globalization in the contemporary era have had a profound impact on the educational sector. The realms of both schooling and higher education have experienced significant developments, including privatization and corporatization, which align with the neoliberal model of education that is prevalent in today's globalized world. These developments provide an opportunity for educators to reflect on the trajectory of educational reforms in the era of contemporary globalization. The application of the aid and development regime's notion of education as an economic investment has also been significant, especially for the countries of the Global South. Global educational declarations, such as EFA, are also central developments that display the influence of globalization on education. Although many of the key trends in both schooling and higher education are connected to the influence of neoliberalism, it is important to keep in mind that other models of education exist. As many critical scholars point out, neoliberal globalization can be resisted and altered. Educators should both recognize the impact of neoliberal globalization and consider different ways in which to organize the world, including within the realm of education.

Notes

1. Although non-formal modes of education are salient in many countries, the bulk of the research available is on formal education. Therefore, I have focused on the two main areas of formal education: schooling and higher education. Schooling refers to education at the basic (or primary) and secondary levels, while higher education covers all postsecondary education.
2. This view was reflected in the Social Efficiency Movement in the USA in the early 1900s, in which schooling was seen as a form of social control (Kliebard, 2004). This movement was also closely tied to structural-functionalism. To a certain extent, the experience of the USA is evident in the global social efficiency movement, although it goes beyond a basic level of social control to a restructuring of society through education.
3. User fees are still common in many countries in the Global South, although a number of countries throughout the African continent have begun to abolish user fees as a means to facilitate universal access.
4. The *QS* ranking was part of the *THE* ranking before the two split in 2009. Other ranking mechanisms include *U-Multirank* in Europe, *SCImago Institutions Rankings*, and *Webometrics*.

5. China has two projects aimed at developing world-class universities. Project 211 was launched in 1995 with an emphasis on 100 HEIs and involves funds from both central and provincial sources as well as from affected HEIs. The focus of Project 985, which was established in 1998, was to develop 39 HEIs to compete on global HEI ranking measures.
6. One notable university in this realm is the King Abdullah University of Science and Technology in Saudi Arabia, which is a public institution created for the express purpose of competing with other elite institutions (Portnoi & Bagley, 2011).
7. Prior to the era of development that ensued in the post-WWII era, when the needs of people in the Global South became a focus, education, which was then under colonialism, had a different purpose. It was meant primarily to keep colonized people repressed, while allowing them to gain sufficient skills to support the colonial regime (Samoff, 2013). Colonial regimes were not the only providers of education in colonies, however. During colonialism and the early years of independence, missionaries provided a broader range of subjects for study. In addition, missionary schools served to indoctrinate local peoples into dominant Western religions (Shields, 2013).
8. The descriptions provided here are generalizations and pertain primarily to the poorest countries of the world. Wide variation exists between countries in the Global South, which is one reason that having only two terms to distinguish between country types (i.e., developed and developing) is problematic. Nevertheless, I provide these general notes to offer a background for the reader.
9. As I explain, however, higher education has historically not been the focus of the aid and development regime.
10. During the Cold War, the USA and its allies were concerned about communism, due mostly to concern about their chief adversary, the Soviet Union. Therefore, any opportunities to educate people around the world for democracy and capitalism were welcomed.
11. The hidden curriculum refers to the subtle socialization that occurs through education, such as the concept of rules and authority, as well as capitalist ideals, such as individualism. Although structural-functionalists would consider hidden curriculum to be important and positive, this concept has often been used to provide critique of the functionalist system from a conflict theory or neo-Marxist perspective.
12. Although critiques have arisen for Psacharapoulos' ROR analysis (see, e.g., Bennell's (1998) assertion that ROR analysis did not hold true for Asian countries), Psacharapoulos' findings served as a foundation of development thinking, particularly at the WB.

13. See http://www.girleffect.org/why-girls/ for an example of a corporate–INGO partnership related to girls' education. The Nike Foundation created a series of 'Girl Effect' videos in collaboration with INGOs, launching a campaign alongside the MDGs.
14. See http://en.unesco.org/gem-report/.
15. Indeed, the EFA movement has been posited as an example of a policy that stems from the global agenda for education and is driven by global governance institutions (Mundy, 2006).
16. See Chap. 5 for a further discussion of the policy borrowing and lending process and Chap. 6 for examples of how policy borrowing plays out in practice.

CHAPTER 5

Educational Reform Processes in a Globalized World

National educational policies, or reforms, are increasingly influenced by global trends, as discussed in Chap. 4, particularly in the Global South, where the influence of global governance institutions is strong. Importantly, however, policies may be developed and implemented at any level of locality within education. For instance, HEIs might have campus-specific policies (e.g., a smoke-free environment), while schools might have individual policies about where and when parents may drop off and pick up their children. Policies could also be effected in state or provincial jurisdictions, for example, in federal systems in which states or provinces may determine the minimum number of days of instruction that children must receive in schools each year. In this book, the focus of discussion and analysis is *public policy*, or policy that is the domain of national governments. 'Policy' can be defined as 'the dynamic and value-laden process through which a political system handles a public problem' (Fowler, 2009, p. 5). Policies are designed to alleviate societal problems and are key drivers of innovation and change.

Policymaking involves multiple actors, especially given the global context in which policies are created, implemented, and assessed. As discussed in Chap. 2, various actors and stakeholders are involved in the processes of educational reform: (a) global governance institutions, including IGOs, regional organizations, bilateral organizations, IMOs, and INGOs; (b) TNCs; (c) nation-states; (d) communities, policy implementers, and individuals; and (e) think tanks, special interest groups, and lobbyists. The

© The Editor(s) (if applicable) and The Author(s) 2016

L.M. Portnoi, *Policy Borrowing and Reform in Education*,
DOI 10.1057/978-1-137-53024-0_5

policymaking process offers opportunities for all interested parties to discuss problems and formulate potential solutions, although not necessarily with equal access.

In this chapter I provide an understanding of policy and how it works, while I focus on the policy borrowing and lending processes that occur across borders in Chap. 6. Below, I first discuss the parameters of policy and reform, including the meanings of these terms and the policy climate in which policies are created. I also introduce the interdisciplinary field of policy studies that has developed to study this complex phenomenon. In the next section, I cover models and theories of public policy formation and implementation, including the influential policy process model, several additional competing and complementary models, and three emerging models. I also present the Four Stages of Policy Borrowing model (Phillips & Ochs, 2003) that developed in the field of comparative and international education, specifically. In the implementation section that follows, I cover two of the chief strategies that have been used for implementing policies, forward mapping and backward mapping, followed by a discussion of a synthesized approach that involves both strategies. I also present the importance of 'street-level bureaucrats' who are involved with putting policies into practice on the ground level. I then consider the debate about whether policy implementation involves coercion versus the expression of stakeholder agency. Finally, I focus on the globalization of educational policies.

Policy Matters

Educational reform stems from policy, and, as described in detail below, policies take on numerous forms, purposes, and functions. The policymaking process is not neutral but, rather, takes place within a multifaceted policy climate that involves multiple stakeholders. Given the complexities of the policymaking process, policy studies has evolved as an interdisciplinary area of study focused on understanding policy and the policymaking process.

Unpacking the Meaning behind Policy and Reform

The term 'policy' is used synonymously with 'reform' to refer to government-provided guidelines for addressing issues of public concern. Policies (or reforms) are often codified into laws, although they do not need to be formed into legislation to be implemented, especially if they derive from governmental sources and connect resources to implementation or prescribe punitive measures for non-compliance. Policies comprise both (a) formal texts (e.g., laws and regulations) designed to further a government's goals and outcomes and (b) the effects of these actions on society. In essence, policies and laws serve to purposefully regulate society and individuals' behavior. Although reforms are designed to engender consistent behavior, they are rarely implemented as intended, as I discuss in the section on policy implementation.

Policy can be understood as a process or set of processes rather than a bounded entity. According to sociology of education professor Stephen Ball (2006), a suite of policies forms a 'policy ensemble' that is framed by a policy discourse and sets the stage for what can and should be included in a policy. In a general sense, public policy constitutes the measures that governments deem important to undertake for the betterment of society; therefore, public policy is 'entangled with the notions of public and social issues, the solutions to these, and the role of the state in providing these solutions' (Ward et al., 2015). Public policy symbolically represents the values that government and, by proxy, citizens hold at a given historical moment. In essence, policies allow governments the opportunity to publicly declare what is important in their societies. Also important is what governments choose not to do; that is, silence or inaction on certain societal concerns displays a government's stance on the significance of particular issues (Dye, 2012; Kraft & Furlong, 2014; Rizvi & Lingard, 2010).

Policies guide movements within a particular social, political, or economic milieu to alleviate problems or conditions that the public believes require government intervention. Three main conditions typically lead governments to conclude that their involvement is necessary: (a) when there has been a marked shift in public opinion (political), (b) when there are circumstances for which the government must take a stand on what is 'right' in the absence of public instigation (moral or ethical), and (c) when the free market economy does not engender desired results or produces uneven results (economic) (Kraft & Furlong, 2014). Governments clearly play an important role in the policymaking process, yet this role is not simply benevolent; notions of authority and power factor into decisions about educational reforms, which reflect the norms and values of the government (Rizvi & Lingard, 2010). Policies represent both a means to resolve problems and a normative force that attempts to engender alignment with government mandates (Ward et al., 2015). Importantly, for the government's authority to be maintained, the populace must consent to the policies being formed (Rizvi & Lingard, 2010).

Symbolic and Material Policies

Public policies serve to highlight governments' values and objectives. The underlying motivation for governments to initiate a policy is ostensibly to alleviate societal problems that citizens believe require government intervention. Policies are created within a contested political terrain, however, and therefore reflect multiple additional motivations. Political maneuvers might lead to governments adopting policies without the intention of implementing them. Policies that serve a strategic purpose such as political expediency are symbolic. Symbolic policies are typically abstract and lack concrete language for implementation. In contrast, material policies are generally more clearly articulated and provide provisions for implementation and monitoring. Material policies are intended to have a longer-term impact, and may serve to address societal problems.

Two central types of policies are the symbolic and the material (Rizvi & Lingard, 2010). Symbolic policies serve to legitimize the importance of certain issues and often stem from political motivations. These policies, which tend to be abstract and lack concrete strategies for implementation, often have a strategic, rather than a practical, impact. Governments typically do not possess the commitment to carry out symbolic policies and often allocate very limited resources for their implementation. They may, however, serve as a step toward a material policy. Material policies are usually clearly articulated, with specific mechanisms provided for implementation (including funding and other resources) and monitoring. A material policy may be either distributive (of resources) or redistributive when there is a need to intervene to forge greater equity in society, as with affirmative action measures (Rizvi & Lingard, 2010). The main distinction between the two types of policies is that governments generally intend to implement material policies, while they often have no plans to implement symbolic policies.

The Policy Climate

Policies are developed and implemented within contested political, social, cultural, and economic environments. The prevailing climate influences which problems rise to the top and which can realistically be undertaken, given the existing environment. Thus, most policies are necessarily transitory in nature and are constantly evolving as circumstances change. As David Easton (1965), a political scientist, stated in his seminal work on politics, policies represent an 'authoritative allocation' of society's values, which demonstrates the relative strength and influence of particular policy imperatives that rise to the top in a given society at a specific historical point. Because policies 'unfold in nested contexts' in this complex policy terrain, they 'provide the stage for political dramas' (Ward et al., 2015, p. 8). Politics and power differentials have an impact on the conflict that is inherent in the complex terrain of the policymaking process. Given that reforms are developed in these contested environments, it is not always clear whose values the policies represent (Rizvi & Lingard, 2010).

A variety of motivations exist for developing public policies in this policy climate. In both domestic and global contexts, crises are one of the most significant triggers for policy activity. For example, global financial crises have led to legitimizing neoliberal schooling practices, such as accountability and high-stakes testing in an effort to develop human capital to serve instrumental purposes and improve the economy (Keating, Preston, Burke, Van Heertum, & Arnove, 2013). These developments are related to the economization of education model that critical education scholar Joel Spring (2015) critiques, as discussed in Chap. 4. Policies may also result from 'crises' that policymakers or governments create. When necessary, problems are 'manufactured' ex post facto to allow for the legitimacy of a policy that the government wishes to implement. For example, a government might seek to institute a national education curriculum and use poor educational results (which may be skewed and spun) to develop a sense of crisis around education so that policymakers and the public are 'primed' to seek the very reform that the government envisages.

In many cases, additional motivations factor into policymakers' decisions about which policies to support, including their need to gain legitimacy, return favors that resulted in their election, or appease voters prior to an upcoming election. Elected officials who are tasked with developing and implementing public policy often need to balance their endorsement of particular policies. On the one hand, they need to cater to the preferences of their base, while, on the other hand, they are mindful of the general population's influence (Kraft & Furlong, 2014).

Policy Studies

Given the importance of policies for setting the agenda for change, attention has increasingly been placed on the study of policy as a formal area of inquiry. Policy studies developed as a subdiscipline of political science in the late 1950s and early 1960s as a field of inquiry focused on understanding policies and the policymaking process. The subdiscipline of policy studies was originally closely tied to governmental needs for data on policy development and effectiveness and has evolved to include the study of government actions in the policy arena. Currently, research is conducted in policy studies for a number of reasons, including to develop basic scientific knowledge, to make policy recommendations, and to understand challenges to implementing policies. Although the area of policy studies is often associated with the domain of political science, it is an interdisciplinary endeavor (much like Global Studies). Public administration, sociology, economics, public policy, and other disciplines have strands focused on policy studies, and some universities offer stand-alone programs in policy studies.

The study of policy involves several different types of activities. Some studies cover the full policymaking process cycle, from agenda setting to implementation to evaluation, while others focus on specific aspects. Some scholars and policymakers study particular issues to gain a better understanding of which reforms may be viable alternatives and what the consequences of implementing a reform might be. They may use case studies to understand how public policies are developed and why they succeed (or fail). Other scholars study the content of public policy, as well as the impact that outside forces (e.g., social, economic, political) have on it and vice versa (Dye, 2012). Another activity is policy analysis, through which policies are evaluated for effectiveness as well as for expected (and unexpected) consequences.

Research in policy studies is a shared enterprise that involves HEI researchers and government analysts. Those tasked with creating and effecting policies are increasingly involved in policy analysis, and many governments have full sets of staff researchers focused on studying policies, their impact, and their implementation. HEI researchers typically conduct analysis *of* policy (to understand a policy and why or how it came about), whereas policymakers conduct analysis *for* policy (for policy development). Analysis for policy typically lacks a critical angle because it stems only from government sources (Gordon, Lewis, & Young, 1977) and, therefore, may be tailored toward government purposes and goals without taking multiple perspectives into account.

Theories and Models of Public Policymaking

When shaping or analyzing public policies, including those that pertain to education, policymakers, scholars, and practitioners draw from an array of approaches. In this section of the chapter, I first highlight one of the most common approaches to understand the policymaking process, the policy process (or stages) model, which provides a straightforward understanding of how educational policies are shaped, implemented, and assessed. Next, I discuss several complementary and competing models of the policymaking process, including rational choice, incrementalism, institutionalism/neoinstitutionalism, systems, group choice, public choice, and elite models or theories. In the section that follows, I briefly present three emerging approaches that have gained prominence in policy studies more recently: the streams model, the punctuated equilibrium model, and the advocacy coalition framework. Many of the theories or models included in the discussion were originally developed in the USA or Europe and have been adapted and employed in multiple countries around the globe. In the final section of this portion of the chapter, I discuss David Phillips and Kimberly Ochs' (2003) model of policy borrowing that emerged in the field of comparative and international education to address educational reform, specifically. The theories and models that I cover do not represent an exhaustive list; rather, they demonstrate the variety of approaches that may be employed to develop or assess educational reforms. I describe each approach separately for clarity, although policymakers or policy analysts may use multiple approaches in practice.

The Policy Process Model

Educational reform processes are similar to those of other public policy arenas (e.g., social welfare, healthcare) in which reforms or policies move from ideas to implementation to evaluation in a cyclical fashion. This cyclical policy process model evolved from Harold Lasswell's (1948, 1951) work during the early years of policy studies and incorporates both the stages of policymaking and the stakeholders involved. The model takes a rational perspective and presents a logical sequence of activities that occur as policies are developed, implemented, and evaluated. Although the stepwise account of the policymaking process has been critiqued as overly simplistic and deterministic, it provides a practical, descriptive account of the key stages in the policy cycle. Moreover, policy or reform processes are now thought to be continuous and constantly evolving. From this perspective, various stages in the policy cycle are viewed not as discrete entities but, rather, as overlapping components in most cases. Once a policy works its way through all of the stages (or even skips over some), it often continues through the cycle once again (Kraft & Furlong, 2014).

The first stage in the policymaking process is *problem identification*, in which nation-states or their populaces identify problems that require government intervention. Some of these problems may be new on the policy agenda, while others may be variations or corollaries to existing issues. The second stage is *agenda setting*, during which problems are defined and framed (or spun). Importantly, the definition of problems contributes to the solutions that might be used to address them (Kraft & Furlong, 2014). During the agenda-setting phase, the causes of a problem are also investigated as a means to develop solutions that may be used in the next phase of the policy cycle. The agenda-setting phase involves political maneuvering in which various groups (i.e., elites, government officials, the public, and special interest groups) vie for influence over the way the agenda is set. Dye (2012) suggests that the question of who has the power to get a policy issue on the agenda is more important than the solutions created. In certain cases, interested parties may decide that issues of concern could cause unrest or negative consequences that would outweigh the benefits of instituting policies to address them. In other instances, comparisons to other countries[1] or policy items may be made to legitimize the importance of addressing a particular problem and as generating 'buy in' for intervening on a given issue.

Once the agenda has been set and decisions have been made to address a particular problem, the third stage of *policy formulation* begins. During this phase, policymakers use policy analysis to develop a set of policy goals and actions that the government will undertake to address the identified problem. Government bureaucrats often engage in policy analysis to a large degree because they have the expertise to analyze various options to determine economic or social costs and the potential effectiveness of a reform, although consultations between government officials and other interested sets of stakeholders often occur. The fourth stage of the policymaking process is *policy legitimation*, in which governments 'sell' the policies that they seek to enact and develop political support for them. To this end, policies are justified and rationales are provided for why specific reforms are being developed, and messages may be crafted for various sets of interested parties (e.g., school principals and parents).

The fifth stage, *policy implementation*, is often the most complex and is the subject of a separate section below. This phase involves three complementary activities: (a) organization, in which resources, offices, and modes of program administration are established or specific laws are generated; (b) interpretation, in which policy directives are transferred into language that will resonate with the parties who are involved with implementation (e.g., principals, teachers, office staff, students); and (c) application, in which policies are enacted (Kraft & Furlong, 2014). In this stage, the impact of governmental policies may be observed. Notably, governments' efforts to implement the policies they create involve another set of negotiations.

The impact and consequences (intended or unintended) that arise from policy implementation are assessed during the sixth stage, *policy or program evaluation*. At this point in the policy cycle, outcomes are measured and tested to ascertain whether the policy is achieving the government's goals and addressing the problem at hand. Governments often make assessments regarding success or failure and whether a reform has been worth the money invested. They also determine whether the reform should be continued, cut, or expanded. In the final stage, *policy change*, governments adjust their goals based on the assessments undertaken as well as the prevailing social and political climate. From this point, as the reform is modified through incremental change or a new reform takes its place, the policy cycle begins again.

This process-oriented view of policymaking appears relatively straightforward when set out in descriptive fashion, yet complexities emerge at each step of the process. Problems that require government intervention evolve over time, and potential solutions may be fleeting because the context is ever-changing (McLaughlin, 2006).

Competing and Complementary Theories and Models of Public Policy

In addition to the policy process model, several other competing and complementary theories or models exist that represent different ways to approach the processes of policy formation and analysis. Several of the key models are discussed below.

Rational Choice Theory

Rational choice theory (also known as the rational-comprehensive model) evolved after WWII and is an influential perspective on public policy that draws from political science. Grounded in both psychology and economics, rational choice theory posits that people are rational actors who make decisions based on self-interest and the possibility of economic gain. In this view, individuals are motivated by their own needs and goals but realize that they cannot obtain everything that they desire. Therefore, they calculate the costs and benefits of their actions prior to making decisions. Critics of rational choice theory have suggested, however, that not all individuals are motivated by self-interest and that their actions may vary over time. In addition, the theory does not account for the possibility of collective action.

According to rational choice theory, policymakers must select policy options in which the benefits will outweigh the costs for the greatest societal gain (Dye, 2012). The theory suggests that policymakers consider how people are likely to act based on the current societal context and values prior to creating policies. Selecting policies using a rational model requires understanding society's values, having a full grasp of all of the policy alternatives possible, and knowing all potential consequences of policy actions as a means to weigh the costs and benefits of policy options. Thus, it is not practical in most applications (Kraft & Furlong, 2014). In addition, policies already in place have typically involved a great deal of investment of time and other resources, and therefore, it may not be feasible to begin with a new policy in most instances of policymaking. For this reason, incrementalism emerged as an alternative approach to policymaking.

Incrementalism Model

The incrementalism model stems from Charles Lindblom's (1959) critique of rational choice theory. According to Lindblom, although the rational choice model may be useful for making small-scale changes, it is not effective in the complex social and political environments in which most public policies, including those in education, are created. The incrementalism approach suggests that policymakers make decisions to adapt existing policies in an incremental manner due to time and resource constraints related to researching policy alternatives and their potential outcomes. In this 'muddling through', to which Lindblom refers, policymaking essentially involves building on prior policy development. Changes are made to modify existing policies to expand, contract, or add on, as needed, often through trial and error. Rather than conducting an exhaustive analysis that takes considerable time and may lead to inaction, policymakers use an incremental model to search for the best option that they can find at the time that involves minimal changes and conflict. Aaron Wildavsky (1964) and Michael Dempster and Wildavsky (1979) further developed Lindblom's model and the notion of incremental changes based on existing policy, applying the model to the budgetary process in particular.

Proponents of the incrementalism model suggest that policy is evolving and that it changes over time. The incremental approach allows policymakers to simplify the policymaking process by focusing only on feasible policy options that are already in place. The incrementalism model also offers a way for minor changes to be made without lasting implications and unintended consequences that might accompany a radical change. Existing policies may be retained to a large degree due to the investment that has already been made in them, their influence, or the regard that the public holds for them. In this sense, incrementalism is a conservative approach because it accepts the legitimacy of existing policies and does not allow for innovation or radical changes (Dye, 2012). Alternatives that may be effective or beneficial may not be considered if an incremental approach to policymaking is employed. Although incrementalism is still used in policymaking decisions, other theories and models have become more prominent in recent years.

Institutional and Neoinstitutional Theory

According to institutional theory, institutions are central to the policymaking process. This theory, which has its roots in political science, highlights government structures and how they affect decision making in terms of facilitating or impeding the policymaking process (Kraft & Furlong, 2014). Institutional theory focuses on the legal and structural dimensions of public policy. An institution, or structure, may be either an organization (e.g., a legislative body) or a rule. When analyzing public policies, institutional theorists might consider the structures and rules that exist to legitimize policy and determine those that are involved in developing policy. In other words, they might analyze which groups are part of the policymaking process based in institutions and which groups are left out. Institutional theory suggests that governments authoritatively determine policy, apply policy universally, and use coercion to do so.

Understanding the role of institutions is an important part of the policymaking process because these structures provide the framework in which policies are made and enacted. The study of institutions was central to political science after WWII, although, in the 1960s, the sciences shifted the focus to individual behavior. Neoinstitutionalism (Meyer, 1977) offers a revival of institutionalism to a certain degree and focuses greater attention on rules or norms that guide behavior and the resulting patterns of behavior that emerge. Rules and norms may be formal (e.g., policies, laws) or informal guidelines for how individuals should function within institutions and society. As noted in Chap. 4, neoinstitutionalism is one of the dominant theories used to understand the apparent convergence, or isomorphism, in educational reforms across countries in a globalized world.

Systems Theory

Systems theory, which stems from political science, is founded on the notion that the structural, political, social, and economic context (or *policy environment*) in which policy choices are made is central to the policymaking process. The *structural* environment is the political and governance system in a given country, while the *political* environment entails qualitative components, such as public opinion, attitudes, and values. The *social* environment includes the demographics of the populace, as well as its social structure, and the *economic* environment involves wealth distribution, inflation, growth rates, and similar factors. Through their activities and institutions, governments address the demands that develop from these four environments.

Easton (1965) pioneered this way of thinking about policy studies and focused primarily on the 'inputs' and 'outputs' of the policymaking process, similar to a biological model, which employs a reactive strategy in which government involvement leads to an adjustment in the system. *Policy inputs* come primarily from two sources: (a) demands, or problems that individuals or groups present to further their interests, and (b) support, or the acceptance of the legitimacy of government's actions that the public demonstrates when they comply with laws or vote in favor of policies. *Policy outputs* are the policies, laws, or guidelines that emerge from the policymaking process. Over time, policy outputs result in *policy change*, which addresses the problem that demanded government intervention in the first place (Kraft & Furlong, 2014). *Feedback* based on policy changes may lead to retaining a specific policy or new demands for change. This model has been criticized as simplistic because the inner workings of the system are not explained. Therefore, it is no longer in widespread use, although the model's concepts and terminology are still part of public policy parlance (Birkland, 2010).

Group Theory and Public Choice Theory

Both group and public choice theory focus on the influence of groups in the policymaking process. Group theory emphasizes relationships and interactions among groups as central in the political sphere. From a group theory perspective, individuals become powerful forces in policymaking when they form groups; thus, politics and the policymaking process are seen as a struggle between groups (Dye, 2012). Individuals tend to join, either formally or informally, with others who share similar interests to influence the policies that are developed and implemented. A group's relative influence is dictated by factors such as the size of the group, their economic power, their cohesion (or lack thereof), and the strength of their organization. Group theory suggests that governments seek to manage the conflict between groups to develop positions of compromise that translate into policy initiatives. Public policy represents a form of equilibrium that results from these compromises. Similar to systems theory, group theory is a reactive model because governments respond to the demands that influential groups place upon them and negotiate changes within this terrain of competing groups.

Public choice theory, developed by Nobel Prize winner James Buchanan and colleagues, is related to group theory because it focuses on collective action. Rather than emphasizing group competition and compromise, public choice theory is an economic theory that assumes that individuals are self-interested parties who act based on their individual interests. The theory recognizes that government is necessary to perform certain functions, especially the provision of public services (Dye, 2012). According to public choice theory, people pursue their self-interests whether they are operating in the marketplace or in politics. They join with others who can help them achieve their own goals. The benefit of collective decision making motivates individuals to join with other people to influence policymaking through shared agreement about outcomes that will be beneficial to individuals within the group.

Elite Theory

Another way to understand policy formation is through elite theory (Dye, 2012; Dye & Ziegler, 2011). According to this theory, cultural, political, and economic elites strongly influence public policy because their values and priorities rise to the top. In elite theory, the public is perceived as not desiring involvement and not having a full understanding of policies and their implications. Therefore, an elite group that is not representative of the masses and often comes from a high socio-economic status shapes public policy within the group's domains. Importantly, elites are not always influential in the same way in all circumstances because the dominance of different groups of elites varies in different spaces (Kraft & Furlong, 2014). However, elite theory suggests that elites remain a powerful force in public policymaking. In effect, they serve to shape public opinion rather than to respond to the needs of the masses.

Elite theory emphasizes a hierarchical policymaking process with a top-down approach in which leaders create policies and lower-level workers carry them out (Dye, 2012). Like incrementalism, elite theory represents a conservative approach because elites desire to keep change minimal to maintain their own status and influence as well as the policies that reflect their values. Elite theory assumes that there is a consensus to which elites subscribe regarding which values are important in society. New members of elite groups must be willing to accept this consensus to maintain the societal system that the elites have developed (Dye, 2012).

Emerging Models of the Policymaking Process

Although many of the theories and models described earlier are still used, three emerging models have gained prominence in recent years: the streams model, the punctuated equilibrium model, and the advocacy coalition framework.

Streams Model

The streams model expands on Michael Cohen, James March, and Johan Olsen's (1972) 'garbage can' metaphor of organizational choice, which suggests that 'organized anarchies', such as universities, are a 'collection of choices looking for problems, issues and feelings looking for decision situations in which they might be aired, solutions looking for issues to which they might be the answer, and decision makers looking for work' (p. 2). For the authors, choice opportunities constitute a garbage can into which all potential problems and solutions are deposited. Cohen et al. suggest that decisions are the outcome of four streams within an organization, which are relatively independent from one another: (a) problems, or concerns that require intervention; (b) solutions, which are answers that actively seek questions; (c) participants, which vary over time and result in new choices; and (d) choice opportunities, in which decisions are made.

John Kingdon (2010) adapted this model for the study of public policymaking and presented it in a book originally published in 1984. Kingdon's model of public policy comprises three parallel streams: (a) the problem stream, involving urgent issues that require attention, which are identified through a subjective and political process; (b) the policy stream, which often involves a predetermined solution that has been developed in anticipation of a problem's coming to the fore; and (c) the politics stream, which provides the motivation to implement (or not implement) a policy due to the political context and public opinion. According to Kingdon, those who seek to influence policy attempt to join the streams during a 'window of opportunity' in which there is the greatest possibility of policy change. However, the existence of an opening does not guarantee that a change will occur (Birkland, 2010). This model differs from the earlier rational model of policymaking because it recognizes the 'messiness' of policymaking, which often does not occur in a logical or stepwise fashion. The model also provides a clear understanding of how the environment, especially the political context, serves to limit or constrain policy choices.

Punctuated Equilibrium Model

Drawing from the terminology of evolutionary biology, Frank Baumgartner and Bryan Jones (2009) developed a model that accounts for long periods of time that are relatively stable with limited policy changes, followed by periods of abrupt, profound change accompanied by destabilization. As connected to group theory, these changes are often associated with the fluctuation of power of various groups involved in the policymaking process, which upsets the equilibrium of the system (Birkland, 2010). Several components comprise punctuated equilibrium theory, which was originally put forth in Baumgartner and Jones' book, published in 1993. *Disproportionate attention* implies that issues either receive significant attention from policymakers or stagnate because they do not; at the same time, *bounded rationality* suggests that policymakers need to focus on a small number of issues at any given time.

Group dynamics within the policymaking process are also key to the punctuated equilibrium model (Cairney, 2011). First, groups vie for influence with regard to *framing*, or how a policy will be positioned and 'sold' to various constituencies. Second, groups have varying degrees of influence. *Power* and *agenda setting* are key components of the policymaking process because groups have the opportunity to shape the agenda based on their relative degrees of influence, which may change over time.

Third, a *policy monopoly* occurs when specific groups are given the opportunity to frame an issue for an extended period of time. When groups wish to break a monopoly, they may seek the favor of policymakers from another part of the policy spectrum to help achieve their goals through *venue shopping*. The punctuated equilibrium model helps us to understand how reforms may stagnate over time, while also experiencing bursts of activity.

Advocacy Coalition Framework

Established by Paul Sabatier and Hank Jenkins-Smith, the advocacy coalition framework provides an understanding of the policymaking process that involves multiple actors, ambiguity, and various ways of developing policy depending on the issue (Jenkins-Smith & Sabatier, 1994; Sabatier, 1998; Sabatier & Jenkins-Smith, 1993). Coalitions, which comprise government officials, researchers, and other interested parties, are groups of people who share similar enough values that they will act in concert to enact policy aligned with their beliefs (Cairney, 2011). The advocacy coalition framework offers a long view of the policymaking process that may involve multiple years for policy ideas to come to fruition. This framework involves three types of beliefs: (a) *core*, or fundamental, beliefs that are broad, normative, and not likely to change; (b) *policy core* beliefs that are more specific and also unlikely to change; and (c) *secondary aspect* beliefs that relate to specific policy topics and are the most likely to change.

According to the advocacy coalition framework, policymaking takes place in issue-specific networks, called subsystems. Within these subsystems, coalitions (usually two to four) vie for positioning to influence the particular policy realm of that subsystem. These negotiations are mediated by a policy broker within each coalition. Events that transpire within one subsystem have an impact on the others because they are all connected within the larger system (Birkland, 2010). The broader system in which subsystems operate involves both stable (e.g., legal structure, core social values) and dynamic (e.g., public opinion, demographic or socioeconomic changes) elements, which operate symbiotically to constrain or facilitate policy development. Over a protracted period of time, usually ten years or more, policy change may take place based on the work of advocacy coalitions. The advocacy coalition framework also allows for the possibility that events outside the subsystem may lead to significant and swift policy change through 'shocks', which may be internal, when core beliefs are challenged, or external, when a major event (e.g., a global economic crisis) occurs that allows one coalition to assert its influence over others (Cairney, 2011). After a shock, competition between various coalitions starts anew.

Each of the various approaches to understanding or assessing the policymaking process provides a specific lens through which to view its complexities. Although each theory or model offers its own perspective, what these differing approaches have in common is that they view the policymaking process as value laden and as occurring within the context of the political, economic, and social conditions that prevail at a given time. These various conceptualizations of policymaking also highlight the multifaceted nature of the process.

The Four Stages of Policy Borrowing Model

Within the field of comparative international education, the study of policy borrowing and lending has been an especially robust area of inquiry and is the focal point of Chap. 6. Phillips and Ochs (2003) developed a model[2] that involves four stages of policy borrowing (Fig. 5.1), which has proved to be an enduring framework for understanding how educational policies

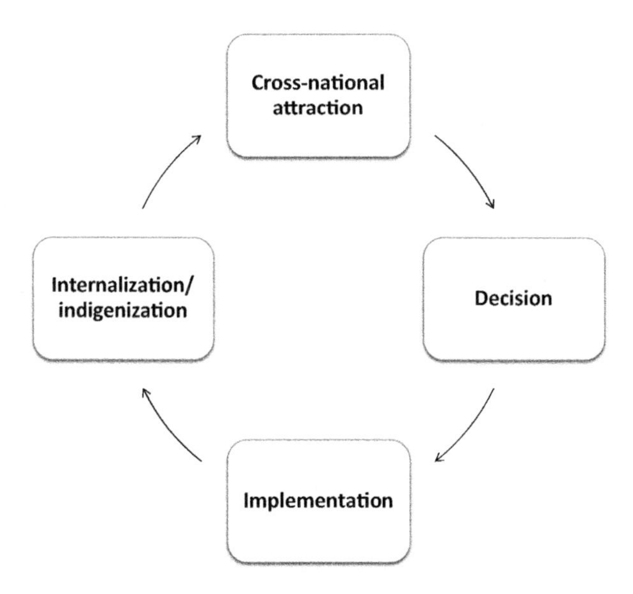

Fig. 5.1 Four stages of policy borrowing model (adapted from Phillips & Ochs, 2003)

move across national borders. Although policy borrowing and lending will be discussed in more detail in the next chapter, I introduce the model here to highlight its contribution to the theoretical literature on public policymaking. This composite model of policy borrowing offers a lens for understanding all four stages through which policies intentionally borrowed from another country move: (a) cross-national policy attraction, (b) decision, (c) implementation, and (d) internalization/indigenization (Ochs, 2006; Phillips, 2005; Phillips & Ochs, 2003).

In the *cross-national policy attraction* stage, with impulses and externalizing potential as its two main components, context plays a crucial role. The contextual and local situational factors that lead to borrowing are called *impulses*. Impulses may include factors such as (a) internal dissatisfaction, resulting in various stakeholders involved in education's seeking a change, (b) systemic collapse, which may follow a war or natural disaster, in which there is a profound failure or deficiency that needs to be addressed, (c) negative external evaluation, such as those related to higher education rankings or international achievement tests, (d) economic changes or new competition, (e) political imperatives, such as compliance with global norms or changes during elections, (f) the desire for innovation, and (g) political change, for example, after a new regime has been installed. The second component of the attraction stage is *externalizing potential*; here, impulses lead governments to search for international models to solve national problems. According to Phillips and Ochs (2003), there are six different types of 'loci of attraction', or components of a reform, that may be borrowed[3]: (a) a guiding philosophy or ideology (e.g., 'diversity' and 'world class'), (b) ambitions or goals to be achieved as outcomes of the policy, (c) strategies for achieving goals, (d) enabling structures (e.g., funding, administration, human resources) needed to support change, (e) educational processes, such as styles of teaching and regulations that govern education, and (f) techniques, or particular pedagogical strategies or methodologies.

In the second stage, *decision*, the government begins the process of change. According to the policy-borrowing model, four types of decision rationales[4] are common. First, governments might use a theoretical rationale, in which they align with particular philosophies or ideals at an abstract level, making implementation challenging (see below). Second, governments may employ a realistic or practical rationale in which there is an immediate problem to solve and for which an assessment has been made regarding the feasibility of implementation. Third, the quick-fix rationale involves making a decision when it is an immediate political necessity, often based on the suggestion of international advisors, without having a sense of the feasibility of carrying out the reform. Finally, Phillips and Ochs (2003) label an additional rationale as 'phony'. In this case, the government, often led by a single politician, chooses to make a change that has limited possibility of being implemented.

Once the focus of a reform has been decided, policy borrowing moves to the third stage of the model, *implementation*, in which policies are carried out within the context of the country that has borrowed the policy. Change is mediated in this environment by 'significant actors', which may be individuals, groups, or institutions involved with implementation. These parties may be beneficial to the implementation process, especially in a decentralized system; however, they may also resist the reform and delay (or circumvent) change (Phillips, 2005). The final stage, in which the model comes full circle, is called *internalization* or *indigenization*. At this stage, the reform has been adapted into the borrower country's education system, and its outcomes may be assessed. Four layers comprise this stage of assessing the reform: (a) impact on system/modus operandi, in which the motives and objections of policymakers are analyzed, (b) absorption of external features, which involves examining how and to what extent external features have been adapted into the borrower's context, (c) synthesis, through which the borrowed reform becomes part of the overall policy landscape of the receiving country, and (d) evaluation, to assess the outcomes of the reform and determine whether the cycle should begin anew. Phillips and Ochs' model provides a clear way to trace the development of policy borrowing.

Implementing Educational Reforms

Implementation is one of the most complex components of the policymaking process. Policymakers are often unable to anticipate how policy implementers or the intended targets of reforms will interact with the policy (Birkland, 2010). Ensuring implementation is challenging because 'policies embody values, theories of intervention, and orientations to social and educational issues that may or may not conform to the ideas, interests, and ideals of the actors' involved with implementation (Malen, 2006, p. 27). Policies are always incomplete, and (re)formulation often occurs when they are implemented within local contexts. Power relations and the relative influence of various actors come into play as policy responses go through additional sets of negotiations while reforms are being implemented in the prevailing political, social, and economic contexts (Ball, 1994). For these reasons, discretion is involved in implementing policies at the local level, as I describe below.

Implementation Strategies

Governments and reformers have historically employed two main strategies for policy implementation: (a) a top-down approach, also known as the technical-rational perspective or forward mapping, and (b) a bottom-up approach, also known as mutual adaptation or backward mapping (Bates, Lewis, & Pickard, 2011; Datnow, 2006; Dyer, 1999; Elmore, 1979–1980). The technical-rational perspective, developed by Berman and McLaughlin (1978), is a top-down approach to implementation that focuses on central planning, coordination, organization, and control and that largely ignores the context in which policies are implemented.

In his seminal work, Richard Elmore (1979–1980) labels this top-down approach 'forward mapping' and explains that it follows a technical-rational process that dictates expectations for implementation along with specific satisfactory outcomes. This strategy begins with the assumption that those involved in the implementation process are nested within a hierarchical organizational structure and that implementation involves exercising authority and control. Elmore suggests that forward mapping's premise that policymakers are central to implementation is a myth because they generally have very little influence over implementation within local environments. Therefore, when policymakers employ a top-down strategy, there is often an 'implementation gap' between what policymakers expect to occur and what transpires due to the disconnection between policymakers and those who are tasked with implementing policy (Cairney, 2011). Despite the challenges of top-down implementation strategies, they have remained salient in the literature and in practice (Natesan & Marathe, 2015).

In contrast, the bottom-up approach, which Elmore (1979–1980) labels 'backward mapping', involves a dispersed strategy for policy implementation that highlights collaboration between those who create policies and those who implement them. Backward mapping calls into question the assumption that developing a logical process with clear outcomes will lead to successful implementation. Elmore's analysis, which has been widely cited throughout the policy studies literature, takes into account that there will be multiple influences on policy implementation that policymakers cannot anticipate. The backward mapping process has also been called 'mutual adaptation' and offers a flexible, dynamic, and multidimensional approach in which the social, political, and organizational structures of educational or other policy environments are taken into account (Datnow, 2006).

In essence, the backward mapping strategy involves a system of reciprocity in which a certain level of discretion is delegated to lower levels and can be understood as a shared approach to policy implementation. Instead of relying on a hierarchical model of authority, backward mapping maximizes discretion at the point where it is most useful and with those closest to the problems being addressed (Elmore, 1979–1980). The use of such a dispersed model is likely to be effective because those who are tasked with implementing an educational reform may see it as a shared response rather than as a change imposed upon them (Bates et al., 2011). Elmore further suggests that reforms would be more successful if policymakers were to consider the lowest level of behavior desired by on-the-ground implementers (also known as 'street-level bureaucrats') and move up from that behavior to the policy level, not only at the stage of implementation but also while developing the policy.

Before turning to the role of street-level bureaucrats, it is important to recognize that policy studies, while still influenced by top-down and bottom-up approaches, increasingly relies on synthesized approaches that combine these two in one form or another. One of the prominent models within the synthesis literature is the advocacy coalition approach (introduced earlier in this chapter), which combines an understanding of the top-down constraints that delimit behavior with the centrality of implementers' actions to both policymaking and implementation. The policy network approach, in which a large number of mutually dependent actors (both those in power and those who implement policy) interact in a series of encounters involving negotiation, offers another way to consider a combined top-down and bottom-up approach (Hill & Hupe, 2014). Another synthesized conceptualization is 'multilevel governance', which posits that power is dispersed across the policymaking process. Multilevel governance operates under the assumption of blurred boundaries between various formal and informal nodes of power and authority. As such, the lines between policymakers and implementers are considered flexible (Cairney, 2011). Multilevel governance also helps to explain how policies are enacted within global environments in which policy actors who share a certain level of responsibility for policymaking are connected across country boundaries.

The Influence of Street-Level Bureaucrats

From a backward mapping perspective, one of the most significant influences on policy implementation is the influence of street-level bureaucrats (Lipsky, 2010). Originally published in 1980, Michael Lipsky's seminal text on street-level bureaucrats focuses on the discretion of front-line workers who interact with citizens in public service positions. Street-level bureaucrats include teachers, police officers, social workers, and other public service representatives. According to Lipsky, street-level bureaucrats operate in a context of multiple policy pressures and do not have the full resources (e.g., time, money, and information) needed to comply with all of the policy imperatives that govern their work. Policies that they are expected to implement may also not fully address the contextualized situations that these workers confront on a daily basis. To cope with these competing demands, street-level bureaucrats exercise their discretion to comply while also maintaining their professional autonomy.

Lipsky (2010) contends that 'the decisions of street-level bureaucrats, the routines they establish, and the devices they invent to cope with uncertainties and work pressures, effectively *become* the public policies they carry out' (p. xiii). Therefore, the role of street-level bureaucrats is critical in policy implementation. Even when policymakers insist on employing a top-down implementation strategy, it will not guarantee that a policy will be carried out as intended. Policy implementation may be more successful if street-level bureaucrats sense that they have some autonomy in implementing policy because there may be a 'mediation effect' in which their willingness to implement a policy increases with their realization that they will be able to adapt it to the needs of their constituencies (Tummers & Bekkers, 2014). In this way, policymakers may have an opportunity to (re) exert their influence over street-level bureaucrats if they recognize their function in policy implementation. Street-level bureaucracy in this context is a normative concept, even though discretion is involved, because policymakers can use their understanding of the construct to more successfully implement policies.

The notion of street-level bureaucrats has proven to be highly relevant and endures in the policy literature (see, e.g., Brodkin, 2011, 2012; Hupe & Buffat, 2014; Maynard-Moody & Portillo, 2010; Meyers & Lehmann Nielson, 2012; Smith, 2012). To a large extent, the discretion of street-level bureaucrats is assumed to be an inevitable component of policy implementation (Gofen, 2014; Hupe & Hill, 2007; Tummers &

Bekkers, 2014), and this assumption has led to dispersing ownership of policy implementation in many applications. For example, Deborah Rice (2013) argues that decentralization in many welfare nation-states around the world was largely due to the influence of the street-level bureaucracy. Although Lipsky's work was focused on coping rather than disobedience, another strand of literature in this area has focused on active resistance, known as 'divergence' (Brodkin, 2003). The extent to which street-level bureaucrats have the ability to influence policy implementation is an enduring issue. In the realm of education, global trends to adopt neoliberal tenets in schooling and higher education provide an opportunity to explore whether policy 'consensus', or isomorphism, results from coercion, agency, or a combination of the two.

Shaping Policy Implementation Consensus: Coercion or Agency?

One of the fundamental issues of policy implementation is the degree to which coercion versus agency is involved on the part of those who implement policies. Implementers must consider a policy to be aligned with their value systems to desire to enact it; however, this alignment can be manufactured through a process that replicates consensus. This process of 'winning over' those who must implement policies so that their views align with policymaker or governmental perspectives may be considered a coercive process. Consent is often manipulated through stakeholder consultations, while, at the same time, the intended educational reforms are presented as 'common sense' or inevitable (Harvey, 2009). Market-oriented educational reforms fall into this category because neoliberal tenets have become so ingrained in the way that educators operate that they may not be able to shift the focus. Even if they are aware of the detrimental aspects of such reforms, educators often find themselves complying with the implementation of policies with neoliberal components (Ward et al., 2015). These prevailing neoliberal discourses are 'deliberately and constructively (re)used, (re)emphasised and (re)iterated until they enter the public consciousness and become reified' (Ward et al., 2015, p. 7) and, therefore, become common sense. In this view, policy consensus is manufactured, which may be especially true in cases in which policies emanate from global governance institutions based in the Global North.

At the same time, policy implementation is often contested, operating in a 'political space in which dominant policy discourses are not simply accepted at face value, but may be challenged, nuanced, reformulated, and changed' (Ward et al., 2015, p. 6). Although considerable time, effort, and resources typically go into the process of developing and implementing educational reforms, policymakers' control over the application of policies is often constrained in practice. For this reason, Stephen Ball, Meg Maguire, and Annette Braun (2012) suggest that education policy implementation involves 'ad-hockery, borrowing, re-ordering, displacing, making do and re-invention' (p. 8). When local stakeholders, including administrators, teachers, and parents, take an active role, they serve as agents who exercise their power to influence the course of policy implementation (Braun, Maguire, & Ball, 2010; Rizvi & Lingard, 2010).

Policy implementation is not an either/or proposition. It may be both coercive and malleable, depending on the context. Additionally, those charged with implementing policies may practice strategic compliance in which they support the policy symbolically while choosing their own methods of implementation or non-implementation. As will become clear in Chap. 6, symbolic adherence to global trends and norms is a common mechanism for countries to appropriate global policies into their own contexts, especially when the reforms are dictated by global governance organizations and essentially forced upon them. Although the policy context is circumscribed by the impact of neoliberal educational reforms, such policies are not put into practice in the same way within countries. In the complex and contested environment of policy implementation, 'no one policy gets implemented or is successful everywhere all of the time' (Honig, 2006, p. 25). Vernacular globalization ensures that policy outcomes vary based on the local context. The importance of context contributes to the existence of coercion alongside agency and resistance.

The Globalization of Educational Policymaking

Although the development of public policies remains, to a certain extent, a national endeavor, policymaking no longer takes place within the confines of the nation-state. Policies have always involved negotiations between various groups with different ideals and values; the difference is that these negotiations now take place in a global environment. The framing of policy texts relies on discourses that are no longer bounded by national contexts, and agenda setting occurs with global developments in view (Rizvi & Lingard, 2010). As detailed in Chap. 2, a variety of global actors have an impact on educational policy, especially in the case of countries in the Global South, for which global governance institutions may dictate policy as a condition of receiving aid. Nation-states have varying degrees of sovereignty and capacity to resist the current dominant (neoliberal) form of globalization due to their relative geopolitical strength. The ascendancy of neoliberalism plays a significant role in shifting the education policy discourse toward reforms that align with its tenets, such as human capital development and lifelong learning, as described in Chap. 4. In addition, the current neoliberal environment of policymaking leads to a 'policy by numbers' approach that emphasizes accountability (Rose, 1999), which aligns with Joel Spring's (2015) notion of the audit state. The global economic climate also factors into policymaking around the world, as national governments no longer have full control over their economies.

Given the new globalized policy environment with its neoliberal emphasis, the purpose of education and whose values it represents must be interrogated and reassessed (Rizvi & Lingard, 2010). At the same time, it is important to keep in mind that there is nothing inevitable about the shifts that have taken place. They represent the dominant discourse of the era in which we live. Although the nation-state's role is evolving, it remains vital to national policy discourse. Local actors continue to mediate changes in their own political, social, cultural, and economic contexts (Appadurai, 1996; Rizvi & Lingard, 2010). Thus, the challenge in this new globalized policy environment is to stimulate new ways of thinking about educational reform.

Conclusion

Policymaking and policy implementation are contested and value-laden processes that involve multiple actors with competing agendas. Policies, or reforms, have various purposes and functions, depending on who proposes them and which groups have influence at a given time in history. From a governmental perspective, policies serve to regulate behavior and alleviate societal problems. They also have a normative effect in that governments seek to shape the focus of the policy agenda. At the same time, the political environment of the policymaking process results in numerous actors expressing their own perceptions of problems and solutions. Specific aspects of the policymaking process may be explored through a variety of theories and models, including the Four Stages of Policy Borrowing model. One of the most critical areas of the policymaking process is implementation, particularly because policymakers often have limited control over it. The street-level bureaucrats who implement policies play a significant role. With the understanding of the policymaking process provided in this chapter in view, I now turn to policy borrowing and lending, around which comparative and international education scholars have developed a rich set of literature focused on education.

Notes

1. See Chap. 6 for a full discussion of how and why policies are borrowed from other countries.
2. Phillips and Ochs (2003) drew upon prior scholarship on policy borrowing in developing their model. Additional research and theoretical ideas are included in Chap. 6.
3. The authors drew upon their earlier work (Ochs & Phillips, 2002), which focused on policy attraction, and outlined these six aspects of policy that might be borrowed. These six components were part of their structural typology of cross-national attraction in education, which they incorporated into the composite policy-borrowing model discussed here.
4. Motivations for policy borrowing and lending are discussed in more detail in Chap. 6, along with examples of reforms that illustrate concepts from the model.

CHAPTER 6

Mapping Educational Policy Borrowing and Lending

In today's globalized world, educational policies are increasingly borrowed and lent in multiple directions. Current educational policy borrowing activity has its roots in early investigations through which reformers endeavored to learn from afar. Although comparative and international education (CIE) did not became a discrete area of study until the late 1950s, documentation of educational policy borrowing dates back to the 1800s. Early policy borrowing initiatives involved government officials traveling to other countries with the purpose of learning from foreign educational systems and importing structures or practices back home. For example, during the Meiji Restoration in the late 1800s, Japan actively sought to borrow features from the USA and European countries to modernize and improve its educational system after a period of relative isolation during the Tokugawa Shogunate (Phillips & Schweisfurth, 2014). Reliance on policy borrowing and lending has intensified due to globalization, increased competition resulting from neoliberal economic policies, and the establishment of post-WWII global governance institutions that serve as the core of the aid and development regime (see Chap. 2). These governance organizations allow for greater flow and exchange of ideas in all policy realms, including education. Given technological advances and the interconnectedness of the world, policymakers now have multiple ways of learning about educational innovations that take place in other

© The Editor(s) (if applicable) and The Author(s) 2016

L.M. Portnoi, *Policy Borrowing and Reform in Education*,
DOI 10.1057/978-1-137-53024-0_6

countries, and policy borrowing and lending have become increasingly commonplace in the policymaking process.

Why would countries borrow or lend policies? Policy borrowing and lending are not neutral, and underlying political and economic impulses are present. Common motivations and rationales for policy borrowing and lending include the desire to adopt recognized global trends (e.g., standardized testing in schools and world-class universities) and to gain legitimacy at the time of a regime change by bringing in initiatives from elsewhere. In some cases, policies may be expressly borrowed or sought. For example, if a country is experiencing a problem with poor quality in its higher education system, its leaders may seek to borrow quality-assurance policies from other 'successful' countries to address this issue. Policies also may be explicitly lent, sometimes forcefully, as with policy diffusion (or the spreading of policies), due to the influence of global governance institutions. Although some countries may look to these organizations for resources and 'best practices', the international development and aid regime often facilitates a coercive form of lending. As I discuss below, a continuum of voluntary versus coercive transfer exists in the movement of policies across borders, and receiving countries may be required to adopt particular reforms or initiatives based on donor agency recommendations as a condition of obtaining funding. These circumstances are more common for countries in the Global South, given these countries' geopolitical position and need to accept donor funding.

Despite the geopolitical power that rests in the Global North, policy borrowing and lending processes do not simply represent a one-way exchange from the Global North to the Global South. Policies may flow between countries within the Global North or the Global South or between countries in different regions or geopolitical domains. In addition, nation-states and local constituents continually challenge the normative nature of reforms driven by global governance institutions that often promote 'best practices' that have become commonplace, whether or not there is evidence of their effectiveness (see below). Policies may be actively disregarded or resisted, or stakeholders may reformulate them in the local environment through vernacular globalization, leading to a policy that only vaguely resembles the one that was lent (Appadurai, 1996; Ball, 2012; Lingard, 2000; Portnoi, Rust, & Bagley, 2013; Rizvi & Lingard, 2010). In essence, the debate about coercion versus agency that I discuss in Chap. 5 plays out at the international level, with global governance institutions engaging in coercion and national governments and other local actors exerting agency.

Building on the understanding of the policy process that I present in Chap. 5, the focus of this chapter is on policy borrowing and lending across nation-state borders, adding a global layer to the policymaking and implementation literature. In this chapter, I map out the policy borrowing and lending processes and include in the discussion related terminology, motives, and rationales for policy borrowing and lending that nation-states undertake; policy diffusion and 'best practices' lending; and the continuum of policy transfer. I also present five illustrative cases that provide a window into how policy borrowing and lending transpire. The chapter concludes with a section on the complexities of policy borrowing and lending, including the varying directions of transfer, local agency as a means to resist global trends, and indigenization of policies into the local context.

Understanding Policy Borrowing and Lending

The terminology that scholars and policymakers use to describe the processes through which policies move across borders includes 'policy transfer', 'policy borrowing', 'policy lending', 'policy attraction', 'policy learning', and 'policy diffusion'. These terms differ in nuanced ways and must be differentiated to better understand these processes (Phillips, 2005; Phillips & Ochs, 2003; Silova, 2012; Steiner-Khamsi, 2004, 2012). 'Policy transfer' is an all-encompassing term that scholars from various disciplines, most notably political science, frequently use to describe the processes through which policies travel from one country to another, regardless of whether they are lent, borrowed, or imposed (Cairney, 2011). Two central forms of policy transfer are policy borrowing and policy lending. CIE scholars who write from a culturalist perspective (see Chap. 4) generally prefer to use the combined term 'policy borrowing and lending', rather than 'policy transfer', because it captures the nuances of the process more accurately (e.g., Silova, 2012; Steiner-Khamsi, 2012)

'Policy borrowing' implies that countries explicitly seek to appropriate a policy and tailor it to the local context, whereas 'policy lending' connotes that governments or global governance organizations provide policies to a receiving country with or without consent (Samoff, 2013; Silova, 2012). CIE scholar Florian Waldow (2012) suggests that policy borrowing generally involves a greater focus on the receiving country as opposed to policy lending, in which the originating country is often more central, particularly when a policy has been successful. In the case of policy borrowing, policymakers often interact with representatives from countries that employ a specific policy and may even conduct site visits. They are generally overtly seeking to import a policy and may appropriate the text of policies from other countries as a model.

'Policy lending' often occurs when a country receives international attention due to positive results on international metrics and implicitly lends its policies to other countries by way of model or example. For instance, elements of the US higher education system are often lent to other nation-states, due to the perceived effectiveness of the system, particularly given its dominance on global university rankings. A more direct, or coercive, form of lending occurs when nation-states or global governance institutions place conditions upon other countries, generally through the aid and development regime. Such coercive lending typically affects countries in the Global South the most because they often must accept specific reforms as a means to receive aid or donor assistance.

The term 'policy attraction', which is sometimes used interchangeably with 'policy borrowing' in the literature, refers to a more precise component of policy transfer—the stage in which a borrowing country becomes interested in appropriating a policy from another country, as depicted in the Four Stages of Policy Borrowing and Lending model (Phillips & Ochs, 2003) that I describe in Chap. 5. For this reason, scholars' use of the term 'policy attraction' as a blanket term to cover several processes is no longer common in the literature. The notion of 'policy learning' stems from the realm of political science and refers to the use of data or other forms of information to make policy decisions (Cairney, 2011). Policy learning focuses, in large part, on the stage of the policy process that I describe in Chap. 5 (policy formulation) in which policymakers purposefully gather information to make informed choices based on past policy experience or predictions about new policies. In some cases, this learning may involve the exploration of alternatives present in international contexts, which may occur through visits to another country or through observing and reading relevant documents remotely. Because policy learning focuses on making data-driven decisions, it may result in a policy *not* being adopted because policymakers deem it to be unfeasible or undesirable in the local context.

The term 'policy diffusion', the subject of a more extensive discussion in a separate section below, stems from the sociology and anthropology literature and refers to the spread of similar policies throughout the world

(Burde, 2004; Jakobi, 2012), such as standardized testing in schools. Policy diffusion is a normative concept because it fails to recognize that actors are involved in transferring policies and rests on the assumption that 'best practices' will be automatically adopted throughout the world (Dale & Robertson, 2012; Silova, 2012). Those who work from a world culture theory perspective, in contrast to culturalist CIE scholars, are more likely to use this term to describe learning from elsewhere.

Throughout this book, I have chosen to use the term 'policy borrowing and lending' (or the shorthand 'policy borrowing') to refer to the processes through which governments and global governance institutions share policies between and among countries. Although the processes involved in policy borrowing and lending are more complex than this terminology implies, and the term 'policy transfer' would often be more accurate as a blanket descriptor, I use these terms because they are ones mostly commonly employed to refer to these sets of processes in the CIE literature (Steiner-Khamsi, 2012). I acknowledge that using the abbreviated term 'policy borrowing', as I do in this book, is problematic in some ways because it may appear to connote that countries always have a choice when adopting a reform from elsewhere. I use this term intentionally, however, because, even when policies are forcefully lent, receiving nations and their constituents have agency, especially during the implementation phase, as I explain in Chap. 5 and discuss later in this chapter.

The Policy Borrowing and Lending Continuum

The complexities involved in policy borrowing and lending have led scholars to conceptualize variations in these processes along a continuum, with voluntary borrowing on the left and coercive lending on the right (see Fig. 6.1). Each component of the continuum is associated with particular motivations and rationales, which I introduce here and discuss in more detail in the section that follows. Writing from a political science perspective, David Dolowitz and David Marsh (1996, 1998, 2000) developed the original continuum of policy transfer, which includes, from left to right, lesson drawing, middle ground, obligated, and conditional positions. Lesson drawing is similar to the notion of policy borrowing, and policymakers voluntarily and actively employ this strategy when there is a public problem or a sense of dissatisfaction with the current state of affairs related to a specific issue. If policymakers ascertain that modifying a current policy to alleviate the problem or issue is not feasible or desirable, they may turn

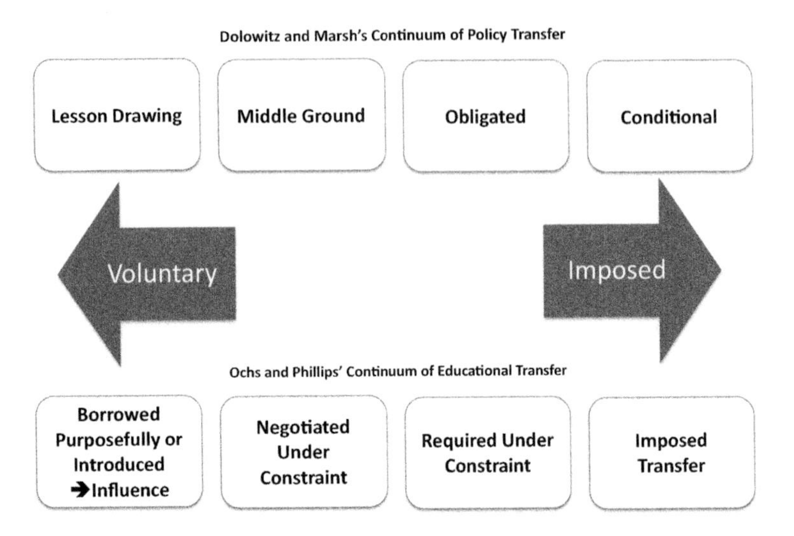

Fig. 6.1 The policy borrowing and lending continuum (adapted from Dolowitz & Marsh, 1996 and Ochs & Phillips, 2004)

to other countries for an entirely new policy that may be imported and adapted within the local context (Dolowitz & Marsh, 2000). Voluntary transfer often stems from political activity, such as an upcoming election, and serves to legitimize a new policy because governments or policymakers can often demonstrate that it has worked elsewhere.

On the other end of the spectrum is coercive transfer, in which countries are essentially compelled to implement a certain policy. For example, a country may force its policies on another through war or occupation, as with the imposition of the Western education model during the colonial period. In the conditional position, toward the coercive end of the continuum, global governance institutions, such as the International Monetary Fund (IMF) and the World Bank (WB), may impose policies as a condition of receiving loans or other funding. Nation-states may need this funding so desperately that they are willing to implement the desired reforms to obtain it (Cairney, 2011). The obligated form of transfer is less direct and is positioned to the left of conditional transfer. This form of transfer is the result of treaties and other conventions that countries have adopted, which requires them to enact certain policies in their countries. For example, nation-states that sign on to Education for All (EFA) conventions agree to develop policies designed to achieve universal primary education.

The middle ground position involves elements of both coercive and voluntary forms of transfer. In some cases, governments might have concerns about their nation-states' falling behind their competitors on influential international measures of educational quality (e.g., global university rankings, Programme for International Student Assessment [PISA] test results) and decide that they have no choice but to voluntarily adopt 'best practice' policies to address these deficiencies (Dolowitz & Marsh, 2000). They may elect to follow global trends whether or not they are appropriate for the local context, especially if they believe that doing so will bring international recognition or legitimacy to their education systems. In other instances situated in the middle ground, there may be a form of indirect coercion, when policies from one country result in a negative impact on another, such as the fiscal austerity measures of certain European Union countries that have an impact on others.

CIE scholars Kimberly Ochs and David Phillips (2004) adapted the Dolowitz and Marsh (2000) continuum of educational policy borrowing and lending and termed it a 'continuum of educational transfer'. Their version of the continuum mirrors the general notion of a range of positions along a continuum from voluntary to coercive. They label the coercive end of the continuum 'imposed transfer', which includes policies that are forcibly imposed upon countries. To the left of imposed transfer is 'required under constraint', which applies to defeated or occupied countries that must adopt certain policies due to the current political context. The middle component of the Ochs and Phillips continuum is 'negotiated under constraint', as with policies required by agreements with bilateral organizations or IMOs, aligned with Dolowitz and Marsh's obligated transfer. Policies in this realm may not be required, but rather are negotiated between the country and donors (Ochs & Phillips, 2004). The voluntary end of the continuum includes both policies that are 'borrowed purposefully' and those that are 'introduced through influence'. The former is similar to lesson drawing on the Dolowitz and Marsh continuum, while the latter is an addition to the original model. According to Ochs and Phillips, policies introduced through influence are transferred 'naturally' when professionals from one country visit another for professional development or exchanges (e.g., of teachers or nurses) and then bring practices back to their home countries when they return.

Aside from the nuances in wording and the addition of policies introduced through natural transfer via the exchange of people and ideas, the Ochs and Phillips (2004) continuum differs from that of Dolowitz and Marsh (2000) because Ochs and Phillips position the impact of global governance organizations more neutrally at the middle of the continuum, whereas Dolowitz and Marsh place this type of transfer toward the coercive end of the spectrum. In addition, 'natural' transfer due to the exchange of people and ideas across borders may inadvertently exert a neocolonial influence because it is more likely that ideas from the Global North will trickle down into countries in the Global South rather than vice versa (Rizvi & Lingard, 2010). Nevertheless, conceiving policy borrowing and lending processes as a continuum provides a useful way to understand the various influences that may be involved in importing policies from one location to another.

Motives and Rationales for Policy Borrowing

Given the political nature of policy borrowing and lending, a variety of motives and rationales exist for the educational policy borrowing and lending activities that nation-states undertake.[1] Although multiple rationales are often intertwined in developing educational reforms, in this section, I describe these various motives separately for clarity. In the next section, I focus on a specific form of lending—policy diffusion—followed by a section in which I present five illustrative cases through which scholars have traced policy borrowing and lending processes related to specific reforms. These examples serve to demonstrate a variety of motivations and the complex ways in which policy borrowing and lending take place in practice.[2]

Early attempts to understand the motivations for policy borrowing or 'learning from elsewhere' tended to center on broad generalizations regarding rationales for undertaking investigations of educational reforms. For example, Phillips (2000) developed a typology of motivations, which includes: (a) rigorous scientific investigations for academic purposes, (b) a response to popular views that other countries have superior approaches to education, (c) politically motivated assessments that contrast reforms from other countries with the ones at home, and (d) highlighting of perceived deficiencies at home via exaggerated evidence from abroad. Over the past 15 years, the policy borrowing and lending literature within CIE has flourished, and numerous journal articles and several books focused on this area of scholarship have been published (e.g., Chisholm & Steiner-

Khamsi, 2009; Phillips & Ochs, 2003; Steiner-Khamsi, 2004; Steiner-Khamsi & Waldow, 2012). Recently, research has begun to focus on the actors who are involved in the policymaking process as well as coercive and prescriptive lending (Steiner-Khamsi, 2012), such as that which occurs through policy diffusion and 'best practices' lending (see the next section). Through these research endeavors, scholars have explored a variety of motivations for the adoption of policies, most of which are within the political realm.

In cases of intentional policy borrowing, political motivations typically prevail in the policymaking process. In such instances, policies are not necessarily borrowed because they are good or successful but, rather, because they serve a political function (Halpin & Troyna, 1995; Steiner-Khamsi, 2004; Waldow, 2012). Jeremy Rappleye (2012) refers to explicit policy borrowing as 'political production' and uses the analogy of theater to explain how policy borrowing is often a carefully scripted and orchestrated endeavor that is staged for the purposes of engendering specific policy outcomes. This view of the political production of intentional policy borrowing is connected to both the streams model and the advocacy coalition framework models that I introduce in Chap. 5 because the focus is on the political actors and their motivations (Rappleye, 2012). As Phillips (2000) suggests, in many cases, governments seek to implement a policy because there is a perceived deficiency at home. Rappleye states that government actors may seek to highlight a 'crisis' through 'public staging' so that other policymakers and the public are more receptive to the policy that the government wishes to adopt. The intended policy is often selected in advance in such cases, serving as a cover for something the government already intended to do (Cairney, 2011). The effect of the manufactured crisis is to lead to the desired policy intervention.

Within the political production of policy borrowing, scholars have identified several common motivations. Often, policy borrowing is used to generate a 'quick fix' solution when a country needs to adopt a policy due to an impending event of significance, such as an election or anniversary (Chakroun, 2010; Ochs, 2006; Phillips & Ochs, 2003). In such cases, policies are often symbolic rather than material (see Chap. 5) because they are being used for the purpose of short-term appearances rather than long-term effects (Robertson & Waltman, 1992). Another form of symbolic policy borrowing involves adopting a policy (or agreeing to do so) because it fulfills a specific purpose or mandate in either the national or international context, such as the need to align with international conventions

(Morais de Sá e Silva, 2012; Silova, 2004). As with a 'quick fix' solution, this form of symbolic policy borrowing typically is not undertaken with the intention of implementation. Symbolic policy reforms involve 'policy talk' rather than action (Cuban, 1998); as such, they may result in a change in the policy discourse without lasting effect. Although the original policy borrowed may be symbolic, employing an international example might provide an opportunity to inspire change and encourage innovation in the local context (Steiner-Khamsi, 2012).

Another commonly employed political motivation for policy borrowing is gaining legitimacy, which may be deemed necessary at times of governmental transitions or when other politically significant events have occurred (Chisholm, 2012; Green, 1993; Halpin & Troyna, 1995; Spreen, 2004; Steiner-Khamsi & Quist, 2000). In such cases, decisions regarding which policy to borrow are not based on contextual factors and whether the policy will be successful but, rather, on political expediency (Rappleye, 2012). References to practices from elsewhere, also known as externalization,[3] add legitimacy in such cases. Political actors reference 'best practices' that appear to be international standards to help build domestic alliances in support of policy adoption, especially when the policy terrain is particularly contested (Steiner-Khamsi, 2012). Externalization may involve positioning borrowed policies as evidence-based and, therefore, valid. References to elsewhere may generate pressure and build advocacy coalitions within the local environment, especially through 'scandalizing' practices at home by comparing them to 'successful' policies elsewhere (Phillips, 2005; Steiner-Khamsi, 2004).

Paradoxically, however, the desire to borrow policies to gain political legitimacy may lead to policies being borrowed that were not effective in the original location (Chisholm, 2012; Halpin & Troyna, 1995; Steiner-Khamsi & Quist, 2000). Yet, the impulse to reference from elsewhere is often so strong that it does not matter whether the policy has been successful in other contexts. In such cases, the driving force is not necessarily problems in the home environment that warrant attention, but, rather domestic politics (Rappleye, 2012; Steiner-Khamsi, 2012). In these instances, externalization stems from internal pressures, not what is happening in the countries from which reforms are borrowed. For example, governments may use external policy referencing to shift blame away from their failures (Waldow, 2012). To gain legitimacy, the degree to which a borrowed educational reform seems to connect, at least symbolically, to the educational environment of the receiving country is the most important consideration. A borrowed reform is often viewed as neutral, which makes it a politically expedient choice because it provides an opportunity to build coalitions around the reform in the local environment (Steiner-Khamsi, 2012).

Political motivations are also an integral part of the lending process. Lending educational reforms often provides an opportunity to extol the virtues of a country's education system in comparison to others (Ochs, 2006; Steiner-Khamsi, 2004). Nation-states that lend policies often gain stature and recognition, as is the case with Finland's educational system, which has been lauded for its success with student achievement, as manifested in performance on international assessments, such as PISA. Countries throughout the world have sought to emulate Finland's policies and practices, whether or not they intended to implement their reforms fully or sought to adopt them symbolically. Focusing on these 'star' educational systems causes countries to adopt features related to reforms that may not resonate with the realities in either the lending or the borrowing country (Steiner-Khamsi, 2012). In other words, countries may incorporate features that that are connected with 'success' without any clear evidence that they have been effective or that they are able to be translated into the receiving environment. In other cases, countries seek to explicitly lend policies for the purposes of gaining legitimacy in the home country. Often, such lending, which CIE scholar Gita Steiner-Khamsi (2004) refers to as 'export for survival', occurs at times of protracted domestic political contestation when countries or politicians need to gain legitimacy for a reform (which may, in fact, be homegrown) by showing that it has been adopted elsewhere.

As is evident, politics and geopolitical positioning are integral to the process for both the countries that borrow policies and those that lend them (Ball, 1998; Rappleye, 2012; Samoff, 2013; Steiner-Khamsi, 2004; Takayama, 2012). Countries from the Global North tend to be lending countries due to their stature and role in global governance institutions, and nation-states of all kinds seek to borrow from this group of influential countries (Samoff, 2013; Steiner-Khamsi, 2004). Nation-states from the Global South that rely on donor funding, however, are generally more constricted in their policy choices due to the conditions associated with loans and other aid they receive. For this group, suggestive or coercive lending through global governance organizations is more common (Harvey, 2003; Nguyen, Elliot, Terlouw, & Pilot, 2009; Samoff, 2013), as I discuss in more detail in the next section. Rising or middle-range countries, such as those that are considered to be newly industrialized countries or BRICS (Brazil, Russia, India, China, and South Africa; see Chap. 2), may be in an intermediary position in which they have some autonomy but may still choose to borrow from Global North countries and employ referencing of international 'standards' for symbolic reasons (Chisholm, 2012; Rappleye, 2012).

Policy Diffusion and 'Best Practices' Lending

Policy diffusion, the spread of similar policies throughout the world, may be considered to be a broad rationale for policy borrowing and lending. Policy diffusion is closely connected to the notion of convergence espoused by world culture theorists that I discuss in earlier chapters of this book. In education, clear examples of policy diffusion include the standardized testing and lifelong learning movements, both of which accompany the shift toward neoliberalism as a standard economic model worldwide (see Chap. 4). Similar to the notion of neoliberalism that purportedly operates under the 'invisible hand' of the market, policy diffusion is often presented as a process 'without an agent' (Dale & Robertson, 2012). As noted, in Ochs and Phillips' (2004) continuum of educational transfer, for example, policy diffusion is positioned as a middle ground in which internationally recognized 'best practices' are adopted into local environments.

The policy borrowing and lending processes that contribute to the diffusion of educational reforms, however, do not transpire unprompted. Instead, actors who may be seeking to borrow policies to comply with international expectations (i.e., countries in the Global South) or to position their countries' reforms as models to be lent (i.e., countries in the Global North) often drive educational reform. Global governance institutions—Intergovernmental Organization (IGOs), regional organizations, bilateral organizations, IMOs, and INGOs, as I outline in Chap. 2—also are key actors in the spread of educational reforms across the globe.

The influential role of global governance institutions in policy diffusion connected to 'best practices' lending warrants special attention. Anja Jakobi (2012) considers these institutions to be 'central nodes for policy diffusion' and suggests that they facilitate policy transfer in four main ways: (a) by disseminating ideas, (b) by establishing standards, (c) by coordinating policies within an international network, and (d) by providing financial resources. Using a world culture perspective, Jakobi shows how global governance organizations have succeeded in establishing norms that have resulted in an emphasis on lifelong learning throughout educational systems in much of the world. Considered from a neutral world culture theory perspective, policy diffusion performs an important function in that it allows the transfer of 'best practices' to nation-states that have educational problems in need of reform (Jakobi, 2012; Rappleye, 2012; Silova, 2012). In this view, benign global governance organizations serve the purpose of establishing internationally recognized structures and practices that nation-states should adopt. This perspective stems from an assumption that rational decision making occurs (Steiner-Khamsi, 2012) and appeals to policymakers who are seeking a pragmatic response to policy problems by relying on what has worked in other countries.

The underlying premise built into the world culture theory approach holds that there is a commonly accepted and legitimate 'blueprint' for improving education globally (McNeely, 1995; Silova, 2012). This inherent premise leads to certain reforms being deemed 'best practices' or 'international standards' '*as if* there existed a clearly defined set of standards, policies and practices that are universally shared' (Steiner-Khamsi, 2012, p. 4). Rappleye (2012), Dana Burde (2004), and Steiner-Khamsi (2004, 2012) question the 'imagined' convergence of educational policy reforms. In most cases, no universal agreement of scholars and policymakers around the world exists with regard to what reforms are best. Yet, 'popular' policies often become normative—in other words, they are deemed to be best practices simply because they come from the Global North or are lauded by global governance institutions. The impact of diffusion becomes clear when 'late adopter' countries that are part of a second or third wave of adopting a reform refer to 'global' reforms in staging their policy processes, without referencing the specific origin of these policies (Morais de Sá e Silva, 2012; Steiner-Khamsi & Stolpe, 2006).

Scholars who write from a critical stance and raise concerns about 'best practices' lending typically do not contest the fact that some policies have spread through diffusion and the influence of global governance institutions.[4] Instead, these scholars problematize the view of global governance institutions as benign and recognize their normative influence (e.g., Auld & Morris, 2014; Ball, 2012; Burde, 2004; Klees, 2012; Samoff, 2013; Silova, 2012). Critical scholars demonstrate that a causal link exists between the uniformity of policy in national contexts and global governance organizations, not because of agreement regarding best practices but, rather, due to their role in consultancy, research, and policy oversight, especially through providing aid in the Global South (McNeely,

1995; Silova, 2012). They also note the economic motivations inherent in coercive lending that results from conditions for receiving aid. When reforms are adopted under such circumstances, they are often transient because they may be dropped if external funding does not continue or if donors move on to other reforms as part of the conditions of receiving aid (Steiner-Khamsi, 2012).

In addition, the normative approach of world culture theory and 'best practices' lending is entangled with notions of modernity that involve a belief in progress and scientific forms of inquiry (Silova, 2012). Educational policy borrowing and lending have come to be seen as central to achieving progress on global mandates, such as EFA. 'Evidence-based' policymaking is central to this modern agenda, which highlights scientific objectivity and detaches reforms from their ideological underpinnings (Auld & Morris, 2014; Ozga & Lingard, 2007; Steiner-Khamsi, 2012; Waldow, 2012). To encourage and justify the diffusion or explicit lending of 'best practices', global governance institutions and others who espouse the adoption of particular reforms throughout the world marshal 'scientific' evidence related to their effectiveness. Although some of this evidence comes from world culture theorists, most stems not from CIE or other scholarly domains but, rather, from think tanks or 'knowledge banks', namely, the WB, the IMF, and the Organisation for Economic Co-operation and Development (OECD).

Even though these organizations may laud objective scientific investigations, they frequently provide the very evidence that promotes the reforms they are recommending. These organizations gloss over the limitations inherent in their work and conduct research that is 'reductionist; downplays context and non-educational factors; tends to confirmation bias; [and] uses correlations to infer causality' (Auld & Morris, 2014, p. 149). Despite its claimed objectivity, research conducted by think tanks and knowledge banks is also typically driven by a neoliberal ideology that equates education with an economic investment that leads to the production of human capital. Through conceptualizing educational policy borrowing and lending in technical and instrumental terms, the focus becomes how one-size-fits-all policies may be transferred effectively, with limited reference to the local context (Silova, 2012).

Countries typically adopt these 'best practice' policies from the Global North without fully considering their origin or impact. In contrast to the typical policy process model that I describe in Chap. 5, in which problems lead to the need for reforms, Steiner-Khamsi suggests that governments (especially those in the Global South) may create local problems in line with 'best practice' solutions even if they were not inherent or pronounced concerns in the local environment. Further, Rappleye (2012) notes that uncritically adopting policies from elsewhere often means that governments are not taking into account the political production of policymaking. In other words, borrowed policies may be taken at face value without policymakers and the public recognizing the political origins and staging that may have occurred when the original policies were constructed.

Critical scholars also interrogate the assumption inherent in normative policy diffusion discussions that suggest that all countries are equal players on the world stage. The diffusion of norms taken for granted as 'best' calls into question which countries and organizations have control and which have the opportunity to decide what norms are accepted. Clearly, a country's stature and geopolitical position has an impact on whether it has the luxury of choosing to borrow (or lend) policies, and nation-states that accept prescribed policies as a condition of receiving aid are party to a coercive form of transfer. Early iterations of policy diffusion in education are tied to colonialism and the connected belief in the superiority of the cultures and practices of Global North countries (Spring, 2015; Steiner-Khamsi, 2012). As I note in Chap. 4, some would argue that the imposition of global educational trends involves a new form of colonialism, or neocolonialism (Crossley & Tikly, 2004; Harvey, 2003; Nguyen et al., 2009; Samoff, 2013). Despite the oppression inherent in 'best practices' lending that hails from Global North countries and global governance institutions, nation-states have agency to resist the imposition of these reforms or to adapt 'internationally recognized' practices to their local circumstances, as I discuss in more detail below.

Illustrative Cases of Policy Borrowing and Lending[5]

Below, I briefly introduce five cases of educational policy borrowing and lending, which represent different motivations and rationales for reform. The case of Outcomes-Based Education (OBE) in South Africa reflects an intentional effort to borrow a policy at a time of profound political change, in which an external reference to a new educational policy was expedient for the purposes of legitimacy. This policy was, however, implemented. In contrast, England's short-lived Masters in Teaching and Learning (MTL) provides a clear example of phony policy borrowing, in which the reform was adopted prior to a general election and then later dropped. The transfer of adapted education (the term used for industrial education in the Gold Coast) from the USA to colonial Ghana reflects both active lending and active borrowing for the purposes of political legitimacy. International assessments, such as PISA, represent a clear case of policy diffusion because they have an impact on countries all over the world. Japan is offered as an illustrative case in which PISA results affected educational policy, yet in unexpected ways due to the involvement of a variety of actors. Conditional cash transfers (CCTs) are an example of 'best practices' lending, albeit a complex one. Although CCTs originated in the Global South and have been transferred between countries within the Global South, they are reflective of the neoliberal ideas of the Post-Washington Consensus (PWC) due to the involvement of global governance institutions and other donors. At the same time, the Opportunity NYC (New York City) project appropriated the CCT reform only to later serve as a key exporter of the policy.

Outcomes-Based Education

OBE is an educational reform that involves policymakers organizing the educational system around outcomes or goals in specific curricular areas. Once goals are established, the curriculum and other components of education are designed around them to ensure that all students meet the intended outcomes. South Africa's implementation of OBE in the post-apartheid era serves as an interesting example of a case in which a policy was borrowed through international referencing, followed by a later attempt to conceal the international origins of the policy. As South Africa was making the transition to a democracy in the early 1990s, the entire system of schooling was being redeveloped in a highly politically charged era of transformational change (Jansen, 2004; Spreen, 2004). South Africa needed to adopt a policy that involved strong international references to gain legitimacy, especially given the contested political terrain of the post-apartheid era. At the same time, the country needed a 'quick fix' solution due to its transitional nature and the need to signal a change, both to be accepted internally and to establish itself on the global stage (Spreen, 2004).

Although it may have been a symbolic policy at the beginning, OBE was implemented in large part in South Africa. During the early phases of OBE policy borrowing in South Africa, government officials made trips to

Australia, New Zealand, and Scotland to study OBE and made multiple references to international examples in policy documents. After OBE was indigenized into the local environment, as in the final stage of Phillips and Ochs' (2003) Four Stages of Policy Borrowing Model, international references began to dissipate, as questions were raised with regard to the efficacy of transferring OBE to South Africa. The implementation of OBE was controversial, and the government gradually began to eliminate references to other countries in policies, curriculum guides, and other documents (Spreen, 2004). In this way, South Africa sought to make it clear that OBE was an appropriate policy for the country and claimed it as a thoroughly indigenized policy.

Masters in Teaching and Learning Degree

England's brief adoption of an MTL degree for newly qualified teachers displays a case of phony, superficial policy borrowing for symbolic purposes. Unlike OBE, however, the symbolic MTL degree was dropped shortly after implementation. The MTL reform was announced in 2010 immediately prior to the country's general election. Although England's PISA results were above average, educators, parents, and policymakers were concerned about educational quality, and the government sought to improve education by enhancing teacher qualifications (Chung, Atkin, & Moore, 2012). Based on the accolades that Finland's education system, which is progressive and student-centered in nature, had received due to that country's strong PISA test results, England sought to borrow Finland's teacher preparation model, in which all teachers have an advanced university degree. England launched the government-funded MTL program for this purpose. The government borrowed the MTL reform, even though there was no evidence to support the notion that having a master's degree leads to higher-quality teachers or better educational results (Chung et al., 2012).

The MTL program's philosophy mirrored that of the Finnish education system, in which teaching is student-centered, and English teachers were trained to use progressive education as a foundation in the MTL program. The reform addressed only part of the education system (teacher preparation), however, without changing the context of the schooling environment. Schools in England remain standards-based with yearly national exams; therefore, the MTL curriculum did not align with the realities of the schooling system. In this sense, the MTL was a short-term solution to a long-term problem (Chung et al., 2012). The short-term political motivations for adopting this reform added to its ineffectiveness. For these reasons, the MTL reform was not sustained and was discontinued before the first cohort finished, although the government committed to funding the first group to complete the program.

International Assessments

As I discuss in Chap. 4, standardized international assessments, such as OECD's PISA, have gained increasing influence as countries compare their achievements and strive to perform better. Keita Takayama (2012) traced the impact of PISA on the Japanese education system. According to Takayama, at the time that the 2003 PISA results were released, Japan was experiencing a contested educational environment in which a new governmental reform, called *yutori*, had been introduced. The *yutori* reform, which was modeled on global curricular standards that stem from the OECD, involved a shift from traditional teacher-centered instruction to constructivism and streamlining curricular content by 30 %. Interestingly, the Japanese government did not use international references or divulge connections between the *yutori* reform and the OECD model when it was implemented (Takayama, 2012). In a case of 'silent borrowing' (Waldow, 2009), references to the OECD were not used when the *yutori* reform was enacted. Takayama stated that the lack of international referencing was due to the fact that the OECD model of schooling places an emphasis on competition and economic productivity that would have been at odds with the movement under way at the time to make Japanese schools less competitive and more humanizing.

The 2003 PISA results, which showed that Japanese youths' performance had dropped, changed the environment. They provided an opportunity for criticism of the *yutori* reform, and the government then sought to emphasize the connections between the model used in the *yutori* reform and the OECD, given that the organization also administers the test. Various actors responded to this situation in differing ways. The educational minister and Ministry of Education, Sports, Science and Technology took the opportunity to introduce a new national assessment. In line with Rappleye's (2012) political production model, Takayama (2012) suggests that the government used the media to develop a manufactured sense of crisis to gain legitimacy for this reform, which already was one of its objectives. The government also moved toward the economization of education model that I discuss in Chap. 4. Takayama also shows how progressive scholars used the PISA results in a different way: They highlighted the inequalities that the results showed between students from different economic and social backgrounds. Progressive scholars also used the positive view of Finland, based on its PISA results, to argue for importing elements of the progressive Finnish education system into the Japanese context. This case displays how international lending of standardized assessments—even though this lending may not have been intentional—entered the Japanese educational context and then was refashioned and used in different ways by various actors within the local environment.

Adapted Education

In a historical case of policy borrowing and lending, the US model of industrial education for African Americans was transferred to Achimota College in the Gold Coast, which is now Ghana. Achimota was the centerpiece of the British government's colonial master plan (Steiner-Khamsi & Quist, 2000). In this environment, adapted education focused on manual and agricultural training, reflecting the purpose of the colonial government for the African population, which it deemed mentally inferior. Interestingly, the Achimota case reflects both policy lending and policy borrowing activity. On the lending side, a US philanthropic society, the Phelps-Stokes Fund, was active in spreading the industrial education model and was central to diffusing the US model to colonial Africa (Steiner-Khamsi & Quist, 2000). On the borrowing side, the British colonial government sought a policy through which it could gain legitimacy for its discriminatory education system for Africans by using external references within a contested political environment. Although missionary education was prevalent at the time and was focused on industrial, agricultural, and manual training, British colonial officials sought to borrow a different policy because their focus was on facilitating the colonial economy through training Africans for their assigned role in the system rather than for religious conversion (Steiner-Khamsi & Quist, 2000).

In this case, a reference from elsewhere was needed to help validate the implementation of the racist colonial policy. Borrowing from the USA was politically expedient because the country had no history as a colonial power. Through the policy borrowing and lending process, however, the US model was 'decontextualized, locally modified, and indigenized in an attempt to appease opponents of a strictly agricultural model of education' (Steiner-Khamsi & Quist, 2000, p. 279). The US model was combined with the British model of education to create an environment in which Africans would be prepared for working in rural areas, with some emphasis on Africanization. Another noteworthy aspect of the Achimota case is that industrial education was beginning to be criticized in the USA at precisely the time when the reform was borrowed. This fact was inconsequential, however, because a reform is always contested in, and indigenized into, the local context (Steiner-Khamsi & Quist, 2000).

Conditional Cash Transfers

CCTs represent a global reform movement that has spread to more than 40 countries, providing an example of a 'best practice' reform. Echoing the PWC, CCT programs are focused on poverty alleviation through increasing educational opportunities for children. They operate from the premise that children in many countries are not able to attend school due to their families' financial circumstances, which do not allow the families to pay for direct or indirect costs of schooling or require them to work instead of attending school (Morais de Sá e Silva, 2012). CCTs provide a temporary financial subsidy—typically cash incentives provided on the condition that children regularly attend school and/or visit health clinics—that encourages educational attainment while also providing an opportunity to break the cycle of poverty in the longer term. Governments offer these programs to targeted populations that are most in need rather than providing blanket subsidies, although many countries' CCT programs are national in scale. International donors, including bilateral aid agencies, IMOs, and private foundations, are involved in funding nearly 50 % of CCT programs (Morais de Sá e Silva, 2012), while governments fund the remaining balance.

Michelle Morais de Sá e Silva (2012) conducted an analysis of three CCT cases that display differing aspects of the policy borrowing and lending process: Opportunity NYC, Subsidios Condiciondos a la Asistencia Escolar (Bogota, Columbia), and Bolsa Familia (Brazil). In Bogota and New York, CCTs are localized efforts, while Brazil's program is federal. In the Opportunity NYC context, CCTs are contingent upon both school attendance and improved standardized test performance. Supported by the Rockefeller Foundation, former New York City mayor Michael Bloomberg and deputy mayor Linda Gibbs traveled to Mexico to learn about CCT programs and to consider the possibility of implementing CCTs in New York. The CCT model was eventually adopted because it aligned with Harvard education professor Roland Fryer's ideas regarding behavioral incentives, which had been piloted in NYC schools previously (Morais de Sá e Silva, 2012). In the NYC Opportunity case, the language of CCTs was very different from that used in countries from the Global South and, thus, had to be adapted to the local context. For example, the words 'incentive' and 'customer service' were used, connoting an economic spin on the policy, as opposed to the use of words that indicated the social service approach that many countries undertake.

According to Morais de Sá e Silva's (2012) analysis, this instance of policy borrowing provides an example of using an external policy to gain legitimacy for an initiative that was already under development in the local context; in other words, use of a reference from elsewhere served as a cover for an educational reform that the city already had planned to implement. Once CCTs were in place, New York City sought to solidify the reform's legitimacy. Despite a lack of evidence regarding the efficacy of Opportunity NYC and CCTs in New York, government officials sought to transfer the policy to other countries in a further effort to gain legitimacy for the policy, in particular to secure funding at home. Opportunity NYC succeeded in becoming internationally recognized by foundations and IMOs. This case provides an interesting example that involves borrowing from one country (Mexico) and repackaging the reform in the local context to later lend to other countries. It also shows how the stature and geopolitical position of a country from the Global North factors into the positive reception of a reform abroad, no matter its origin.

The Subsidios program in Bogota was designed as a specialized CCT program to augment the national CCT framework due to low school completion rates in the city, particularly for impoverished communities. This program offered a complex set of payment options to different portions of the city as an experiment to discern the best strategy moving forward. An additional objective contributed to the adoption of CCTs in Bogota: Borrowing from the Mexican and Brazilian models, which were receiving positive acclaim in donor communities, provided an opportunity to impress the Inter-American Development Bank from which the government sought a loan (Morais de Sá e Silva, 2012). Whereas policymakers in the Opportunity NYC project used external references to gain support for a policy that was already under development locally, Subsidios evoked external references to add legitimacy to the policy and garner donor support. In Brazil, the Bolsa Familia program resulted from the consolidation of several cash transfer programs under one umbrella. CCTs have enjoyed a long history in Brazil, and the policy was 'homegrown' rather than borrowed (Morais de Sá e Silva, 2012). In this case, international donor involvement was prevalent, and Brazil was a lending country, often serving as a consultant or forming cooperative relationships with other countries in the Global South. This case demonstrates a situation in which policies were transferred among a group of countries, albeit with oversight from lenders.

Complexities in Policy Borrowing and Lending Processes

The illustrative examples I provide above demonstrate that policy borrowing and lending are complex processes that involve strong political dimensions. As with the policymaking process more generally (described in Chap. 5), policy borrowing and lending are value laden and political. Various actors are involved, and there are different motivations for borrowing and lending policies, which are often based on the local political environment and the geopolitical position of the borrowing and/or lending country. Analysis of policy borrowing and lending processes reveals a number of important and interconnected implications, including varying directions of policy transfer, local agency to resist global trends, and indigenization of policies into the local context.

Multiple Directions of Policy Transfer

Although normative discussions about policy convergence suggest the prominence of policy diffusion and 'best practices' lending from global governance organizations and the Global North to the Global South, the fuller range of scholarship on policy borrowing and lending demonstrates that educational reforms are lent or borrowed in multiple directions. As noted, the assumption that most policies are lent from the Global North to the Global South is false. Policies increasingly circulate between and among countries in the Global North, between and among countries in the Global South, between Global North and Global South countries, or in a 'triangular' fashion, involving transfer from two countries, at least one of which is from the Global South, to a third country (Abdenur, 2009). As reflected in the case of CCTs, a policy that emanates from a country in the Global South (albeit with donor support) may emerge in the

Global North and then be repackaged for further dissemination in various countries.

The aid and development regime began to recognize the multiple directions involved in policy borrowing and lending in the late 1990s and early 2000s when 'South-South' policy transfer, or cooperation, became an increasingly popular concept. Continued use of this terminology in aid and development circles raises questions regarding why global governance agencies would encourage South-South transfer. Scholars have suggested that the aid and development regime employs the language of South-South cooperation as a guise for continued 'best practices' lending—for example, by encouraging less developed countries to borrow 'internationally recognized' policies from other countries in the Global South that have previously adopted these reforms (Morais de Sá e Silva, 2009; Steiner-Khamsi, 2009). Steiner-Khamsi suggests that, 'in most cases, we deal with a North-South-South transfer or West-East-East transfer, whereby donors in the North or West, respectively, have designed a standardized reform or intervention package for the global South' (p. 257). In this way, policy borrowing and lending becomes a mechanism through which dependency of the Global South on the Global North continues, even if it gives the appearance of a South-South transfer.

Significant policy borrowing and lending activity has taken place between and among countries in the Global South in recent years (Chisholm, 2012; Steiner-Khamsi, 2009), and not all such lending is coercive. In some cases, countries in the Global South actively seek to borrow from other countries that share a similar geopolitical position as a form of resistance (Chisholm & Steiner-Khamsi, 2009; Morais de Sá e Silva, 2009; Nazmul Islam & Anwar, 2012). For example, Global South countries, such as Jamaica and Namibia, have actively sought support from Cuba for building teacher capacity (Hickling-Hudson, 2004). Collaboration also

South-South Transfer

Despite the relatively strong geopolitical position of countries in the Global North, not all policies flow from the Global North to the Global South. 'South-South' transfer connotes the process through which policies are borrowed and lent between countries in the Global South. In some cases, countries in the Global South intentionally initiate cooperation with other countries of a similar geopolitical stature as a means to counter dominant global policies that stem from the Global North. In other instances, policies that one country from the Global South borrows from another actually stem from policies that have already circulated in the Global North or reforms that global governance institutions seek to advocate. In this way, these organizations continue to maintain authority with regard to the reforms that countries in the Global South undertake, to a large degree, while maintaining the guise of transfer between countries in the Global South.

occurs from South-East or East-South, as in the case of multiple forms of cooperation between South Africa and India (Soudien, 2009).

Cooperation among countries in the Global South may also occur on a larger scale. One of the most notable examples of such cooperation is the INGO called BRAC, which began in Bangladesh in 1972 (BRAC, 2015). BRAC manages multiple programs related to sustainable development in the Global South and has expanded its operations into Afghanistan, Haiti, Liberia, Myanmar, Pakistan, the Philippines, Sierra Leone, South Sudan, Tanzania, and Uganda. In the realm of educational policy, BRAC is known for its teacher training initiatives (Nazmul Islam & Anwar, 2012) and non-formal primary education model, which predated the EFA movement (Chabbott, 2009a). Another example of cooperation is Cuba, which has disseminated resources related to teaching, adult literacy, and scholarships to other countries in the Global South (Hickling-Hudson, Gonzalez, & Preston, 2012). Although the influence of global governance institutions that hail from the Global North is clearly strong, existing research demonstrates that it is not all-encompassing, and policy borrowing and lending within the Global South is increasingly present and influential.

Local Agency to Resist Global Trends

When considering the policy borrowing and lending environment, it is important to keep in mind that nation-states and local constituencies have agency to resist global trends (Appadurai, 1996; Burde, 2004; Samoff, 2013). Given this ability to resist, it becomes clear that policy diffusion characterized by 'best practices' lending is an important, although not a monolithic, force. In most cases of policy borrowing, there is a strong interplay between global and local forces because even coercive lending is not simply a one-way process. For example, Joel Spring (2015) suggests that the spread of the economization of education model, with its emphasis on human capital development, involves both imposition and choice. Although some countries may find it difficult to avoid adopting this increasingly standard model, other countries' governments may strategically adopt the model for their purposes. In one instance of the latter, Peru strategically adopted the economization of education model in the early twentieth century to bolster its industrialization process and, thus, focused on skills and jobs-based education (Spring, 2015). Alongside this economization of education model, mass education and mass literacy remained key areas of focus in Peru.

As I discuss in Chap. 5, there is a balance between coercion and agency. Even when policies are coercively lent or espoused through 'best practices' lending, their homogenizing effects are always reshaped in the local environment (Ball, 2012; Luke & Luke, 2000). Critical education scholars Allan Luke and Carmen Luke highlight a both/and approach that recognizes the influence of global forces (and policies) alongside local agency. This both/and approach is connected to the notion of vernacular globalization. Hybridity, in which a new educational reform has global elements while retaining a local character, is likely to result in any case of international policy borrowing and lending (Appadurai, 1996; Chisholm, 2012; Lingard, 2000; Spring, 2008). With coercive lending, hybridity represents a hallmark of agency and resistance to dominant global trends. These developments are always mediated in the local context, especially through the role of street-level bureaucrats who shape implementation.

Indigenization of Policies into the Local Context

Since the early stages of policy borrowing, context has been a vital concern for educational scholars who recognize that there are no standard solutions for borrowing educational reforms due to the local adaptations that necessarily occur (Appadurai, 1996; Ball, 2012; Lingard, 2000; Portnoi et al., 2013; Rizvi & Lingard, 2010). Sadler's (as cited in Phillips, 2000) famous caution from 1900 about the importance of context still resonates. Nonetheless, countries often visit other nation-states and become enthralled with a reform without considering contextual factors (Phillips, 2000). Similarly, movements to adopt 'best practices' often disregard social, political, and economic variations in contexts that are of critical importance to policy implementation and the ultimate success of a policy

(Rizvi & Lingard, 2010; Silova, 2012; Steiner-Khamsi, 2004). Not surprisingly, reforms are more successful if transferred to a similar context, which puts countries in the Global South at a disadvantage when adopting 'best practice' reforms that originate in the Global North.

No matter whether policies are forcefully lent or intentionally borrowed, reforms are indigenized as they are brought into the local context, as depicted in the final stage of the Four Stages of Policy Borrowing and Lending model (Phillips & Ochs, 2003). In the case of OBE in South Africa, for example, the general 'internationally recognized' policy that emanated from countries in the Global North was adapted to the South African context, particularly with regard to the educational outcomes that were made relevant to the local context. Even when policies are intentionally borrowed, they are not copied and are always reinterpreted in the local context due to the political environment (Steiner-Khamsi, 2012). For example, Ka-Ho Mok (2012) demonstrates that the governments of Malaysia and Hong Kong each developed a different regulatory framework to monitor transnational higher education. Hong Kong actively promotes transnational higher education as a way to alleviate educational inequalities, while Malaysia is more reticent to encourage transnational higher education due to quality concerns. Therefore, Malaysia has developed a centralized quality-assurance mechanism to regulate transnational higher education, while Hong Kong relies on program providers to measure quality. Mok indicates that the variations between the policy imperatives about transnational higher education in these two countries stem from differing political motivations. This example highlights the importance of the (political) context in which educational policies are enacted.

Conclusion

Policy borrowing and lending are multifaceted processes, and educational reforms flow in multiple directions. These processes always contain a political dimension and are related to specific motivations or rationales for reform, ranging from quick fix to symbolic to legitimization. Normative scholarship on policy diffusion, emanating from world culture theorists, suggests that there is significant convergence in educational policies worldwide. Critical scholars have problematized this approach, noting that there is a continuum of voluntary versus coercive transfer. Nation-states from the Global North and the global governance institutions that originate in these countries have taken on the responsibility of setting global policies with the assumption that their policies are 'best practices' worthy of adoption, while they deem countries in the Global South to be in need of the support of the aid and development regime. A great deal of the flow of policies, therefore, stem from coercive forms of 'best practices' lending. Although policy diffusion has clearly occurred, critical scholars acknowledge that politics and geopolitical positioning are always involved. In other words, policies are adopted not because they are the 'best' based on shared international standards but, rather, due to the influence of global governance organizations in the current context. They are also adopted for political expediency based on the domestic climate. At the same time, it is important to recognize that governments and other local constituents, even those in the Global South, have agency to resist dominant trends. Policies, whether borrowed or lent forcefully, are refashioned in the local context, where they become indigenized.

Notes

1. Policy diffusion and 'best practices' lending driven by global governance organizations are the subject of a separate section below.
2. Whereas this chapter includes examples for illustrative purposes, Chap. 7 provides a comprehensive synthesis of patterns and trends in relevant literature on policy borrowing and educational reform.
3. Externalization, or the use of an external reference society, stems from Niklas Luhmann's system theory approach (Rappleye, 2012; Silova, 2012).
4. Steiner-Khamsi (2004, 2012) is particularly skeptical of policy diffusion and refers to convergence in policy *discourse* rather than policy *action*.
5. See the original texts for full descriptions of the policy borrowing and lending processes involved.

CHAPTER 7

Patterns of Educational Reform and Policy Borrowing

Since the inception of formal systems of education, nation-states have undertaken educational reforms to improve their systems. Many of these reforms were developed from within, while others drew upon learning from the experiences of other countries. Given the heightened nature of contemporary globalization, educational policy borrowing and lending across country borders has increased, as I explain in Chap. 6. In this context, educational reforms are borrowed and lent for a variety of purposes, not only for the express purpose of improving educational structures and practices. Countries that desire to improve their educational systems continue to seek out reforms that have been successful elsewhere, while, in other cases, governments may opt to enact borrowed policies for political expediency. As noted, governments are not the only actors in an increasingly globalized world. Given the influence of global governance institutions, 'best practices' lending is a central component of educational reform worldwide.

In keeping with governments' and organizations' increased use of policy borrowing and lending, the research on educational reforms that take place in international contexts has proliferated over the past 15 years. Most of the scholarly literature focuses on educational reforms that have taken place within the period of contemporary globalization since the end of World War II (WWII), although a number of scholars investigate historical cases of policy borrowing and lending. Some of this educational reform research is situated within comparative and international education (CIE),

© The Editor(s) (if applicable) and The Author(s) 2016

L.M. Portnoi, *Policy Borrowing and Reform in Education*,
DOI 10.1057/978-1-137-53024-0_7

generally, and/or the policy borrowing literature, specifically, while other research extends to complementary domains within education and beyond.

The central purpose of this chapter is to provide an overview of the key patterns evident in the research literature on educational reforms in international contexts. These patterns, which I have discerned through a systematic analysis of existing literature, relate to various stages of the policy process, including agenda setting, policy attraction, policy borrowing, and implementation. Five interrelated patterns repeatedly appear throughout the extant scholarship on educational reforms across the globe. The first pattern is the neoliberal market orientation that is manifested within many of the educational reforms that countries around the world have undertaken, especially over the past 30 years. The manifestation of neoliberal reforms connects to the second pattern of educational reform—that most of the policies emanate from external sources, especially when they are pushed through 'best practices' lending. The third pattern is that the context into which reforms are borrowed or lent is often overlooked or not considered fully. A related fourth pattern is that policymakers typically fail to pay sufficient attention to those who have the crucial task of implementing reforms. Finally, the fifth pattern is that nation-states and implementers adapt reforms to their local contexts through vernacular globalization. After presenting these patterns, in the final section of the chapter, I reflect on the educational reform lessons that emerge from a systematic examination of existing scholarship on educational reform and policy borrowing throughout the world.

Educational Reform Patterns in a Globalized World

In this section, I provide a brief overview of each of the five patterns that are evident in the literature on educational reforms worldwide. The discussion includes several illustrative examples for each pattern.

The Manifestation of Neoliberal Market-Oriented Principles

One of the overarching patterns evident in the literature on educational reforms across the globe is the neoliberal market orientation that is woven into the majority of reforms that various countries have undertaken—either by choice or by imposition—since the 1980s. As noted in Chap. 2, the agreement forged at the Bretton Woods Conference in 1944 solidified the importance of a global free market economy and led to the spread of capitalism and the opening (or liberalization) of trade and markets in most corners of the world. During the postwar reconstruction period, the Keynesian free market economic system existed alongside the welfare state, in which governments provided significant social services to their citizens (see Chap. 2). As previously discussed, after the economic downturn of the 1970s, welfare states declined, and neoliberalism, a form of capitalism that prescribes decentralization, privatization, and deregulation, became the dominant economic paradigm throughout the world.

As neoliberalism has intersected with globalization, widespread changes have occurred that have had an impact on all sectors of society, including education. As noted in Chap. 4, through the influence of neoliberalism and the aid and development regime's application of human capital theory, education has become synonymous with producing human capital to improve nation-states' economic competitiveness on the world stage. In this section, I discuss the research on the two main ways in which neoliberalism is reflected in education reforms that have taken place across the globe. The first way is the adoption of neoliberal reform packages that are aimed at improving economic competitiveness, while the second is the development of human capital for the post-Fordist global knowledge economy.

Numerous educational systems around the world have experienced sweeping educational reforms since WWII, especially in the countries of the Global South, many of which gained their independence from colonial powers during the period of contemporary globalization. A systematic review of the existing literature provides evidence that a wide range of countries throughout the world have adopted neoliberal educational reform packages since the late 1970s, including Australia (Doherty, 2009; Lingard, 2010; Marginson, 1997a, 1997b; Savage & O'Connor, 2014; Whitty, Power, & Halpin, 1998), Brazil (Arnove, 2015; Arnove, Franz, & Torres, 2013; Barreyro, Rothen, & Santana, 2014; Fortes, 2015; Hales, 2012), India (Clarke, 2003; Goswami, 2013; Mukhopadhyay, & Sriprakash, 2013; Tooley & Dixon, 2006; Verger & VanderKaaij, 2012), South Africa (Allais, 2003; Fataar, 2006; Naidoo & Muthukrishna, 2014; Spreen & Vally, 2006; Stenvoll-Wells & Sayed, 2012), and the UK (Evans, 2011; Furlong, 2013; Lingard & Sellar, 2012; West & Pennell, 1997; Wilkins, 2015).

Given the dominance of neoliberal globalization across the world today, it is not surprising that a strong market orientation is contained within these reform packages that are designed to improve educational systems for economic competitiveness. For example, Rosa Buenfil (2014) demonstrates how Mexico's *Modernización Educativa* educational policy, which was in effect from 1988 to 1996, reflected several tenets of neoliberalism, which the country had adopted in the 1980s under the label of 'social liberalism'. Aligned with neoliberalism and influenced by the aid and development regime, *Modernización Educativa* portrayed education as an investment and a means for skills development to improve the economic environment of the country (Buenfil, 2014). In Thailand, a suite of policies instituted in 2008 included several neoliberal schooling reforms, such as school-based management and quality assurance (Hallinger & Lee, 2011). Similarly, Singapore instituted an array of neoliberal educational policy reforms, such as decentralization and standardized testing, from the 1970s to the 1990s, with the express purpose of maintaining a globally competitive edge during the time period in which the country's economic system was experiencing market liberalization (Gopinathan, 2001).

Through the New Senior Secondary (NSS) school reform in Hong Kong, the government sought to increase the country's economic competitiveness (Chow, 2014). The NSS policy, which replaced the former elitist British system in 2009, was based on the internationally recognized International Baccalaureate Diploma Programme (IBDP) curriculum that was developed in the 1960s. Reformers expected that this curriculum would improve quality, leading to a greater ability to be globally competitive. South Korea borrowed a variety of market-oriented reforms, including school choice, accountability, and standardized testing. Youl-Kwan Sung (2011) explores how the South Korean government borrowed 'loanwords' from the USA and the UK when externalization was desirable for political expediency, in keeping with politically motivated policy borrowing, as discussed in Chap. 6. These loanwords eventually translated into concrete policies. South Korea's import of the loanwords 'choice' and 'diversity' provides an interesting case because the original intent was to democratize education by improving educational outcomes for the full spectrum of South Korean society after 30 years of dictatorship, which ended in 1990. Despite these words' initial connotations of democratizing education, they have become associated with conservative, neoliberal aspects of educational reforms. Through 'selective filtering', words such as 'choice' were later used to validate opportunities for the privileged, such as having the choice to attend an elite high school (Sung, 2011).

A second area in which neoliberal tenets have manifested in educational reforms is the emphasis on developing human capital for the global knowledge economy. Many of these reforms are tied to producing workers who are capable of functioning effectively in the post-Fordist economic environment described in Chap. 2. For example, Qatar's government initiated a reform, 'Education for a New Era' in 2001, which was designed to improve the quality of its educational system and to prepare its citizens to function in the global knowledge economy. Neoliberal principles are evident in various aspects of this reform. One of its most transformational aspects, which ties directly to neoliberalism, is its decentralization of the school system, which was previously centrally run through the Ministry of Education. With the reform, all government schools were transferred to the semi-autonomous structure of 'independent schools', which function much like charter schools in the USA (Nassar et al., 2014). Another significant change initiated by Education for a New Era was a shift from the Ministry's subject-based curriculum to standards-based education that uses the Qatar National Curriculum Standards and includes standardized testing at each grade level. Standards-based education in Qatar brought the country's educational system into alignment with the accountability movement that has dominated market-based schooling reforms in the Global North (see Chap. 4). It also provided an opportunity for students to develop 'soft skills', such as flexibility and working with diverse people, which are purportedly needed in the post-Fordist economy.

In Singapore, the full spectrum of education, from preschool to university education, was restructured during the 1990s, with an emphasis on students' developing skills and capabilities for the post-Fordist working environment, such as innovation, flexibility, creativity, entrepreneurship, and a commitment to lifelong learning. The government was concerned about the country's and its citizens' keeping up with the changes that accompany market liberalization, such as a growing service sector and a technology-driven economic environment (Gopinathan, 2001). As another case of developing a country's citizenry for the global knowledge economy, Botswana's 1994 'Revised National Policy on Education' is aligned with the need to cultivate workers for the post-Fordist economy. According to the policy, the desired worker, a lifelong learner, would have skills that align with the demands of the post-Fordist economic environment, such as innovativeness, creativity, flexibility, and independent thought (Tabulawa, 2009). This reform represented Botswana's response to globalization and a desire to create 'self-programmable' learners who would later become the workers needed to drive the increasingly competitive economic environment (Tabulawa, 2009).

Wing-Wah Law (2004) discusses how Taiwan and Hong Kong adopted market-oriented educational reforms to enhance their competitiveness in the global economy. These reforms emphasized 'transnational' skills, such as English and information and communications technology. As in other jurisdictions, Taiwan and Hong Kong focused on promoting lifelong learning, developing skills for critical thinking, and working with multicultural groups. To achieve these changes designed to prepare students to function in the global knowledge economy, the curriculum in both jurisdictions was restructured to move away from subject-based teaching that involves rote learning to competency-based education that includes areas such as personal and social skills as well as post-Fordist skills related to foreign languages and technology (Law, 2004).

This emphasis on preparing citizens for the global knowledge economy is seen throughout higher education as well. For instance, Michael Dobbins and Christoph Knill (2009) researched the Bologna Process, which they characterize as Europe's answer to globalization and the demands of the new global knowledge economy. The Bologna Process derives from the 1999 Bologna Declaration, in which nearly 30 signatory countries established a common European Higher Education Area to harmonize degree structures and enhance mobility between countries in the European Union (EU). The Bologna Process rests on voluntary agreements and does not prescribe a particular form of governance. Nevertheless, in their research on Central and Eastern European countries, Dobbins and Knill found that market-oriented strategies dominate the Bologna Process. In addition, the European Commission actively promotes the integration of market-oriented features into the Bologna Process, such as lifelong learning for economic productivity. These countries, which had previously been governed by communist regimes, went through dramatic structural and political changes, moving from state centrism to marketization. A strong market orientation was evident in their higher education systems, with the 'aim of increasing the accountability, efficiency, and viability of HE institutions' (Dobbins & Knill, 2009, p. 425) to function in the global knowledge economy.

National qualification frameworks (NQFs) for vocational education and training (VET) are a related phenomenon in which industry partners become involved in helping to define the skills that learners should develop to participate in the global knowledge economy. According to Chakroun (2010), in the countries where NQFs started (Australia, Ireland, New Zealand, and the UK), NQF policies focused on education in which learners obtain vocational qualifications. As the reform has spread throughout the world, NQFs have increasingly become tied to all levels of education, including secondary schooling, VET, and higher education. Borhene Chakroun's (2010) research on NQFs in EU partner countries (e.g., the former Soviet Republics) show that there is a 'global consensus' regarding the need for VET reforms and that NQFs are being championed as a way to modernize VET and to infuse principles of lifelong learning into this area of education. Through NQFs, stakeholders (i.e., industry partners) are involved in setting and standardizing qualifications and learning outcomes, thus allowing VET to be responsive to the needs of the labor market in the post-Fordist economy.

Taken together, the research on educational reforms in international contexts contains a strong manifestation of neoliberal policies and tenets, from decentralization to school choice to standardized testing. Further, many educational reforms focus on preparing citizens for the global knowledge economy as related to governments' interests in remaining economically competitive. Neoliberal reforms have swept countries in both the Global North and the Global South, indicative of the second pattern in educational borrowing and lending: the externally driven nature of most educational reforms worldwide.

Employing External and 'Best Practice' Reforms

A clear pattern exists in the literature with regard to the origin of many education reforms: A significant number of reforms emanate from external sources, with some borrowed and others lent. As noted, some policies are intentionally borrowed from one or more specific countries. Qatar's 'Education for a New Era', which stemmed from a government mandate for a long-term strategy for investing in the increasingly important knowledge-based economy, is based on intentional borrowing. The Qatari government actively sought out assistance from the US-based Research and Development (RAND) Corporation to develop a 'world-class' school system to ensure a better future for the country (Nassar et al., 2014). One of the central components of 'Education for a New Era' was standards-based education, which Qatar borrowed from the USA, the reference society of origin. The adoption of a standards-based education led to numerous curricular changes, as well as changes to instruction, which had been based on subject matter in Qatar.

Historically, policy borrowing and lending have involved this type of one-to-one transfer (Silova, 2012). With increased globalization, however, the processes of educational policy borrowing and lending are changing. Many educational policies that travel across borders essentially become 'global' reforms that no longer have a clear reference society of origin (Steiner-Khamsi, Silova, & Johnson, 2006; Steiner-Khamsi & Stolpe, 2006). This type of reform often involves 'best practices' that circle the globe due, in large part, to the influence of global governance institutions, as discussed in Chap. 6. Global governance organizations that serve as the core of the aid and development regime are often involved directly in prescribing reforms and funding them (Jakobi, 2012; McNeely, 1995; Mundy, 1998; Punchi, 2001; Samoff, 2013). These organizations include International Monetary Organization (IMOs), such as the World Bank (WB) and the International Monetary Fund (IMF); bilateral agencies, such as United States Agency for International Development (USAID) and the UK's Department for International Development; and Intergovernmental Organizations (IGOs), such as United Nations Educational, Scientific and Cultural Organization (UNESCO) and the Organisation for Economic Co-operation and Development (OECD). In addition to these traditional aid and development regime actors, International Non-governmental Organizations (INGOs) are increasingly involved in 'best practices' lending.

Global Educational Reforms

Over time, the origins of many educational reforms that circulate around the world have become obscured. Although some countries seek to borrow a specific policy that was developed in one clear reference society, many of the policies that are being borrowed and lent around the world increasingly have taken on a 'global' nature because they have circulated throughout several countries and their origins are no longer clear. Global governance institutions are also advocating specific reforms, typically known as 'best practices', to multiple countries, which results in the absence of any one country to serve as the reference society for a reform. Although the impact of these global reforms is powerful and is manifested throughout the world, they are not monolithic. Countries can and do resist these reforms or borrow them with adaptations for the local environment.

Indonesia's 'active learning' policy is an example of an externally driven, 'best practice' reform. The policy was part of the wave of learner-centered education (LCE) reforms that aid agencies have recommended since the 1970s, when human rights movements and rights-based conventions gained prominence (Song, 2015). LCE, which has been instituted in both schooling and higher education, draws upon constructivist notions, which do not view teachers as the center of the classroom; rather, learners and their needs, experiences, and interests become the focus. Sopantini Heyward (2014) posits that Indonesia's adoption of active learning was undertaken primarily for purposes of compliance with and conformity to international expectations. Indonesia's first active learning reform was introduced in the late 1970s and has been followed by various iterations of active learning in each successive national education curriculum. These reforms draw upon the 'best practices' of the Global North and have enjoyed extensive government and donor agency support, including specialized structures for implementation. Nevertheless, the reform has had limited impact on everyday teaching practices in Indonesia, primarily because active learning is not aligned with the country's existing educational culture (Heyward, 2014), as I describe in more detail in the section on context below.

Following global trends, when Cambodia reformed its educational system in 1996 through the Education Investment Plan 1995–2000, one of the specific changes was to institute LCE, which is called 'child-centered pedagogy' in this context. The Ministry of Education developed the reform with backing and recommendations from UNESCO, UNDP, and the Asian Development Bank (Song, 2015). LCE reforms, whether as separate policies or part of major education policy packages, have been implemented in countries as diverse as India (Smail, 2014; Sriprakash, 2010), Tanzania (Bartlett & Mogusu, 2013; Vavrus & Bartlett, 2012), and Turkey (Aksit, 2007; Sak, Erden, & Morrison, 2015).

Another 'best practice' reform espoused and funded by the WB, regional banks, and other IMOs in the 1980s and 1990s was OBE. OBE originated in Global North countries, such as Australia, Canada, England, and New Zealand, and spread to dozens of other countries (Jansen, 2004). In the case of Kyrgyzstan, OBE was both sought and imposed, as the reform was pushed by the Ministry of Education and USAID. In the Global South, much of the spread of OBE was due to the influence of the aid and development regime and imposed lending. In the case of South Africa, presented in Chap. 6, however, the post-apartheid government intentionally sought out the 'best practice' of OBE at a critical political juncture (Jansen, 2004; Spreen, 2004). Kyrgyzstan, Mongolia, and Kazakstan were 'late adopters' of OBE at a time when it had already become a global reform and was reaching its 'burnout' stage (Steiner-Khamsi et al., 2006).

The same was true for South Africa, which adopted OBE even though it was declining in support in many of the original countries in which it had been enacted (Spreen, 2004). In the cases of Kyrgyzstan, Mongolia, and Kazakstan, the countries were primed for introduction in these post-Soviet countries due to their concerns about quality and corruption (Steiner-Khamsi et al., 2006). In addition, although the three countries' contexts and incorporation of OBE differ, the reform served to reinforce and revitalize principles that had been common under socialism, namely, planning, accountability, and surveillance. OBE's inherent focus on data and evidence-based research appealed to the governments of these post-Soviet countries (Steiner-Khamsi et al., 2006).

Although IMOs, IGOs, and bilateral agencies are the most prominent actors involved in circulating 'best practice' reforms, INGOs have increasingly become engaged in propagating these global reforms. Daniel Friedrich (2014) coined the term 'microlending' for this type of educational transfer, in which reforms may have the appearance of being grassroots movements. These reforms, however, are espoused by powerful INGOs, which are typically based in the Global North. The influence of microlending policies that INGOs push is not a direct imposition, as was the case with Structural Adjustment Programs (SAPs). Microlending entails well-intentioned educators seeking to improve educational quality through instituting reforms derived from the global INGO network. Despite their interest in improving education, Friedrich suggests that reformers who engage in microlending typically do not investigate the underlying causes of the problem that they seek to address but, rather, choose pre-packaged solutions that circulate among these global networks.

Argentina's *Enseñá por Argentina* (Teach for Argentina) program serves as an example of a type of reform that circulates through microlending. *Enseñá por Argentina* is part of the Teach for All campaign that the Clinton Global Initiative started in 2007 and involves a mix of democratic and neoliberal ideals. Modeled on Teach for America and Teach First in the UK, the Teach for All movement targets low-income and other disadvantaged populations while at the same time championing free market ideals (Friedrich, 2014). Teach for All has now spread to more than 35 countries (Teach for All, 2015). In the case of Argentina, Freidrich (2014) stated, 'By borrowing the language of grassroots change grounded on the will of individuals participating in NGOs, *Enseñá por Argentina* engages in a narrative of educational reform seen as apolitical, in the sense of it being commonsensical to the point of becoming incontestable' (p. 318).

In this way, the reform's origins are concealed, and it gains prominence as a global reform, despite the fact that there may be no evidence to suggest that it is truly an effective reform.

Regional organizations also participate in 'best practices' lending, and this form of lending takes place in both the Global South and the Global North. Some of this lending is imposed, while, in other instances, adherence to international norms is voluntary. In the case of the Bologna Process, for example, EU member countries' involvement in harmonizing credentials is highly voluntary. Nevertheless, the process is governed by a normative form of isomorphism, or convergence, in which countries feel compelled to do what their counterparts are doing (Dobbins & Knill, 2009). Even though there is not full convergence and each higher education system remains unique, the desire to conform is strong. Countries in the Global South may feel obligated to conform to international standards, yet countries in the Global North are not immune to the pressure to conform.

Another aspect of the pattern of employing externally driven reforms is related to the motivation to use external referencing to gain legitimacy for reforms, as I discuss in Chap. 6. Linda Greveling, Hilda Amsing, and Jeroen Dekker (2014) use the term 'framing' from media and communication studies similar to the way that CIE scholars use 'externalization' to signify the act of using external references to 'sell' the government's preferred policy. In their study of comprehensive school reforms, Greveling et al. found that the government of the Netherlands intentionally sought out the reform and used framing that involved international examples, particularly Sweden and Italy, to convince their audiences of the benefits of comprehensive education. Comprehensive schools were a global reform, or 'best practice', at the time of the Dutch reform in the 1970s. Dutch schools were designed to provide all children with equal educational opportunity by postponing school choice in the early phase of secondary education (which countries such as the USA refer to as middle school or junior high school), rather than to sort students into specific school tracks, some of which lead to a university education and some of which do not, at an early age. Greveling et al. demonstrate that, while the government used international examples to glorify and legitimize the reform, the teachers' union used the Belgian and English examples as a means to resist the reform, as these countries offered a 'double system' of comprehensive schools alongside traditional schools. In this way, teachers used international examples to sensationalize and caution against the reform, which was never implemented.

In most cases, however, the government is the main actor involved in using international referencing. In the case of South Korea, referenced earlier Sung (2011) showed how 'loanwords' were borrowed from the USA and the UK due to the 'perceived superiority' of educational policies from English-speaking countries. Once these English loanwords have been adopted in the receiving country, they 'acquire the symbolic power necessary to create the need to borrow within the new cultural context' (Sung, 2011, pp. 534–535). Sung found that, although these loanwords were not based on an objective measure of what is 'better', political tensions within the domestic environment nevertheless led to adoption of the associated policies.

Keita Takayama (2007) found that some government leaders, scholars, and media came together to intentionally create a sense of crisis around the *yutori* educational reform that was put into place in the 1990s (introduced in Chap. 6). Despite the fact that Japanese education had achieved international acclaim, many stakeholders in Japan were concerned about the reform's reduction in rote learning methods and 'relaxation' of educational pressures for Japanese children, which they feared would lead to declining achievement and international competitiveness. In this instance, the Japanese government borrowed the US discourse about the 'crisis' of education to provide an opportunity to revise the *yutori* reform. In the case of the NSS reform in Hong Kong, the government specifically referenced international 'best practices' when marketing the policy (Chow, 2014). In another instance, Australia borrowed standards-based education with accountability measures from the state of New York without attention to research that showed that these practices were ineffective (Reid, 2011). In such cases, policy borrowing is not a rational process based on evidenced needs but, rather, is a politically expedient strategy, as I discuss in Chap 6.

Overlooking the Importance of Context

Given that many reforms are adopted simply because they are perceived to be 'best practices' or because they fulfill political needs, another pattern evident in policy borrowing and lending is that many reforms are undertaken without considering the context into which the new policy will be brought. As noted in Chap. 6, CIE scholars have been cautioning against decontextualized policy borrowing and lending for many years. In the early days of policy borrowing, Sadler (as cited in Phillips, 2000) warned of the challenges of moving reforms across borders without ensuring that the context was primed to receive it, and numerous scholars of policy borrowing have echoed this concern (see, e.g., Phillips, 1989; Halpin & Troyna, 1995; Philips & Ochs, 2003; Silova, 2012). In the literature on policy borrowing and lending, 'context' may be perceived in a number of ways. In one view, context is conceptualized broadly, as when researchers consider the ineffectiveness of copying a reform directly from one country to another, such as from an established country in the Global North to a country in the Global South. Another view of context involves different cultures of schooling. A third issue related to context is a lack of consideration in regard to whether the educational infrastructure is designed for or prepared to support the reform. I discuss examples of all three types of contextual mismatch below.

Broad contextual issues come into play in many cases of policy borrowing and lending. For example, in regard to the German dual system–in which learners study in vocational schools while simultaneously gaining experience via industry partnerships, that has been lent throughout the Global South via German aid programs, Theodore Lewis (2007) found that 'The imported model invariably comes up against a set of assumptions different from those of the original, and that these discrepancies deter it from taking hold' (p. 463). Copying a reform from one country to another can be especially ineffective with a quick implementation cycle. For example, Chakroun (2010) notes that, when NQFs for VETs are transported as a policy package into a new context without sufficient time for adjustments, these reforms are 'not necessarily useful in satisfying the policy aspirations for which they were adopted in the first place' (p. 199). Because NQFs are tied to the goals of VETs within the institutional context of the receiving country, translation problems are likely to occur if an NQF from another country, especially a country of a completely different type, is brought into the new environment (e.g., from the Global North to the Global South). Although countries seek to have their VET systems aligned with the needs of the local labor market, there remains a significant gap between what VET can offer and what industry demands, especially in countries in the Global South. Chakroun suggests that, to combat these issues, intentional policy borrowing with a clear implementation plan and realistic timetable would be more effective.

Anthony Chow (2014) offers another case of contextual mismatch in the receiving country, arguing that the Hong Kong government overlooked fundamental contextual differences between the countries in which the IBDP had been implemented and the local environment when proposing the aforementioned NSS reform. The IBDP curriculum was created for the children of international diplomats from Global North countries. The post-independence environment in Hong Kong was completely different from that of most Global North countries, and the NSS curriculum was not designed to adjust to the diversity in ability levels and languages within Hong Kong schools. Teachers and administrators in these schools also critiqued the NSS reform for borrowing the model of IBDP superficially, without borrowing its substance (Chow, 2014). Moreover, although the reform was designed to reduce learner stress and make teaching more effective, students would have needed to be in school for ten hours per day to successfully complete the curriculum (Chow, 2014). These cases highlight the challenges of implementing a reform wholesale without considering the broad context into which the reform will be transferred.

In other cases, the educational reform proves to be a mismatch for the cultural context of the schooling environment of the receiving country. LCE provides a clear example of this kind of misalignment. In her review of 72 studies on implementation of LCE throughout the world, Michele Schweisfurth (2011) found that the schooling environment was very important to the receptivity of both teachers and learners in regard to a new method of education. Teachers are perceived as authority figures in many countries, and it has proven to be difficult for educators in cultures where hierarchies are prevalent and obedience is expected to align these contextual factors with LCE, as it transfers a certain degree of power from teachers to students.

Similarly, Heyward (2014) found that reforming teacher practice in Indonesia based on 'best practices' pushed by donor agencies that were touting active learning was ultimately unsuccessful due to inattention to the mismatch of the policy with the prevailing local context. Teachers in Indonesia viewed active learning as signifying a lack of respect for authority. Given the traditional, bureaucratic culture prevalent in Indonesia and Indonesian schools, active learning did not resonate with educators, students, or parents (Heyward, 2014). Likewise, the existing high-stakes national examination at the conclusion of the schooling system was incongruent with the foundation of active learning and, therefore, promoted continual use of traditional 'chalk-and-talk' methods of teaching (Heyward, 2014). In this vein, Cambodia's 1996 child-centered pedagogy reform has experienced limited success with implementation, despite the fact that teachers overwhelmingly support it (Song, 2015). Although the policy has been in place for nearly 20 years, classroom instruction in Cambodia remains teacher centered and textbook based. Sopheak Song found that teachers fail to implement the policy, in part or in full, because they have been trained to teach using a traditional teacher-centered approach. Not surprisingly, they retain their conventional beliefs and training, despite the introduction of a new policy.

The case of the England's brief attempt to develop an Master's in Teaching and Learning (MTL), which I introduced in Chap. 6, further demonstrates the importance of considering the receiving country's educational culture and context. Given Finland's stellar PISA test results, the UK sought to adopt the Finnish model of teacher preparation, which requires that all teachers have a university credential (Chung, Atkin, & Moore, 2012). England created the government-funded MTL program, which was progressive and student centered in nature, for this purpose. This government-funded program began in April 2010 and was open to all newly qualified teachers. The progressive curriculum associated with the MTL, however, was not in alignment with the standardized testing prevalent in schools in England, where students are tested yearly beginning in the early primary grades. The government failed to recognize that the MTL was an attempt to overlay the Finnish model on top of the existing structure and that the basic underlying principles of the educational systems were incompatible (Chung et al., 2012). Although the government did add distinctly British features (e.g., centralized oversight) to the MTL, the reform was unsuccessful due to both its incongruence with the British model and the lack of genuineness of the reform, given that it was adopted immediately prior to an election (Chung et al., 2012).

A third type of contextual challenge for implementing educational reforms is a lack of attention to the educational infrastructure needed to support new policies. The ability of the receiving country to implement the reform based on its infrastructure should be considered prior to undertaking the reform (Lewis, 2007). Challenges related to infrastructure may occur in any context, although they tend to be most prominent in Global South countries that adopt reforms that were originally designed for resource-rich Global North countries (Song, 2015). For example, with the Cambodian child-centered education reform, the realities of the educational system on the ground—including overcrowding, limited resources, and differing ability levels—prevented the government from effectively instituting its LCE reform, which was modeled on global policies (Song, 2015). In Kenya's free primary education policy, the resulting large class sizes impeded positive educational outcomes (Abuya, Admassu, Ngware,

Onsomu, & Oketch, 2015). Similarly, Lex McDonald and Rasela Tufue-Dolgoy (2013) found that implementing inclusive education in Samoa was challenging due to the lack of structural resources and large class sizes in schools. In such cases, intended reforms are inconsistent with the local realities of the schooling environment. As a result, teachers tend to put into practice limited elements of the reform as they 'adapt, combine, shift, and adopt policy to fit within their workplace constraints' (Song, 2015, p. 43).

Lack of Attention toward Implementers

Another pattern evidenced in the literature is that most reforms are planned with limited attention toward those who must undertake the implementation. Many of the educational reforms that countries seek to implement are complex and would result in significant changes, such as new curricula and new modes of teaching, for the educators involved. Yet, reforms tend to stem from a top-down approach that fails to take into account the views or experience of the educators who will be tasked with implementation. As noted in Chap. 5, top-down approaches are often ineffective because they do not recognize the need for buy-in from educators, or street-level bureaucrats. Further, these reforms are often in tension with the value systems and training that educators have received. As noted, teachers in many countries are likely to have a strong reaction to learner-centered education because it profoundly shifts the power differential between teachers and students (Schweisfurth, 2011). In keeping with this notion, Heyward (2014) found that the government-initiated (and donor-backed) this implementation of active learning in Indonesia lacked efficacy because it did not take into account the educational beliefs of those who were tasked with implementing the policy.

Similarly, the top-down suite of reforms that the Thai government initiated in 2008 were only moderately successful because the government failed to obtain buy-in from educators (Hallinger & Lee, 2011). Essentially, the government's approach of a 'supreme law strategy' for the reform achieved only limited success because policymakers had not attempted to make it 'matter' to those involved with implementation. Likewise, Kenya's free primary education policy might have been more successful if the voices of teachers had been heard during the policymaking process, from agenda setting to planning and evaluation (Abuya et al., 2015). More specifically, the mechanisms through which the goals of the reform were transmitted to teachers were of critical importance to the manner in which teachers received the policy. In this case, the lack of a clear message regarding why teachers were expected to implement the policy interfered with their acceptance of it (Abuya et al., 2015). The authors also found that training to adjust to larger class sizes that accompanied free primary education led to poorer educational quality overall, which ultimately reduced the impact of the reform. In all of these instances, policymakers failed to take into account the voices, beliefs, and experiences of the educators who would implement the reform and may have made it more successful.

A related, common refrain throughout the literature is that top-down reforms generally have very limited training or professional development associated with them. The changes that reforms engender are often profound, which creates a critical, but neglected, need for professional development to support implementation. The language and complexity of the policy often present a challenge at the local level for educators who struggle to understand what they are expected to put into practice (Schweisfurth, 2011). In their study of Samoa's implementation of inclusive education reforms in 2006, McDonald and Tufue-Dolgoy (2013) found that most teachers seemed to be unaware of basic principles associated with inclusive education. Teachers' varying understandings about what inclusive education involves led to differing teaching and learning practices for students with special needs. In Cambodia, Song (2015) found that teachers who are tasked with implementing child-centered pedagogy had only a superficial understanding of the principles of child-centered pedagogy.

In another case, during the various phases of the active learning reform in Indonesia, the educational system did not have sufficient capacity to undertake the reform and to train teachers in this new method, which differs greatly from existing modes of learning in Indonesia (Heyward, 2014). Whereas classrooms had historically been teacher centered, teachers were now expected to reorganize their classroom environments to promote active learning. Further, Philip Hallinger and Moosung Lee (2011) suggest that Thailand's 2008 neoliberal suite of educational reforms have not become deeply ingrained within the educational system because policymakers underestimated the level of skill needed to implement the reforms. These examples highlight the need for adequate training and development for those tasked with implementing reforms.

Differing from the typical top-down approach, Qatar's 'Education for a New Era', which created national standards alongside a decentralized educational system, provided teachers with an opportunity to develop curriculum at the local level. Even though teachers had the opportunity to be involved in developing the curriculum, they were expected to align it with national standards that they were not involved in creating. Teachers were not adequately prepared to undertake the task because professional development was lacking for teachers to obtain the skills for developing the curriculum (Nassar et al., 2014). As a result, teachers developed content that reflected the prior educational system, which was based on subject matter teaching, and did not align the content with the national standards, leading to students' poor results on national standardized tests. Likewise, in Hong Kong, the NSS reform was not effective because it was a top-down approach that did not take into account that the educators charged with policy implementation were not experienced in the new curriculum and in implementing a new change. Teachers were focused on the specialist subject matter knowledge that was central to the former British secondary system in which they had been trained and were not prepared to switch to teaching transferable skills, as required in the new NSS curriculum (Sung, 2011).

Botswana's 1994 reform, which aimed to develop workers for the post-Fordist economy, failed, to a large extent, because teachers did not receive sufficient professional development to support switching from didactic to learner-centered methods, as required by the policy (Tabulawa, 2009). In addition, teachers were not sufficiently prepared to be able to reconcile the inherent tension involved in the expectation to use learner-centered teaching methods while, at the same time, teaching with a highly prescriptive central curriculum. Regarding the child-centered curriculum reform in Cambodia, Song (2015) found that the reform enjoyed limited success because teacher training was superficial and did not reach all implementers. In Kenya, training to adjust to larger class sizes that accompanied free primary education was not sufficient for teachers to be able to adjust to teaching large numbers of students in one class (Abuya et al., 2015). In these cases, policymakers failed to recognize the importance of adequately training teachers and ensuring that conditions in the schooling environment would support implementing a new curriculum, especially when it goes against the principles of other areas of the educational system.

Street-level bureaucrats play a significant role in the success of educational reforms, as I discussed in Chap. 5. Even under ideal circumstances, in which reforms have been adequately planned out with sufficient involvement from and training for implementers, no educational reform is 'teacher proof' (Schweisfurth, 2011). Resistance is also common. For example, the top-down approach of the NSS curriculum in Hong Kong, in which the government neglected warning signs from both donors and local constituents, led to concerns regarding its resonance in Hong Kong on the part of many of the educators who were tasked with implementing the reform (Chow, 2014). After it was implemented, the policy was resisted by street-level bureaucrats and was only superficially put into practice. Similarly, Dyer's (1999) classic study of 'Operation Blackboard' in India, designed to increase the number of school rooms and teachers, indicates that the status quo is entrenched when street-level bureaucrats implementing the reform do not feel as if the policy truly involves them.

Local Adaptations of Global Reforms

The globalized educational environment has produced reforms that are borrowed or lent across multiple countries, resulting in a certain level of policy convergence or similarities in the ways in which education is structured and delivered across the world. The schooling and higher education trends enumerated in Chap. 4 and the research on neoliberal influences in educational reforms discussed earlier in this chapter provide evidence of a move toward the economization model of schooling and a competitive higher education landscape. Despite these trends, a fifth pattern is evident in the literature: Global reforms are adapted and (re)interpreted at the local level through the process that David Phillips and Kimberly Ochs (2003) call indigenization.

As previously noted, even the global reforms that are imposed on countries are adapted into the local context, at the very least through the actions of the street-level bureaucrats who implement them. For example, during the colonial period in India, British colonial powers pressed a number of reforms into Indian education. More specifically, the formal Western system of schooling was imposed to meet the perceived intellectual deficits of the Indian population (Allender, 2009). Even during colonial rule, however, the Western model was adapted to the local context. For instance, during the village education experimentation phase from 1849 to 1854, the British colonial government developed village schools modeled after Western schools, with instruction in local languages. This adaptation led to hybrid indigenous schools in which literacy and numeracy were taught alongside indigenous agricultural practices (Allender, 2009).

Numerous instances of vernacular globalization, in which dominant educational trends are reshaped in local environments, are apparent in the literature. A significant number of peer-reviewed articles and several edited volumes (see, e.g., Steiner-Khamsi, 2004; Steiner-Khamsi & Waldow, 2012; Verger, Novelli, & Altinyelken, 2012) highlight this interplay of the global and local in educational reform. Through studying market-oriented reforms in Taiwan and Hong Kong, Law (2004) concludes that the local context remains a key factor in the success of reform and that global imperatives are tempered by local needs. In Taiwan and Hong Kong, local desires for democratization were a key focus alongside market objectives. Law suggests that global imperatives are always constrained by local players and conditions and that 'economic globalization does not necessarily trivialize democracy, minimize the role of state, or lead to the domination of international over national or other local languages' (p. 517). The local power sharing process allows an opportunity for local players to express creativity and exercise their rights (Law, 2004).

In the case of *Enseñá por Argentina*, Friedrich (2014) discusses how the 'global push for redefining teaching and teacher education encounters local characteristics and histories, thus producing something different' (p. 296). *Enseñá por Argentina* uses the five-week training model common for Teach for All, in which teachers enter classrooms without credentials and with limited training. In Argentina, however, where a stereotype about uncaring and uncommitted unionized teachers is prominent, training for *Enseñá por Argentina* focuses on teachers' learning to be 'transformational' leaders who are present at school each day and are responsible for their students' learning. Training also focuses on the 'mission' to which teachers in this highly Catholic country are called (Friedrich, 2014).

In the Indian context, Antoni Verger and Sanne VanderKaaij (2012) study the development of public–private partnerships (PPPs), a common global reform espoused by key players from the aid and development regime, namely the WB, UNESCO, and the Asian Development Bank. The development community in India had been discussing PPPs for a number of years, mainly in sectors such as infrastructure and water resources, while the discussion of PPPs related to education was more recent (Verger & VanderKaaij, 2012). The authors show that 'there are some parallels between the global and Indian discussion on PPPs, but the translation of the program into the local reality has been very selective and mediated by existing necessities and political interests' (p. 259). For example, although quality is a key concern related to PPPs, and, thus, governments typically regulate them, India's policy leans toward private provision of education with limited monitoring from the government. In addition, typical PPP features, such as school choice and vouchers, are only nominally present in India. Verger and VanderKaaij conclude that the

Indian government's 'discourse on PPPs is far removed from the way the PPP policy stream is being defined globally' (p. 261).

Yet another example of local adaptation of global reforms is South Africa's adoption of OBE, as I discussed in Chap. 6. Carol Anne Spreen (2004) demonstrates how the political environment and resistance to OBE and its vocational emphasis led to the adoption of a hybrid version of OBE that reflected both global trends and local realities. Similarly, CCTs represent a global reform that was adopted into various local contexts in different ways, based on local needs and the existing structure of education. For example, as noted in Chap. 6, in contrast to Latin American iterations of CCTs, NYC Opportunity's version involved using distinctively market-oriented language, such as 'customer service' and 'incentive' (Morais de Sá e Silva, 2012).

Often, as part of the process of indigenization, local governments, policymakers, and street-level bureaucrats resist global reforms. Even though they may comply with or conform to normative trends, local constituents are often involved in reinterpreting the reforms. For this reason, Saravanan Gopinathan (2001) argues that governments maintain relative autonomy, even in a globalized world. Gopinathan posits that, although Singapore has regularly been involved in policy borrowing, the country has intentionally sought to retain its sovereignty and national character, suggesting that 'national politics heavily determine the content of local policies' (p. 33). Even when Singapore adopted a set of reforms that aligned with a market orientation and prepared students for the post-Fordist economy, the government resisted adjusting other elements of its national system. For example, it elected not to follow some of the 'best practice' models that were common at the time, such as comprehensive schooling, which was designed to streamline secondary schooling and make educational opportunity more equal among diverse populations. The government also adopted a modified decentralized system in which a large degree of central control was retained.

In another case, David Johnson (2006) studied the educational change and policy borrowing and lending trajectories of Madagascar, Mauritius, Reunion, and South Africa, and found that these countries resisted imposed global education policies, especially when they were newly independent. Importantly, Johnson found that Global South countries with stronger economies were less vulnerable to imposed reforms and conditions of aid, as was the case with South Africa. This research raises the issue of the importance of the relative geopolitical power of the countries involved in borrowing and lending.

Educational Reform Lessons

Research on educational reforms that take place in various countries around the globe complements the policy borrowing and lending scholarship, providing an understanding of how and why policies are created and put into effect. Several reform lessons may be gleaned from these sets of literature. First, although it seems counterintuitive, many of the reforms that are adopted and put into place around the world are not designed to serve the purpose for which they were intended. Some policies are essentially destined to fail from the start because they are undertaken for symbolic reasons, such as political expediency, and governments have no intention of seeing them through to fruition. All too frequently, education becomes a pawn in a political game. When reforms are instituted as a 'quick fix' solution for political reasons (e.g., an upcoming election), they may interrupt the current educational system for a period of time before the next reform comes along, often with lasting negative consequences.

Educational Reform Lessons

1. Educational reforms often are not designed for the purpose for which they were intended and therefore are destined for failure.
2. Contextual factors play a key role in the development and (successful) implementation of policies.
3. Street-level bureaucrats who will be tasked with implementing policies should be central throughout the policymaking and policy implementation processes through employing a backward mapping approach.
4. Significant attention should be paid to the policy implementation process, as it involves significant time and energy, and is not easily controlled due to the discretion of street-level bureaucrats who implement policies.

Second, even when policies are sought for genuine purposes to address real needs, there are a number of overarching planning issues that may come into play due to contextual factors. For example, if a pre-packaged solution is adopted wholesale, it is not likely to address the educational problems it is meant to alleviate in the receiving country. Further, the infrastructure of the borrowing educational system is a vital component in the effectiveness of the reform for the purposes intended. A major design flaw in much of the educational reform planning is that the receiving system does not have adequate resources to implement the reform. In addition, if a mismatch between the cultural contexts of the educational systems of the two countries exists—for example, when a teacher-centered approach is in place and a new reform requires using learner-centered methodologies—an educational policy is not likely to be implemented. For these and other reasons, educational reforms should be planned with the local context and local constituencies in mind.

Third, street-level bureaucrats should be involved with all stages of policymaking, from agenda setting to policy formation to implementation. They are crucial to successfully implementing policy and are one of the key groups that will be most directly affected by the changes that educational reforms engender. Educators are also close to the ground in terms of understanding the needs and concerns of other affected groups, such as students and parents. Policymakers should be working with educators to ensure that their voices are heard during the agenda-setting and policy-formation process, which would help to support the reform by enabling the buy-in that is crucial for street-level bureaucrats' motivation to implement the reforms. An approach to reform that involves backward mapping (Elmore, 1979–1980), rather than a purely top-down approach, would ultimately prove more effective, even if undertaken only in part because street-level bureaucrats would have greater ownership over the reforms, which would then more closely reflect what 'matters' to them.

Finally, the implementation stage of policymaking clearly warrants greater attention. Implementation cannot be undertaken without careful planning. As Hallinger and Lee (2011) note, change is a developmental process, not an event. A reform does not simply take place; rather, it unfolds over time and takes commitment. Given that change takes time and involves the will to institute reforms, the environment should be prepared to receive the reform in advance. Structural resources and educator training and professional development are key components of readying the environment and people involved to undertake the reform. Greater attention must be paid to advance planning, both for adopting and implementing the reform. If these areas continue to be ignored, policies will continue to be ineffective and fail to serve the purposes for which they are intended.

Conclusion

Planning and implementing educational reforms is a multifaceted endeavor, which is made even more complex when reforms are borrowed and lent across borders. The research on educational reforms reflects five key patterns in educational policy borrowing and lending, which connect to the scholarship on these processes more generally. Taken together, the research on educational reforms and the policy-borrowing literature demonstrate a number of educational reform lessons. Most reforms fail because they are typically not developed with effective planning and foresight. Some reforms are destined to fail from the start because they are symbolic in nature, while others, though material, are unsuccessful because they take into account neither the context nor the importance of those who will be responsible for implementing them. For these reasons, policymakers should take greater care with planning reforms to suit the intended context as well as to ensure that there are adequate resources (human and material) available to implement the reform. Implementation is a key area where more attention must be paid, both to the processes and to the implementers.

CHAPTER 8

Assessing the Impact of Globalization on Education and Educational Policy Reform

Globalization remains a contested concept that both scholars and the public are continually in the process of contemplating. Although the history of globalization is still being debated, as is the meaning of the term itself, what is clear is that globalization's processes are complex. Globalization is a multidimensional process that involves economic, political, cultural, social, technological, and ecological domains. Scholars have developed a number of different ways to understand and view globalization, generally emphasizing one central dimension over the others. In addition, multiple perspectives exist regarding the impact of globalization, particularly in the increasingly interconnected world during the contemporary period of globalization after World War II (WWII). In the realm of education, globalization's impact has been profound, especially due to the dominance of neoliberal globalization, the influence of global governance institutions, and the use of 'best practices' lending.

In this final chapter, I briefly synthesize the themes covered throughout the book and then reflect on two of the book's central emphases: (a) globalization's impact on education and educational reform and (b) alternatives to globalization from above. Through this discussion, I highlight the importance for educators and those from affiliated professions around the world to have an understanding of globalization and its impact upon multiple sectors of society, most specifically education and educational reform.

© The Editor(s) (if applicable) and The Author(s) 2016

L.M. Portnoi, *Policy Borrowing and Reform in Education*,
DOI 10.1057/978-1-137-53024-0_8

Synthesis of Themes

The discussions that I have presented in the chapters in this book cover a wide range of topics related to globalization and its impact on the world, including the realm of education. Five major themes cut across these topics and are evident in multiple ways throughout the chapters. One of the most salient recurring themes is the ascendancy of the dominant form of globalization that exists today: neoliberal globalization. Neoliberal globalization coincides with Manfred Steger's (2013) 'market globalism', which he highlights as the dominant ideology of globalization central in our contemporary world that is infused with neoliberal economic tenets. Central to this perspective is the inevitability of (neoliberal) globalization, also known as the TINA (there is no alternative) mindset. From this perspective, globalization is typically viewed as a benign, inevitable, and irreversible force that is not controlled by anyone or any entity.

The reach of neoliberal globalization has been wide, and it has significantly altered our environment into one that centers around and further engenders competition. The focus of this competition is economic in nature, and other aspects of society, including education, have increasingly become intertwined with national (and global) economic interests. As noted in Chap. 7, neoliberal educational reforms have spread throughout countries in both the Global North and the Global South. Given that neoliberal principles have prevailed in the periods of the Washington and Post-Washington Consensus, the role of the aid and development regime has been prominent in spreading the belief that countries' citizens' attainment of education is synonymous with economic progress and development.

A second prominent theme, which resonates with many of the topics that I present in this book, is the interplay between the global and the local in the era of contemporary globalization. Clearly, globalization, broadly conceived, has engendered many significant changes within the world in which we live. Even though we may not acknowledge it on a daily basis, we are operating within an environment that is no longer circumscribed by national borders. In other words, the contemporary environment has become deterritorialized. National economies are closely interconnected, and technological advances have made it possible to communicate with people across the globe in real time. Accordingly, the citizens of most countries increasingly exhibit a global imaginary, or awareness of the ways in which the world around them is interconnected (Steger, 2013). Despite these interconnections, however, global developments and trends are not monolithic and are frequently interrupted and reinterpreted in local contexts, where local actors remain integral. The centrality of local actors is particularly salient for nation-states. Although their role is changing with contemporary globalization because they are closely connected to other countries around the world in various multifaceted ways, nation-states maintain their sovereignty over their national domains. In fact, the role of nation-states may be even more profound as they interpret and reshape global trends into local environments.

This relationship between the global and the local is connected to the third and fourth themes: the tension between coercion and agency and the relative geopolitical power of the Global North. In today's era of contemporary globalization, governments may feel compelled to respond to normative global trends by complying with or conforming to them, especially given the number of global agreements that are forged on a wide range of topics, including education. In the Global South, compliance is more common, especially due to the influence of global governance institutions and the conditions imposed upon countries that obtain loans. Due to these countries' relatively weak geopolitical positions, which typically stem from the legacy of colonialism and continued neocolonialism, their ability to resist global mandates or trends is often circumscribed. They may, however, exert agency to adapt policies to the local context, especially in the implementation phase.

In contrast, countries from the Global North typically enjoy a relatively strong geopolitical position and may choose whether to conform to these mandates. For example, despite substantial political pressure from other countries in the Global North, the USA chose not to ratify the Kyoto Protocol and the subsequent Doha Amendment, which were binding resolutions aimed at curbing greenhouse gas emissions and limiting the negative impacts of climate change. As noted, however, even countries from the Global North often feel compelled to react to global trends, especially in the competitive environment of neoliberal globalization. For instance, some countries in the Global North may feel obliged to focus on teaching academic subjects (e.g., science, mathematics) that are central to international tests, such as Programme for International Student Assessment (PISA), because they are concerned about reaching a certain stature relative to their peers or maintaining their competitive edge.

A fifth theme appears throughout the latter chapters of this book in particular: Policies are enacted in an increasingly contested political environment in the era of contemporary globalization. Public policies have historically represented the values of the governments that create them; thus, politics have always been part of the policymaking process. Policies are no longer created, however, within a national context—one that is capable of operating independently from the influences of global developments and trends. Policies display governments' interests and motivations, which, with the influence of neoliberal globalization, are increasingly tied to political expediency at the expense of authentic, material reforms that would serve to ameliorate pressing social problems. This growing shift toward reforms, designed, in large part, for political purposes, is central to the competitive neoliberal economic environment. As noted, reforms are regularly created in advance of important events, such as elections or significant anniversaries. These reforms are often symbolic in nature, and governments may have little intention of implementing them as prescribed. In many such cases, reforms from other countries are borrowed as a means for gaining legitimacy regarding policies that governments wish to put into place. These borrowed policies may serve as a cover for specific reforms that governments already sought to enact, especially in the Global North. In the Global South, borrowing 'best practice' policies often serves as a political strategy in which these countries are seen to be aligning with global norms. Whatever their specific motivations, it is clear that governments increasingly enact reforms in a globalized political environment that, in many cases, undermine the impetus for authentic change and the effectiveness of a given reform.

Globalization's Impact on Education and Educational Reform

Given the multiple effects that globalization has had on the world, it is not surprising that education has experienced the impact of changes in the era of contemporary globalization as well. Education, while often organized and administered locally, is no longer an entirely local endeavor. As I discuss in Chap. 4, a number of global trends have an impact on both schooling and higher education, most of which reflect the considerable influence of neoliberal globalization in particular. Schooling has become increasingly decentralized and organized around neoliberal elements, such as accountability and standardized testing. In the realm of higher education, governments increasingly emphasize rankings and internationalization for global competitiveness. In addition, both schooling and higher education reflect a market-oriented approach that aligns with corporatization.

Principles of the 'new public management', in which post-Fordist skills are increasingly valued, are evident throughout all sectors of education. Changes to education, which reflect the 'best practices' espoused by global governance organizations, align with the perceived need to prepare citizens as lifelong learners who will operate within the global knowledge economy and contribute to the overall economic progress of their countries. All of these developments engender an enhanced focus on learning for the instrumental purpose of job preparation, as opposed to learning for the sake of learning.

Although educators who operate with their local contexts often do not fully recognize the origins of the policies that guide their work and the everyday practices they employ, these policies often stem from global sources. Educators may not realize that the foundations of many of the reforms that are undertaken in the education sector are neoliberal in nature and align with the hyperglobalist TINA approach that assumes the inevitability of (neoliberal) globalization. Despite the claims of numerous world culture theorists, many educational reforms are adopted not because evidence has shown them to be the 'best' but, rather, because they stem from normative global trends and global governance institution mandates. In other words, such reforms are often taken for granted as best practices, even though there is no evidence to show that they are effective. These 'global' reforms typically stem from powerful actors, such as Global North countries and global governance organizations, and are, therefore, not questioned. Such imposition, especially on countries in the Global South, could be considered a form of neocolonialism. For these reasons, it is imperative that all types of educators and affiliated professionals from varying country types consider the impact of globalization on education and how some of its negative impacts may be countered or reshaped.

Alternatives to Globalization from Above

The current dominant mode of globalization, neoliberal globalization, has proven to be widespread around the world. The origins of the trend toward neoliberalism as the dominant mode of economic practices lie in the geopolitically powerful Global North. Although this version of globalization from above has become dominant, it is not inevitable or unalterable. Many scholars, activists, and individual citizens have critiqued the negative impacts of neoliberal globalization and have recognized that alternatives exist (i.e., they support alter-globalization). Countering the myth that neoliberal globalization results in greater equality, social justice advocates have pointed to the increasingly marked distinctions between the 'haves' and the 'have-nots' in countries in the Global North and in the Global South and within countries of all types (see, e.g., Firebaugh & Goesling, 2007; Korzeniewicz & Moran, 2007; Stromquist & Monkman, 2014). In many cases, they have also demonstrated that neoliberal globalization can be challenged and reshaped.

Operating from Steger's (2013) 'justice globalism' perspective, these advocates have enacted multiple forms of globalization from below, including formal movements such as the World Social Forum, global protests such as the Battle for Seattle, and multiple individual acts of opposition. Local resistance activities, such as the Chipko movement in India and the Zapatista movement in Mexico, also serve to counter dominant neoliberal trends. These groups and individuals counter neoliberal globalization from above, question its impacts on differing geopolitical areas of the world, and interrogate the role of the aid and development regime in promoting neoliberal reforms. In addition, national governments and other local actors continue to reshape the dominant forms of globalization and global trends that they encounter in their local environments. In this way, vernacular globalization, or globalization from below, takes root.

Resistance and globalization from below have an impact on the educational environment as well. Educators and students, especially those at the higher education level, frequently conduct critical examinations of the reforms that policymakers espouse. Unless governments choose to highlight the ways in which they explicitly borrow policies, however, these critical examinations are often undertaken with an emphasis on the national context. These efforts could have an even greater impact in the future if a significant number of educators and those from associated disciplines were to recognize the myriad ways in which globalization, specifically neoliberal globalization, has an impact upon their everyday working environments. Educators and other professionals in social domains who possess a deep understanding of globalization might question the origin and values represented in seemingly national, or local, educational policies. They might begin to recognize that powerful actors on the global stage have, to a large extent, decided what should matter in education. The normative 'best practice' reforms that governance and global governance institutions from the Global North diffuse through policy lending should be thought of as one way to organize and practice education, not as an absolute. With a growing awareness of the origins of reforms, educators and others concerned with education might recognize the possibility that multiple forms of schooling, such as progressive, student-centered models that focus on social justice, could also exist. They might also imagine a world in which global university rankings would focus on measures related to social justice, not competitive metrics related to academic prowess that stems from, and further fuels, competition.

Conclusion

Globalization has been taking place for many centuries, and the intense interconnectedness of the era of contemporary globalization is not likely to subside. Clearly, globalization has multiple impacts on our everyday lives, including our professional environments. At the same time, the current mode of globalization is not a 'given', and its impacts are not uniform throughout the world. Greater awareness of globalization's impact is therefore crucially important for all types of educators and for those from associated disciplines. Globally aware educators and other professionals from affiliated domains have the opportunity to contribute to forging alternatives to the negative impacts associated with today's dominant form of globalization. Neoliberal globalization has had a strong impact, though alter-globalization can, and should, be an equally strong force for change.

Glossary of Key Terms

Aid and Development Regime The aid and development regime emerged during the reconstruction period that followed World War II (WWII). After two decades of war, former colonial powers sought to ameliorate the effects of colonialism and improve the circumstances in the Global South. The core of the aid and development regime is global governance institutions, such as intergovernmental organizations, international monetary organizations, bilateral organizations, and regional organizations (see Chap. 2). The aid and development regime operates from the perspective of a modern lens that assumes that there is a continuum of development and an ultimate form of progress (that of the Global North) that countries in the Global South should emulate.

Alter-Globalization In contrast to the anti-globalization approach that would reject globalization altogether, those who operate from an alter-globalization perspective would acknowledge the impacts of globalization and suggest that the current dominance of neoliberal globalization is not inevitable. Instead, they would suggest that alternative forms of globalization are possible, including those that are socially just.

Backward-Mapping Approach A backward-mapping, or bottom-up, approach is a dispersed strategy for policy implementation that highlights collaboration between those who create policies and those who implement them (Elmore, 1979–1980). This approach takes into account the multiple influences on policy implementation that policy-

© The Editor(s) (if applicable) and The Author(s) 2016

L.M. Portnoi, *Policy Borrowing and Reform in Education*,
DOI 10.1057/978-1-137-53024-0

makers cannot anticipate. It involves a system of reciprocity in which a certain level of discretion is delegated to lower levels of workers and can be understood as a shared approach to policymaking and policy implementation.

Contemporary Globalization Although many different conceptualizations of the history of globalization exist, most commentators would agree that interconnections between countries around that world have intensified since WWII, in a period that I call 'contemporary globalization'.

Convergence Convergence, also known as isomorphism, is a condition in which the cultures and practices of the world are thought to be becoming increasingly similar around the globe. World culture theorists, who espouse the convergence hypothesis, suggest that educational institutions are a central venue for dispersing global culture. These scholars typically assert that convergence occurs without agents' dictating it, similar to the notion of the invisible hand of the market. World culture theorists suggest that the 'best' ideas and models naturally rise to the top and spread as 'best practices'.

Critical Theory Critical Theory (capitalized) refers to a theoretical paradigm that stems from a group of theorists, including Theodor Adorno, Max Horkheimer, Herbert Marcuse, and Max Weil, who formed the Frankfurt School in 1922 at the University of Frankfurt in Germany. The main thrust of the Frankfurt School theorists' work was to criticize capitalism and its discontents. This group is often considered to be neo-Marxist because, while they drew on Marxism, they added elements in addition to economics, such as Freudian psychology. As a broader range of theories, critical theory (not capitalized) refers to a conglomeration of theories, some of which have modern tendencies (neo-Marxist), while others have postmodern tendencies (post-Marxist). In the realm of critical theory are critical pedagogy, critical feminism, poststructuralism, and numerous other critical orientations.

Deterritorialization Deterritorialization implies that many activities (social, political, economic) occur without the constraints of geographical locations. This condition is thought to be part of globalization and involves the forces of technology to transform our social, political, and economic spheres.

Fordism and Post-Fordism Fordism is characterized by mass consumption and the creation of a consumer culture, which historians generally consider to have developed between the 1940s and the 1970s in highly industrialized countries. During the Fordist period, widespread economic growth and material advancement occurred, along with the emergence of an assembly-line mentality, a fragmented division of labor, and standardized outputs. Since the 1970s, highly industrialized countries have moved into a post-Fordist environment, characterized by an increasingly diverse workforce, greater use of technology, specialization of employment and products based on consumer tastes, decentralization of production, increased diversification in business models, and streamlined management. In post-Fordism, the economy is global, rather than national.

Forward-Mapping Approach The forward-mapping, or top-down, approach is most commonly used with educational and other types of reforms. It stems from a technical-rational perspective that assumes that the hierarchy and authority of the organization will allow expected outcomes to emerge during policy implementation (Elmore, 1979–1980). However, policymakers' expectations typically do not match the complexities of the policy implementation process, leading to the limited success of top-down reforms.

Global Imaginary Due to the increased interconnections that exist within many spheres of society today, many of the world's citizens are developing a global imaginary. This global imaginary, a term coined by Manfred Steger (2013), is a growing awareness of living within a globalized world.

Global North Countries in the Global North (also called 'developed' or 'Western') include wealthy industrialized nation-states, such as those in North America and Europe, plus Japan, Australia, and New Zealand. Critical scholars prefer to use the terms Global North and Global South (see below) to differentiate between the two main types of countries that exist today because this wording breaks from the notions that there is a linear path to development and that one type of country is superior to the other.

Global South Countries in the Global South (also called 'developing') include economically poor countries in Africa, Latin and Central America, and South and Southeast Asia, most of which were former colonies. These countries are generally less industrialized than their counterparts in the Global North and have lower standards of living and per capita income. Using the term Global South represents an acknowledgment of the origins of these circumstances in colonialism and neocolonialism.

Hegemony Hegemony is a set of beliefs and assumptions that assert dominance in a social system without using any real force. Hegemony refers to the form of dominance that the ruling class or group asserts over its subordinate classes. In the international realm, this dominant group is often considered to be Global North/'developed' countries, while the subordinate group is considered to be Global South/'developing' countries. Hegemony legitimates and retains the position of the dominant class or group through the use of ideology.

Ideology An ideology is a set of cultural beliefs, values, and attitudes that underlie and, to some degree, justify and legitimate the status quo or movements to change it. From a Marxist perspective, the dominant ideology represents upper-class views and beliefs and reflects an interest in preserving the privilege of the wealthy. Neo- and post-Marxists, however, would consider issues of race, language, gender, and class as part of ideology.

ICT Revolution The Information and Communications Technology (ICT) Revolution involves significant changes in such key areas as computing, data processing, and telecommunications. The ICT Revolution, characterized by the immediacy of information and contact with others, has led to dramatic changes in the ways in which business and our everyday lives are conducted.

Modernism Modernism has been the dominant theoretical paradigm throughout most of the history of Western thought since the medieval Period through to the 1970s and early 1980s, when postmodernism rose as a new, competing paradigm. Modernism is a particular way of viewing the possibilities and direction of human life. It is rooted in Enlightenment thinking and focuses on rational thought and objective versions of reality. Modernism also assumes that there are stages of progress and that humans (or nation-states) will gain increased freedom as they move through the stages.

Neocolonialism Neocolonialism, also known as neoimperialism, refers to the pressures that dominant nation-states place on newly independent countries from the Global South, which mimic the power they had during the colonial era. With neocolonialism, individual national governments and the 'core' (Global North) countries have reasserted their dominance over 'periphery' (Global South) countries through less direct means, such as controlling their economies through the negative effects of globalization and through the influence of global governance organizations and transnational corporations based in core countries.

In many cases, countries from the Global South have no choice but to accept assistance from their former colonizers; this assistance serves to keep newly independent countries dependent on the former colonial powers.

Neoliberalism Neoliberalism is a conservative economic ideology that supports deregulation, privatization, and the shift away from government involvement in domestic economies. Neoliberalism favors free-market mechanisms, fewer restrictions on business operations, minimal taxation, and property rights. In the free-market economy, neoliberalism assumes that the unrestricted flow of capital will produce the greatest social, political, and economic good. The trend toward neoliberalism began in the Cold War period, becoming prominent in the 1970s and reaching its height in the era of US president Ronald Reagan and British prime minister Margaret Thatcher in the 1980s. The ideology is 'neo'liberal because it harkens back to the days of classical liberal economic theory (e.g., Adam Smith's writings) when the free-market capitalist system took shape.

Normative Normative points of view are based on the underlying assumption that there are standards and norms to which all people (or countries) can and should subscribe. A normative approach typically involves taken-for-granted practices and policies that are accepted as standard based on the influence of the dominant ideology of a given time. In the case of educational reform, normative models are manifested in the 'best practice' reforms that global governance organizations diffuse around the world, even though these practices are typically not evidence-based or suited for the context into which they are borrowed.

Policy Borrowing and Lending Policy borrowing implies that countries explicitly seek to appropriate a policy and tailor it to the local context, whereas policy lending connotes that governments or global governance organizations provide policies to a receiving country, either with or without consent.

Postmodernism Postmodernism is a movement that arose in the 1970s and early 1980s as a response to modernism. Postmodernism is intentionally difficult to describe, as it has no set rules or standard assumptions. In general, postmodernists reject the modernist view that reality is objective and can be measured rationally. They also reject the premise that humans go through stages of progress and encourage alternative views of reality and emphasize voices that stem from marginalized perspectives.

Public Policy Public policies, or reforms, are in the domain of national governments and are designed to alleviate identified social problems. They may be in the form of texts (e.g., laws, regulations) as well as the concrete actions that result from policies and their effects on society. Policies represent governments' values, as they demonstrate the measures that governments deem important to undertake for the betterment of society; in contrast, policy silence on a particular issue indicates that the government does not place value on it.

Street-Level Bureaucrats Street-level bureaucrats are front-line public service workers, such as teachers, policy officers, and social workers. They operate in a context of multiple pressures and cannot fully comply with policymakers' expectations for implementing policies due to limited resources (e.g., time, money, information). To cope with these competing demands, street-level bureaucrats exercise their discretion to comply while also maintaining their professional autonomy (Lipsky, 2010).

Structural Adjustment Programs (SAPs) Global governance organizations, such as the International Monetary Fund and the World Bank, instituted SAPs during the development period of the Washington Consensus (see below). SAPs embrace the free-market model of neoliberalism and call for fiscal discipline, cutting of public spending, tax reform, financial liberalization (market reform), competitive exchange rates, trade liberalization, procurement of foreign direct investment, privatization of state services, deregulation of the economy, and protection of property rights. Global South countries are given loans on the contingency that they follow the tenets of structural adjustment. Although supposedly intended to bring Global South countries out of debt, SAPs, in most cases, have resulted in increased debt and dependency.

There Is No Alternative (TINA) The TINA approach, which is closely tied to neoliberalism, was popularized by British prime minister Margaret Thatcher in the 1980s. The TINA view is synonymous with the notion of the inevitability of globalization. Its proponents suggest that the changes that are occurring in the worldwide economic, social, political, and cultural orders are irreversible and may not be challenged or reshaped.

Vernacular Globalization Vernacular globalization, or globalization from below, suggests that, despite the influence of global forces, trends and developments are always occurring within local contexts that have particular histories and cultures (Appadurai, 1996). Vernacular globalization allows for the possibility that local agents, such as governments, organizations, communities, or individuals, mediate global trends.

Washington Consensus and Post-Washington Consensus The term 'Washington Consensus' began to be used in the late 1970s to refer to the dominant global policies that were emerging from global governance institutions, primarily via Washington. The hallmark of the Washington Consensus was the focus on neoliberalism and the implementation of SAPs (see above) in countries in the Global South. Although the World Bank and the International Monetary Fund were the initial architects of the Washington Consensus and SAPs, this approach became central to the aid and development regime as a whole for many years. Most SAPs failed, however, and led to worsened conditions in the Global South countries in which they were enacted. In the 1990s, the aid and development regime moved toward a focus on poverty alleviation in the Post-Washington Consensus (PWC) era that continues today. The PWC broadens the aid and development regime's emphasis beyond economic development, although providers of loans continue to impose neoliberal reforms as conditional requirements to obtain funding.

References

Abdenur, A. (2009). The strategic triad: Form and content in Brazil's triangular cooperation practices. In L. Chisholm & G. Steiner-Khamsi (Eds.), *South–South cooperation in education and development* (pp. 157–170). New York: Teachers College Press.

Abuya, B. A., Admassu, K., Ngware, M., Onsomu, E. O., & Oketch, M. (2015). Free primary education and implementation in Kenya. *SAGE Open, 5*(1). doi:10.1177/2158244015571488.

Aksit, N. (2007). Educational reform in Turkey. *International Journal of Educational Development, 27*, 129–137.

Allais, S. M. (2003). The National Qualifications Framework in South Africa: A democratic project trapped in a neo-liberal paradigm? *Journal of Education and Work, 16*(3), 305–323.

Allender, T. (2009). Learning abroad: The colonial educational experiment in India, 1813–1919. *Paedagogica Historica, 45*(6), 727–741.

Altbach, P. G., & Knight, J. (2007). The internationalization of higher education: Motivations and realities. *Journal of Studies in International Education, 11*(3–4), 290–305.

Altbach, P. G., Reisberg, L., & Rumbley, L. E. (2009). *Trends in global higher education: Tracking an academic revolution.* Paris, France: United Nations Educational, Scientific and Cultural Organization.

Anderson-Levitt, K. (2003). A world culture of schooling? In K. Anderson-Levitt (Ed.), *Local meanings, global schooling: Anthropology and world culture theory* (pp. 1–25). New York: Palgrave Macmillan.

Andreotti, V. (2006). The contributions of postcolonial theory to development education. In *Development Education Association Thinkpieces.* Retrieved from

© The Editor(s) (if applicable) and The Author(s) 2016

L.M. Portnoi, *Policy Borrowing and Reform in Education*,
DOI 10.1057/978-1-137-53024-0

http://dspace.africaportal.org/jspui/bitstream/123456789/25307/1/The%20contributions%20of%20postcolonial%20theory%20to%20development%20education%20(2007).pdf?1

Appadurai, A. (1996). *Modernity at large: Cultural dimensions of globalization.* Minneapolis, MN: University of Minnesota Press.

Arnove, R. F. (1980). Comparative education and world-systems analysis. *Comparative Education Review, 24*(1), 48–62.

Arnove, R. F. (2015). Globalisation and public education policies in Latin America. In J. Zajda (Ed.), *Second international handbook on globalisation, education and policy research* (pp. 93–104). Dordrecht, Netherlands: Springer.

Arnove, R., Franz, S., & Torres, C. A. (2013). Education in Latin America: From dependency and neoliberalism to alternative paths to development. In R. Arnove, C. A. Torres, & S. Franz (Eds.), *Comparative education: The dialectic of the global and the local* (4th ed., pp. 315–339). Boston, MA: Rowman and Littlefield.

Arnove, R. F., Stromquist, N. P., Fox, C., Levin, H. M., Masemann, V. L., & Epstein, E. H. (2006). Commentary on Carnoy. *Comparative Education Review, 50*(4), 571–580.

Astiz, M. F., Wiseman, A. W., & Baker, D. P. (2002). Slouching toward decentralization: Consequences of globalization for curricular control in national education systems. *Comparative Education Review, 46*(1), 66–88.

Auld, E., & Morris, P. (2014). Comparative education the 'new paradigm' and policy borrowing: Constructing knowledge for educational reform. *Comparative Education, 50*(2), 129–155.

Babb, S. (2010). The social consequences of structural adjustment: Recent evidence and current debates. In G. Ritzer & Z. Atalay (Eds.), *Readings in globalization: Key concepts and major debates* (pp. 127–237). Malden, MA: Wiley-Blackwell.

Bagley, S. S., & Portnoi, L. M. (2012). Expanding the notion of world-class universities. *CIES Perspectives, 159*, 1–2.

Bagley, S. S., & Portnoi, L. M. (2014). Setting the stage: Global competition in higher education. In L. M. Portnoi & S. S. Bagley (Eds.), *Critical perspectives on global competition in higher education* (pp. 1–11). [*New directions for higher education.*] San Francisco, CA: Jossey-Bass.

Bagley, S. S., & Portnoi, L. M. (2016). Examining the discourse on global competition: Vernacular approaches within higher education policy documents. In J. Zajda & V. D. Rust (Eds.), *Globalisation and higher education reforms.* Dordrecht, Netherlands: Springer.

Bajaj, M. (2014). The productive plasticity of rights: Globalization, education, and human rights. In N. P. Stromquist & K. Monkman (Eds.), *Globalization and education: Integration and contestation across cultures* (2nd ed., pp. 55–69). Lanham, MA: Rowman & Littlefield.

Baker, D. (2014). *The schooled society: The educational transformation of global culture*. Stanford, CA: Stanford University Press.

Baker, D., & LeTendre, G. (2005). *National differences, global similarities: World culture and the future of schooling*. Palo Alto, CA: Stanford University Press.

Ball, S. J. (1994). *Education reform: A critical and poststructuralist approach*. Buckingham, UK: Open University Press.

Ball, S. J. (1998). Big policies/small world: An introduction to international perspectives in education policy. *Comparative Education, 34*(2), 110–130.

Ball, S. J. (2006). *Education policy and social class: The selected works of Stephen J. Ball*. London, UK: Routledge.

Ball, S. J. (2012). *Global education Inc. New policy networks and the neo-liberal imaginary*. New York: Routledge.

Ball, S. J., Maguire, M., & Braun, B. (2012). *How schools do policy: Policy enactments in secondary schools*. Abingdon, UK: Routledge.

Barreyro, G. B., Rothen, J. C., & Santana, A. D. C. M. (2014). Policies for evaluation and regulation of higher education in Brazil (1995–2010): Supporting the expansion of private higher education. *Journal for Critical Education Policy Studies (JCEPS), 12*(1), 214–237.

Barthes, R. (1967a). *The death of the author*. New York: Roaring Fork Press.

Barthes, R. (1967b). *Elements of semiology*. New York: Hill and Wang.

Bartlett, L., & Mogusu, E. (2013). Teachers' understandings and implementation of learner-centered pedagogy. In F. Vavrus & L. Bartlett (Eds.), *Teaching in tension: International pedagogies, national policies, and teachers' practices in Tanzania* (Vol. 1, pp. 61–74). Rotterdam, Netherlands: Sense.

Bates, R., Lewis, S., & Pickard, A. (2011). *Education policy, practice and the professional*. London, UK: Continuum.

Baumgartner, F., & Jones, B. D. (2009). *Agendas and instability in American politics* (2nd ed.). Chicago, IL: University of Chicago Press.

Becker, G. S. (1964). *Human capital: A theoretical and empirical analysis, with special reference to education*. New York: National Bureau of Economic Research.

Béland, D. (2010). Globalization and the resilience of the state power. In G. Ritzer & Z. Atalay (Eds.), *Readings in globalization: Key concepts and major debates* (pp. 175–178). Malden, MA: Wiley-Blackwell.

Bell, D. (1973). *The coming of the post-industrial society: A venture in social forecasting*. London, UK: Heinemann.

Bennell, P. (1998). Rates of return to education in Asia: A review of the evidence. *Education Economics, 6*(2), 107–120.

Berman, P., & McLaughlin, M. W. (1978). *Federal programs supporting change: Vol. 7. Implementing and sustaining innovations*. Santa Monica, CA: RAND.

Bhaba, H. (1994). *The location of cultures*. London, UK: Routledge.

Birkland, T. (2010). *An introduction to the policy process: Theories, concepts, and models of policy making* (3rd ed.). Armonk, NY: M.E. Sharpe.

Boli, J., & Petrova, V. (2007). Globalization today. In G. Ritzer (Ed.), *The Blackwell companion to globalization* (pp. 103–124). Malden, MA: Blackwell.

Boli, J., & Thomas, M. G. (1997). World culture in the world polity: A century of intentional non-governmental organization. *American Sociological Review, 62*(2), 171–190.

Boli, J., Ramirez, F. O., & Meyer, J. W. (1985). Explaining the origins and expansion of mass education. *Comparative Education Review, 29*(2), 145–170.

BRAC. (2015). *BRAC*. http://www.brac.net

Braun, A., Maguire, M., & Ball, S. J. (2010). Policy enactments in the UK secondary school: Examining policy, practice and school positioning. *Journal of Educational Policy, 25*(4), 547–560.

Brodkin, E. Z. (2003). Street-level research: Policy at the front lines. In T. Corbett & M. C. Lennon (Eds.), *Policy into action: Implementation research and welfare reform* (pp. 145–164). Washington, DC: Urban Institute Press.

Brodkin, E. Z. (2011). Putting street-level organizations first: New directions for social policy and management research. *Journal of Public Administration Research and Theory, 21*(2), 1199–1201.

Brodkin, E. Z. (2012). Reflections on street-level bureaucracy: Past, present and future. *Public Administration Review, 72*(6), 940–949.

Brown, P., & Lauder, H. (1997). Education globalization and economic development. In A. H. Halsey, H. Lauder, P. Brown, & A. S. Wells (Eds.), *Education, culture, economy and society* (pp. 72–192). Oxford, NY: New York University Press.

Buenfil, R. D. (2014). Global encounters of the universal and the particular in educational policies in Mexico 1988–2006. In N. P. Stromquist & K. Monkman (Eds.), *Globalization and education: Integration and contestation across cultures* (2nd ed., pp. 217–246). Lanham, MA: Rowman & Littlefield.

Burde, D. (2004). International NGOs and best practices: The art of educational lending. In G. Steiner-Khamsi (Ed.), *The global politics of educational borrowing and lending* (pp. 173–187). New York: Teachers College Press.

Cairney, P. (2011). *Understanding public policy: Theories and issues*. New York: Palgrave Macmillan.

Calderon, A. (2012, September 2). Massification continues to transform higher education. *University World News*. Retrieved from http://www.universityworldnews.com/article.php?story=20120831155341147

Cardoso, F. H. (1972). Dependency and development in Latin America. *New Left Review, 74*, 83–95.

Carnoy, M. (1998). National voucher plans in Chile and Sweden: Did privatization reforms make for better education? *Comparative Education Review, 42*(3), 309–337.

Carnoy, M. (2006). Rethinking the comparative—And the international. *Comparative Education Review, 50*(4), 551–570.

Carnoy, M. (2014). Globalization, educational change, and the national state. In N. P. Stromquist & K. Monkman (Eds.), *Globalization and education: Integration and contestation across cultures* (pp. 21–38). Lanham, MA: Rowman & Littlefield.

Castells, M. (1996). *The information age: Economy, society and culture: Vol. 1. The rise of the network society*. Malden, MA: Blackwell.

Castells, M. (1997). *The information age: Economy, society and culture: Vol. 2. The power of identity*. Malden, MA: Blackwell.

Castells, M. (1998). *The information age: Economy, society and culture: Vol. 3. End of millennium*. Malden, MA: Blackwell.

Chabbott, C. (2009a). BRAC goes global. In L. Chisholm & G. Steiner-Khamsi (Eds.), *South–South cooperation in education and development* (pp. 192–209). New York, NY: Teachers College Press.

Chabbott, C. (2009b). *Constructing education for development: International organizations and education for all*. New York: Routledge.

Chakroun, B. (2010). National qualification frameworks: From policy borrowing to policy learning. *European Journal of Education, 45*(2), 199–216.

Cheng, M.-K. (2007). The postindustrial workplace and challenges to education. In M. M. Suárez-Orozco (Ed.), *Learning in the global era* (pp. 175–191). Berkeley, CA: University of California Press.

Chisholm, L. (2012). Education policy borrowing across African borders: Histories of learner-centered education in Botswana and South Africa. In G. Steiner-Khamsi & F. Waldow (Eds.), *World yearbook of education 2012: Policy borrowing and lending in education* (pp. 206–226). New York: Routledge.

Chisholm, L., & Steiner-Khamsi, G. (Eds.). (2009). *South–South cooperation in education and development*. New York: Teachers College Press.

Chow, A. (2014). Replanting the flower in different soil? A critical analysis of education borrowing in Hong Kong. *International Journal of Education, 6*(2), 114–130.

Chung, J., Atkin, C., & Moore, J. (2012). The rise and fall of the MTL: An example of European policy borrowing. *European Journal of Teacher Education, 35*(3), 259–274.

Clarke, P. (2003). Culture and classroom reform: The case of the district primary education project, India. *Comparative Education, 39*(1), 27–44.

Coatsworth, J. H. (2004). Globalization, growth, and welfare in history. In M. M. Suarez-Orozco & D. B. Qin-Hilliard (Eds.), *Globalization: Culture and education in the new millennium* (pp. 38–55). Berkeley, CA: University of California Press.

Cohen, M. D., March, J. G., & Olsen, J. P. (1972). A garbage can model of organizational choice. *Administrative Science Quarterly, 17*(1), 1–25.

Cowen, T. (2004). *Creative destruction: How globalization is changing the world's cultures*. Princeton, NJ: Princeton University Press.

Crossley, M., & Tikly, L. (2004). Postcolonial perspectives and comparative and international research in education: A critical introduction. *Comparative Education, 40*(2), 147–156.

Cuban, L. (1998). How schools change reform. *Teachers College Record, 99*(3), 453–477.

Cummings, W. (1999). The institutions of education: Compare, compare, compare! *Comparative Education Review, 43*(4), 413–437.

Dale, R. (2000). Globalization and education: Demonstrating a 'common world culture' or locating a 'globally structured educational agenda'? *Educational Theory, 41*(2), 117–149.

Dale, R., & Robertson, S. L. (2007). New arenas of global governance and international organisations: Reflections and directions. In K. Martens, A. Rusconi, & K. Leuze (Eds.), *New arenas of education governance. The impact of international organizations and markets on educational policy making* (pp. 217–228). New York: Palgrave Macmillan.

Dale, R., & Robertson, S. L. (2012). Towards a critical grammar of education policy movements. In G. Steiner-Khamsi & F. Waldow (Eds.), *World yearbook of education 2012: Policy borrowing and lending in education* (pp. 21–40). New York: Routledge.

Datnow, A. (2006). Connections in the policy chain: The 'co-construction' of implementation in comprehensive school reforms. In *New directions in education policy implementation: Confronting complexity* (pp. 105–123). Albany, NY: State University of New York Press.

Dempster, M. A. H., & Wildavsky, A. (1979). On change: Or, there is no magic size for an increment. *Political Studies, 27*, 371–389.

Derrida, J. (1966). Structure, sign, and play in the discourse of the human sciences. In A. Bass (Trans.), *Writing and difference* (pp. 278–294). London, UK: Routledge.

Derrida, J. (1967). *Of grammatology*. Baltimore, MD: Johns Hopkins University Press.

Dewey, J. (1907). *The school and society*. Chicago, IL: University of Chicago Press. (Speeches originally delivered 1899).

Dewey, J. (1916). *Democracy and education: An introduction to the philosophy of education*. New York: Macmillan and Company.

Dobbins, M., & Knill, C. (2009). Higher education policies in Central and Eastern Europe: Convergence toward a common model? *Governance, 22*(3), 397–430.

Doherty, C. (2009). The appeal of the International Baccalaureate in Australia's educational market: A curriculum of choice for mobile futures. *Discourse: Studies in the Cultural Politics of Education, 30*(1), 73–89.

Dolowitz, D., & Marsh, D. (1996). Who learns what from whom? A review of the policy transfer literature. *Political Studies, 44*, 343–357.

Dolowitz, D., & Marsh, D. (1998). Policy transfer: A framework for comparative analysis. In M. Minogue, C. Polidano, & D. Hulme (Eds.), *Beyond the new public management* (pp. 38–58). Cheltenham, UK: Edward Elgar.

Dolowitz, D., & Marsh, D. (2000). Learning from abroad: The role of policy transfer in contemporary policy-making. *Governance, 13*(1), 5–24.

Dos Santos, T. (1970). The structure of dependence. *The American Economic Review, 60*(2), 231–236.

Drucker, P. (1959). *The landmarks of tomorrow*. New York: Harper & Brothers.

Drucker, P. (1969). *The age of discontinuity*. New York: Harper & Row.

Dye, T. (2012). *Understanding public policy* (14th ed.). New York: Pearson.

Dye, T., & Ziegler, H. (2011). *The irony of democracy: An uncommon introduction to American politics*. Independence, KY: Cengage Learning.

Dyer, C. (1999). Researching the implementation of educational policy: A backward mapping approach. *Comparative Education, 35*(1), 45–61.

Easton, D. (1965). *A systems analysis of political life*. New York: Wiley.

Elmore, R. F. (1979–1980). Backward mapping: Implementation research and policy decisions. *Political Science Quarterly, 94*(4), 601–616.

Escobar, A. (2011). *Encountering development: The making and unmaking of the third world* (2nd ed.). Princeton, NJ: Princeton Universities Press.

Evans, L. (2011). The 'shape' of teacher professionalism in England: Professional standards, performance management, professional development and the changes proposed in the 2010 White Paper. *British Educational Research Journal, 37*(5), 851–870.

Falk, R. (1999). *Predatory globalization: A critique*. Cambridge, UK: Polity Press.

Fataar, A. (2006). Policy networks in recalibrated political terrain: The case of school curriculum policy and politics in South Africa. *Journal of Education Policy, 21*(6), 641–659.

Firebaugh, G., & Goesling, B. (2007). Globalization and global inequalities: Recent trends. In G. Ritzer (Ed.), *The Blackwell companion to globalization* (pp. 549–564). Malden, MA: Blackwell.

Fortes, L. (2015). The emergence of bilingual education discourse in Brazil: Bilingualisms, language policies, and globalizing circumstances. *International Journal of Bilingual Education and Bilingualism*. doi:10.1080/13670050.2015.1103207.

Foucault, M. (1975). *Discipline and punish: The birth of the prison*. New York, NY: Vintage Books.

Fowler, F. C. (2009). *Policy studies for educational leaders: An introduction*. Boston, MA: Allyn & Bacon.

Freeman, S. (2014). Germany scraps tuition fees. Should Canada follow? *Huffington Post Canada*. Retrieved from http://www.huffingtonpost.ca/2014/10/01/tuition-fees-germany-canada_n_5915500.html

Freire, P. (1970). *Pedagogy of the oppressed*. New York: Continuum.

Freire, P. (1973). *Education for critical consciousness*. New York: Seabury Press.

Freire, P. (1998). *Pedagogy of freedom: Ethics, democracy and civic courage*. Lanham, MD: Rowman & Littlefield.

Friedman, T. (1999). *The Lexus and the olive tree*. New York: Farrar, Straus and Giroux.

Friedman, T. (2005). *The world is flat: A brief history of the 21st century*. New York: Farrar, Straus and Giroux.

Friedrich, D. (2014). Global micro-lending in education reform: *Enseñá por Argentina* and the neoliberalization of the grass roots. *Comparative Education Review, 58*(2), 296–321.

Furlong, J. (2013). Globalisation, neoliberalism, and the reform of teacher education in England. *The Educational Forum, 77*(1), 28–50.

Giddens, A. (1990). *The consequences of modernity*. Stanford, CA: Stanford University Press.

Giddens, A. (2000). *The third way and its critics*. Cambridge, MA: Blackwell.

Global Partnership for Education (2015). *Developing countries*. Retrieved from http://www.globalpartnership.org/developing-countries

Gofen, A. (2014). Mind the gap: Dimensions and influence of street-level divergence. *Journal of Public Administration Research and Theory, 24*(2), 473–493.

Gopinathan, S. (2001). Globalisation, the state and education policy in Singapore. In M. Bray & W. O. Lee (Eds.), *Education and political transition: Themes and experiences in East Asia* (pp. 21–36). Hong Kong: Comparative Education Research Center, University of Hong Kong.

Gordon, I., Lewis, J., & Young, R. (1977). Perspective on policy analysis. *Public Administration Bulletin, 25*, 26–35.

Goswami, M. (2013). Neo-liberalism and higher education in India. *Journal of Research in Humanities and Social Science, 1*(3), 32–37.

Gramsci, A. (1971). *Selections from the prison notebooks*. New York: International Publishers.

Green, A. G. (1993). Magnet schools, choice and the politics of policy borrowing. *Oxford Studies in Comparative Education, 3*(1), 83–104.

Grek, S. (2009). Governing by numbers: The PISA 'effect' in Europe. *Journal of Education Policy, 24*(1), 23–37.

Greveling, L., Amsing, H. T., & Dekker, J. J. (2014). Crossing borders in educational innovation: Framing foreign examples in discussing comprehensive education in the Netherlands, 1969–1979. *Paedagogica Historica, 50*(1–2), 76–92.

Gürüz, K. (2008). *Higher education and international student mobility in the global knowledge economy*. Albany, NY: State University of New York Press.

Hales, S. (2012). The confluence of global and local currents in Brazil's municipal schooling. In A. P. Ortega & B. Schröttner (Eds.), *Transnational spaces and regional localization: Social networks, border regions and local-global relations* (pp. 205–216). Münster, Germany: Waxmann.

Hallinger, P., & Lee, M. (2011). A decade of education reform in Thailand: Broken promise or impossible dream? *Cambridge Journal of Education, 41*(2), 139–158.

Halpin, D., & Troyna, B. (1995). The politics of education policy borrowing. *Comparative Education, 31*(3), 303–310.

Hardt, M., & Negri, A. (2000). *Empire.* Cambridge, MA: Harvard University Press.

Hardt, M., & Negri, A. (2004). *Multitude: War and democracy in the age of empire.* New York: Penguin Books.

Harvey, D. (1990a). Between space and time: Reflections on the geographical imagination. *Annals of the Association of American Geographers, 80*(3), 418–434.

Harvey, D. (1990b). *The condition of postmodernity: An enquiry into the conditions of cultural change.* Oxford, UK: Blackwell.

Harvey, D. (2003). *The new imperialism.* Oxford, UK: Oxford University Press.

Harvey, D. (2009). *A brief history of neoliberalism.* Oxford, UK: Oxford University Press.

Hazelkorn, E. (2008). Learning to live with league tables and ranking: The experience of institutional leaders. *Higher Education Policy, 21*(2), 193–215.

Hazelkorn, E. (2014). Rankings and the global reputation race. In L. M. Portnoi & S. S. Bagley (Eds.), *Critical perspectives on global competition in higher education* (pp. 12–26). [*New directions for higher education*]. San Francisco, CA: Jossey-Bass.

Held, D. (1995). *Cosmopolitanism: An agenda for a new world order.* Cambridge, UK: Polity Press.

Held, D. (2004). *Global covenant: The social democratic alternative to the Washington consensus.* Cambridge, UK: Polity Press.

Held, D. (2010). *Cosmopolitanism: Ideals and realities.* Cambridge, UK: Polity Press.

Held, D., McGrew, A., Goldblatt, D., & Perraton, J. (1999). *Global transformations: Politics, economics and culture.* Stanford, CA: Stanford University Press.

Heyward, S. (2014). *Reforming teaching practice in Indonesia: A case study of the implementation of active learning in primary schools in North Maluku.* Unpublished doctoral dissertation, University of Tasmania, Tasmania, Australia.

Hickling-Hudson, A. (2004). South–South collaboration: Cuban teachers in Jamaica and Namibia. *Comparative Education, 40*(2), 289–311.

Hickling-Hudson, A., Gonzalez, J. C., & Preston, R. (Eds.). (2012). *The capacity to share: A study of Cuba's international cooperation in educational development.* New York: Palgrave Macmillan.

Hill, M., & Hupe, P. (2014). *Implementing public policy: An introduction to the study of operational governance* (3rd ed.). London, UK: Sage.

Honig, M. I. (2006). Complexity and policy implementation: Challenges and opportunities for the field. In Honig, M. I. (Ed.), *New directions in education policy implementation: Confronting complexity* (pp. 1–23). Albany, NY: State University of New York Press.

Huang, S. (2009). Transnationality. In R. Kitchin & M. Thrift (Eds.), *International encyclopedia of human geography* (pp. 404–409). Amsterdam, Netherlands: Elsevier.

Hugonnier, B. (2007). Globalization and education: Can the world meet the challenge? In M. M. Suárez-Orozco (Ed.), *Learning in the global era* (pp. 137–157). Berkeley, CA: University of California Press.

Huntington, S. (1996). *The clash of civilizations and the remaking of the world order*. New York: Simon & Schuster.

Hupe, P., & Buffat, A. (2014). A public service gap: Capturing contexts in a comparative approach of street-level bureaucracy. *Public Management Review, 16*(4), 548–569.

Hupe, P., & Hill, M. (2007). Street-level bureaucracy and public accountability. *Public Administration, 85*, 279–299.

Institute of Education Sciences. (2015). *Trends in international mathematics and science study (TIMSS)*. Retrieved from http://nces.ed.gov/timss/index.asp

International Monetary Fund. (2015a). *Debt relief under the heavily indebted poor countries (HIPC) initiative*. Retrieved from https://www.imf.org/external/np/exr/facts/hipc.htm

International Monetary Fund. (2015b). *Poverty reduction strategy in IMF-supported programs*. Retrieved from http://www.imf.org/external/np/exr/facts/prsp.htm

International Telecommunications Union. (2015). *ICT facts and figures*. Retrieved from https://www.itu.int/en/ITU-D/Statistics/Documents/facts/ICTFactsFigures2015.pdf

Iriye, A. (2002). *Global community: The role of international organizations in the making of the contemporary world*. Berkeley, CA: University of California Press.

Jakobi, A. P. (2012). Facilitating transfer: International organizations as central nodes for policy diffusion. In G. Steiner-Khamsi & F. Waldow (Eds.), *World yearbook of education 2012: Policy borrowing and lending in education* (pp. 391–408). New York: Routledge.

Jansen, J. D. (2004). Importing outcomes-based education into South Africa: Policy borrowing in a post-communist world. In D. Phillips & K. Ochs (Eds.), *Educational policy borrowing: Historical perspectives* (pp. 199–220). Oxford, UK: Symposium Books.

Jenkins-Smith, H., & Sabatier, P. (1994). Evaluating the advocacy coalition framework. *Journal of Public Policy, 14*, 175–203.

Johnson, D. (2006). Comparing the trajectories of educational change and policy transfer in developing countries. *Oxford Review of Education, 32*(5), 679–696.

Johnston, J., & Laxer, G. (2003). Solidarity in the age of globalization: Lessons from the anti-MAI and Zapatista struggles. *Theory and Society, 32*, 39–91.

Jones, P. W. (2004). Taking the credit: Financing and policy linkages in the education portfolio of the World Bank. In G. Steiner-Khamsi (Ed.), *The global politics of educational borrowing and lending* (pp. 188–200). New York: Teachers College Press.

Juergensmeyer, M. (2011, May 6). What is Global Studies? *Global-e: A Global Studies Journal.* Retrieved from http://global-ejournal.org/2011/05/06/what-is-global-studies-3/

Kahn, R., & Kellner, D. (2007). Resisting globalization. In G. Ritzer (Ed.), *The Blackwell companion to globalization* (pp. 662–674). Malden, MA: Blackwell.

Kaldor, M. (2003). *Global civil society: An answer to war.* Malden, MA: Polity Press.

Kamens, D. (2013). Globalization and the emergence of an audit culture: PISA and the search for 'best practices' and magic bullets. In H.-D. Meyer & A. Benavot (Eds.), *PISA, power, and policy: The emergence of global educational governance* (pp. 117–140). Oxford, UK: Symposium Books.

Keating, J., Preston, R., Burke, P. J., Van Heertum, R., & Arnove, R. F. (2013). The political economy of educational reform in Australia, Britain, and the United States. In R. Arnove, C. A. Torres, & S. Franz (Eds.), *Comparative education: The dialectic of the global and the local* (4th ed., pp. 247–292). Boston, MA: Rowman and Littlefield.

Keynes, J. M. (1936). *The general theory of employment, interest and money.* New York, NY: Harcourt Brace.

Kingdon, J. W. (2010). *Agendas, alternatives and public policies* (2nd ed.). New York, NY: Pearson.

Klees, S. (2012). World bank and education: Ideological premises and ideological conclusions. In S. Klees, J. Samoff, & N. P. Stromquist (Eds.), *The World Bank and education: Critiques and alternatives* (pp. 49–68). Rotterdam, Netherlands: Sense.

Klees, S., Samoff, J., & Stromquist, N. P. (Eds.). (2012). *The World Bank and education: Critiques and alternatives.* Rotterdam, Netherlands: Sense.

Kliebard, H. M. (2004). *The struggle for the American curriculum, 1893–1958.* New York: Routledge.

Knight, J. (2002). *Trade in higher education: The implications of GATS.* London, UK: The Observatory on Borderless Higher Education.

Knight, J. (2004). Internationalization remodeled: Rationales, strategies and approaches. *Journal for Studies in International Education, 8*(1), 5–31.

Korzeniewicz, R. P., & Moran, T. P. (2007). World inequality in the twenty-first century: Patterns and tendencies. In G. Ritzer (Ed.), *The Blackwell companion to globalization* (pp. 565–592). Malden, MA: Blackwell.

Kraft, M. E., & Furlong, S. R. (2014). *Public policy: Politics, analysis, and alternatives* (5th ed.). Washington, DC: CQ Press.

Kristeva, J. (1982). *Powers of horror: An essay of abjection.* New York, NY: Columbia University Press.

Kubow, P. K., & Fossum, P. R. (2007). *Comparative education: Exploring issues in international context.* Upper Saddle River, NJ: Prentice Hall.

Labaree, D. F. (2003). The peculiar problems of preparing educational researchers. *Educational Researcher, 32*(4), 13–22.

Lacan, J. (1977). *The four fundamental concepts of psycho-analysis.* London, UK: The Hogarth Press.

Lasswell, H. D. (1948). *Power and personality.* New York: W. W. Norton and Company.

Lasswell, H. D. (1951). The policy orientation. In D. Lerner & H. D. Lasswell (Eds.), *The policy sciences* (pp. 3–15). Stanford, CA: Stanford University Press.

Law, W.-W. (2004). Translating globalization and democratization into local policy: Educational reform in Hong Kong and Taiwan. *International Review of Education, 50,* 497–524.

Lechner, F. J., & Boli, J. (2010). World culture: Origins and consequences. In G. Ritzer & Z. Atalay (Eds.), *Readings in globalization: Key concepts and major debates* (pp. 410–420). Malden, MA: Wiley-Blackwell.

LeVine, R. A. (2004). The global spread of women's schooling: Effects on learning, literacy, health, and children. In M. M. Suárez-Orozco (Ed.), *Learning in the global era* (pp. 121–136). Berkeley, CA: University of California Press.

Lewis, T. (2007). The problem of cultural fit—What can we learn from borrowing the German dual system? *Compare, 37*(4), 463–477.

Li, H. (2010). Higher education in China: Complement or competition to US Universities? In C. T. Clotfelter (Ed.), *American universities in a global market* (pp. 269–304). Chicago, IL: The University of Chicago Press.

Lindblom, C. (1959). The science of 'muddling through'. *Public Administration Review, 19*(2), 79–88.

Lingard, B. (2000). It is and it isn't: Vernacular globalization, educational policy, and restructuring. In N. C. Burbles & C. A. Torres (Eds.), *Globalization and education: Critical perspectives* (pp. 79–108). New York: Routledge.

Lingard, B. (2010). Policy borrowing, policy learning: Testing times in Australian schooling. *Critical Studies in Education, 51*(2), 129–147.

Lingard, B., & Sellar, S. (2012). A policy sociology reflection on school reform in England: From the 'third way' to the 'big society'. *Journal of Educational Administration and History, 44*(1), 43–63.

Lingard, B., Martino, W., Rezai-Rashti, G., & Sellar, S. (2015). *Globalizing educational accountabilities.* New York: Routledge.

Lipsett, S. M. (1959). Some social requisites of democracy. *American Political Science Review, 53*(1), 69–105.

Lipsett, S. M. (1960). *Political man: The social bases of politics.* New York: Doubleday & Company.

Lipsky, M. (2010). *Street level bureaucracy: Dilemmas of the individual in public services.* New York: Russell Sage Foundation (Original work published 1980).

Little, A. W., & Green, A. (2009). Successful globalisation, education and sustainable development. *International Journal of Educational Development, 29,* 166–174.

Luke, A. (2011). Generalizing across borders: Policy and the limits of educational science. *Educational Researcher, 40*(8), 367–377.

Luke, A., & Luke, C. (2000). A situated perspective on globalization. In N. C. Burbles & C. A. Torres (Eds.), *Globalization and education: Critical perspectives* (pp. 275–298). New York: Routledge.

Malen, B. (2006). Revising policy implementation as a political phenomenon: The case of school reconstitution. In M. I. Honig (Ed.), *New directions in education policy implementation: Confronting complexity* (pp. 83–104). Albany, NY: State University of New York Press.

Marginson, S. (1997a). *Markets in education.* Sydney, Australia: Allen and Unwin.

Marginson, S. (1997b). Steering from a distance: Power relations in Australian higher education. *Higher Education, 34*(1), 63–80.

Marginson, S. (2006). Dynamics of national and global competition in higher education. *Higher Education, 52*(3–4), 1–39.

Marginson, S. (2013). Global comparisons and the university knowledge economy. In L. M. Portnoi, V. D. Rust, & S. S. Bagley (Eds.), *Higher education, policy, and the global competition phenomenon* (pp. 29–42). New York: Palgrave Macmillan.

Maxwell, S. (2003). Heaven or hubris: Reflections on the new poverty agenda. *Development Policy Review, 21*(1), 5–25.

Maynard-Moody, S., & Portillo, S. (2010). Street-level bureaucracy theory. In R. F. Durant (Ed.), *Oxford handbook of American bureaucracy* (pp. 252–277). Oxford, UK: Oxford University Press.

McDonald, L., & Tufue-Dolgoy, R. (2013). Moving forwards, sideways or backwards? Inclusive education in Samoa. *International Journal of Disability, Development and Education, 60*(3), 270–284.

McGrew, A. (2007). Globalization in hard times: Contention in the academy and beyond. In G. Ritzer (Ed.), *The Blackwell companion to globalization* (pp. 29–53). Malden, MA: Blackwell.

McLaughlin, M. W. (2006). Implementation research in education: Lessons learned, lingering questions, and new opportunities. In M. I. Honig (Ed.), *New directions in education policy implementation: Confronting complexity* (pp. 209–228). Albany, NY: State University of New York Press.

McLuhan, M. (1962). *The Gutenberg galaxy: The making of typographic man.* Toronto, Canada: University of Toronto Press.

McNeely, C. L. (1995). Prescribing national education policies: The role of international organizations. *Comparative Education Review, 39*(4), 483–507.

Meyer, J. (1997). The effects of education as an institution. *American Journal of Sociology, 83*, 55–77.

Meyer, J. W., Boli, J., Thomas, G. M., & Ramirez, F. O. (1997). World society and the nation-state. *American Journal of Sociology, 103*(1), 144–181.

Meyer, J. W., Kamens, D., & Benavot, A. (2005). *School knowledge for the masses: World models and national primary curricular categories in the twentieth century.* Bristol, PA: Falmer.

Mincer, J. (1958). The investment in human capital and personal income distribution. *The Journal of Political Economy, 66*, 281–382.

Mir, S. (2013). Higher education in the Middle East. In R. Arnove, C. A. Torres, & S. Franz (Eds.), *Comparative education: The dialectic of the global and the local* (4th ed., pp. 89–112). Boston, MA: Rowman and Littlefield.

Moeller, K. (2014). The 'girl effect': U.S. transnational corporate investment in girls' education. In N. P. Stromquist & K. Monkman (Eds.), *Globalization and education: Integration and contestation across cultures* (2nd ed., pp. 71–85). Lanham, MA: Rowman & Littlefield.

Mohrman, K., Ma, W., & Baker, D. (2008). The research university in transition: The emerging global model. *Higher Education Policy, 21*, 5–27.

Mok, K.-H. (2012). International benchmarking with the best: The varied role of the state in the quest for regional education hubs in Malaysia and Hong Kong. In G. Steiner-Khamsi & F. Waldow (Eds.), *World yearbook of education 2012: Policy borrowing and lending in education* (pp. 3–18). New York: Routledge.

Morais de Sá e Silva, M. (2009). South–South cooperation: Past and present conceptualization and practice. In L. Chisholm & G. Steiner-Khamsi (Eds.), *South–South cooperation in education and development* (pp. 39–59). New York: Teachers College Press.

Morais de Sá e Silva, M. (2012). Conditional cash transfers: Paying to keep children in school and conquering the world. Three selected case studies. In G. Steiner-Khamsi & F. Waldow (Eds.), *World yearbook of education 2012: Policy borrowing and lending in education* (pp. 309–335). New York: Routledge.

Morrow, R. A., & Torres, C. A. (2013). The state, social movements, and educational reform. In R. Arnove, C. A. Torres, & S. Franz (Eds.), *Comparative education: The dialectic of the global and the local* (4th ed., pp. 369–378). Boston, MA: Rowman and Littlefield.

Mukhopadhyay, R., & Sriprakash, A. (2013). Target-driven reforms: Education for all and the translations of equity and inclusion in India. *Journal of Education Policy, 28*(3), 306–321.

Mundy, K. (1998). Educational multilateralism and world (dis)order. *Comparative Education Review, 42*(4), 448–478.

Mundy, K. (2006). Education for all and the new development compact. *International Review of Education, 52*(1), 23–48.

Mundy, K., & Manion, C. (2014). Globalization and global governance in education. In N. P. Stromquist & K. Monkman (Eds.), *Globalization and education: Integration and contestation across cultures* (2nd ed., pp. 39–53). Lanham, MA: Rowman & Littlefield.

Myers, M. K., & Lehmann Nielsen, V. (2012). Street-level bureaucrats and the implementation of public policy. In B. G. Peters & J. Pierre (Eds.), *Handbook of public administration* (2nd ed., pp. 305–318). London, UK: Sage.

Naidoo, D. G., & Muthukrishna, N. (2014). Teachers' 'small stories' about curriculum reform in South Africa: 'Square peg in a round hole'. *Journal of Social Sciences, 38*(3), 271–282.

Nassar, R., Zaki, E., Allen, N., Al Mula, B., Al Mutawaha, F., Al Bin Ali, H., et al. (2014). Alignment of teacher-developed curricula and national standards in Qatar's national education reform. *International Education Studies, 7*(10), 14–24.

Natesan, S. D., & Marathe, R. R. (2015). Literature review of public policy implementation. *International Journal of Public Policy, 11*(4/5/6), 219–241.

Nazmul Islam, M., & Anwar, A. (2012). BRAC in Afghanistan: Building South–South partnerships in teacher training. *Prospects, 42*(1), 55–70.

Nguyen, M., Elliott, J., Terlouw, C., & Pilot, A. (2009). Neocolonialism in education: Cooperative learning, Western pedagogy in an Asian context. *Comparative Education, 45*, 109–130.

Noddings, N. (2003). *Happiness and education*. Cambridge, UK: Cambridge University Press.

Nordtveit, B. H. (2009). Western and Chinese development discourses: Education, growth and sustainability. *International Journal of Education and Development, 29*, 157–165.

Ntsohe, I., & Letseka, M. (2013). Quality assurance and global competitiveness in higher education. In L. M. Portnoi, V. D. Rust, & S. S. Bagley (Eds.), *Higher education, policy, and the global competition phenomenon* (pp. 59–72). New York: Palgrave Macmillan.

Ochs, K. (2006). Cross-national policy borrowing and educational innovation: Improving achievement in the London borough of Barking and Dagenham. *Oxford Review of Education, 32*(5), 599–618.

Ochs, K., & Phillips, D. (2002). *Toward a structural typology of cross-national attraction in education*. Lisbon, Spain: Educa.

Ochs, K., & Phillips, D. (2004). Processes of educational borrowing in historical context. In D. Phillips & K. Ochs (Eds.), *Educational policy borrowing: Historical perspectives* (pp. 7–23). Oxford, UK: Symposium Books.

Ohmae, K. (1996). *The end of the nation-state*. London, UK: Harper Collins.

Ohmae, K. (1999). *The borderless world: Power and strategy in the interlinked economy, management lessons in the new logic of the global marketplace*. New York: HarperBusiness.

Ong, A. (1999). *Flexible citizenship: The cultural logics of transnationality*. Durham, NC: Duke University Press.

Organisation for Economic Cooperation and Development. (2015). *About PISA*. Retrieved from http://www.oecd.org/pisa/aboutpisa/

Ozga, J., & Lingard, B. (2007). Globalisation, education policy and politics. In J. Ozga & B. Lingard (Eds.), *The Routledge Falmer reader in education policy and politics* (pp. 65–82). London, UK: Routledge.

Parsons, T. (1959). The school class as a social system: Some of its functions in American society. *Harvard Educational Review, 29*(4), 297–318.

Phillips, D. (1989). Neither a borrower nor a lender be? The problems of cross-national attraction in education. *Comparative Education, 25*(3), 267–274.

Phillips, D. (2000). Learning from elsewhere in education: Some perennial problems revisited with reference to British interest in Germany. *Comparative Education, 36*(3), 297–307.

Phillips, D. (2005). Policy borrowing in education: Frameworks for analysis. In J. Zadja (Ed.), *International handbook on globalisation, education and policy research* (pp. 23–34). Dordrecht, Netherlands: Springer.

Phillips, D., & Ochs, K. (2003). Processes of policy borrowing in education: Some explanatory and analytical devices. *Comparative Education, 39*(4), 451–461.

Phillips, D., & Schweisfurth, M. (2014). *Comparative and international education: An introduction to theory, method, and practice* (2nd ed.). London, UK: Bloomsbury Academic.

Portnoi, L. M., & Bagley, S. S. (2011). Global competition in higher education: Strategies in a glonacal context. *World Studies in Education, 12*(1), 5–33.

Portnoi, L. M., & Bagley, S. S. (Eds.). (2014). *Critical perspectives on global competition in higher education.* [*New directions for higher education.*] San Francisco, CA: Jossey-Bass.

Portnoi, L. M., & Bagley, S. S. (2015, November–December). The AAUP's role in a globalized, competitive higher education landscape. *Academe*, 27–31.

Portnoi, L. M., Bagley, S. S., & Rust, V. D. (2013). Mapping the terrain: The global competition phenomenon in higher education. In L. M. Portnoi, V. D. Rust, & S. S. Bagley (Eds.), *Higher education, policy, and the global competition phenomenon* (pp. 1–13). New York: Palgrave Macmillan.

Portnoi, L. M., Rust, V. D., & Bagley, S. S. (Eds.). (2013). *Higher education, policy, and the global competition phenomenon.* New York: Palgrave Macmillan.

Prebisch, R. (1950). *The economic development of Latin America and its principal problems.* New York: United Nations.

Psacharopoulos, G. (1973). *Returns to education: An international comparison.* Amsterdam, Netherlands: Elsevier.

Psacharopoulos, G. (1985). Returns to education: A further international update and implications. *Journal of Human Resources, 20*(4), 583–604.

Psacharopoulos, G. (1994). Returns on investment in education: A global update. *World Development, 22*(9), 1325–1343.

Punchi, L. (2001). Resistance towards the language of globalization—The case of Sri Lanka. *International Review of Education, 47*(3), 361–378.

Ramirez, F. O. (2003). The global model and national legacies. In K. Anderson-Levitt (Ed.), *Local meanings, global schooling: Anthropology and world culture theory* (pp. 239–254). New York: Palgrave Macmillan.

Rappleye, J. (2012). Reimagining attracting and 'borrowing' in education: Introducing a political production model. In G. Steiner-Khamsi & F. Waldow

(Eds.), *World yearbook of education 2012: Policy borrowing and lending in education* (pp. 121–147). New York: Routledge.

Reid, A. (2011). Policy borrowing will not 'close the achievement gap'. *Social Alternatives, 30*(4), 5–9.

Rhoads, R. A. (2003). Globalization and resistance in the United States and Mexico: The global Potemkin village. *Higher Education, 45*, 223–250.

Rhoads, R. A., Li, S., & Ilano, L. (2014). The quest to build world-class universities: Toward a social justice agenda. In L. M. Portnoi & S. S. Bagley (Eds.), *Critical perspectives on global competition in higher education* (pp. 27–39). [*New directions for higher education.*] San Francisco, CA: Jossey-Bass.

Rice, D. A. (2013). Street-level bureaucrats and the welfare state: Toward a micro-institutionalist theory of policy implementation. *Administration and Society, 45*(9), 1038–1062.

Ritzer, G. (1993). *The McDonaldization of society: An investigation into the changing character of contemporary society.* Newbury Park, CA: Pine Forge Press.

Ritzer, G. (2007). *Modern sociological theory* (7th ed.). New York: McGraw Hill.

Rizvi, F. (2007). Postcolonialism and globalization in education. *Cultural Studies, Critical Methodologies, 7*(3), 256–263.

Rizvi, F., & Lingard, B. (2010). *Globalizing education policy.* New York: Routledge.

Robertson, D. B., & Waltman, J. L. (1992). The politics of policy borrowing. *Oxford Studies in Comparative Education, 2*(2), 25–55.

Robertson, R. (1992). *Globalization: Social theory and global culture.* London, UK: Sage.

Robertson, R. (1995). Globalization: Time-space and homogenity-heterogenity. In M. Featherstone, S. Lash, & R. Robertson (Eds.), *Global modernities* (pp. 25–44). London, UK: Sage.

Robertson, S. L., Bonal, X., & Dale, R. (2012). *WTO/GATS and the education service industry: Global strategy – Local responses.* London, UK: Routledge.

Robinson, R., & White, K. E. (2007). What is globalization? In G. Ritzer (Ed.), *The Blackwell companion to globalization* (pp. 54–66). Malden, MA: Blackwell.

Robinson, W. I. (2001). Social theory and globalization: The rise of the transnational state. *Theory and Society, 30*(2), 157–200.

Robinson, W. I. (2004). *A theory of global capitalism: Production, class, and state in a transnational world.* Baltimore, MD: Johns Hopkins University Press.

Robinson, W. I. (2007). Theories of globalization. In G. Ritzer (Ed.), *The Blackwell companion to globalization* (pp. 125–143). Malden, MA: Blackwell.

Robinson, W. I. (2010). Social theory and globalization: The rise of a transnational state. In G. Ritzer & Z. Atalay (Eds.), *Readings in globalization: Key concepts and major debates* (pp. 195–197). Malden, MA: Wiley-Blackwell.

Rodrik, D. (2011). *The globalization paradox: Democracy and the future of the world economy.* New York: W. W. Norton & Company.

Rose, N. (1999). *Powers of freedom: Reframing political thought.* Cambridge, UK: Cambridge University Press.

Rose, P. (2003). *The education fast track initiative: A global campaign review of progress and recommendations for reform*. Retrieved from http://www.actionaid.org.uk/sites/default/files/doc_lib/145_1_fast_track_initiative.pdf

Rostow, W. (1960). *The stages of economic growth: A non-communist manifesto*. Cambridge, UK: Cambridge University Press.

Roy, A. (2001). *Power politics*. Cambridge, MA: South End Press.

Sabatier, P. (1998). An advocacy coalition framework of policy change and the role of policy-oriented learning therein. *Policy Sciences, 21*, 129–168.

Sabatier, P., & Jenkins-Smith, H. (Eds.). (1993). *Policy change and learning: An advocacy coalition approach*. Boulder, CO: Westview.

Said, E. (1978). *Orientalism*. New York: Pantheon Books.

Sak, R., Erden, F. T., & Morrison, G. S. (2015). Child-centered education: Preschool teachers' beliefs and self-reported practices. *Early Child Development and Care*. doi:10.1080/03004430.2015.1081185.

Salmi, J. (2009). *The challenge of establishing world-class universities*. Washington, DC: The World Bank.

Samoff, J. (2013). Institutionalizing international influence. In R. Arnove, C. A. Torres, & S. Franz (Eds.), *Comparative education: The dialectic of the global and the local* (4th ed., pp. 55–88). Boston, MA: Rowman and Littlefield.

Samoff, J., & Carrol, B. (2013). Education for all in Africa: Not catching up, but setting the pace. In R. Arnove, C. A. Torres, & S. Franz (Eds.), *Comparative education: The dialectic of the global and the local* (4th ed., pp. 403–443). Boston, MA: Rowman and Littlefield.

Sassen, S. (1991). *The global city: New York, London, Tokyo*. Princeton, NJ: Princeton University Press.

Sassen, S. (2012). Cities: A wind won into larger and smaller worlds. *European Educational Research Journal, 11*(1), 1–10.

Savage, G. C., & O'Connor, K. (2014). National agendas in global times: Curriculum reforms in Australia and the USA since the 1980s. *Journal of Education Policy, 30*(5), 609–630.

Schoffer, E., & Meyer, J. W. (2005). The worldwide expansion of higher education in the twentieth century. *American Sociological Review, 70*(6), 898–920.

Schriewer, J., & Martinez, C. (2004). Constructions of internationality in education. In G. Steiner-Khamsi (Ed.), *The global politics of educational borrowing and lending* (pp. 29–53). New York: Teachers College Press.

Schugurensky, D. (2013). Higher education in the era of globalization: Toward a heteronomous model? In R. Arnove, C. A. Torres, & S. Franz (Eds.), *Comparative education: The dialectic of the global and the local* (4th ed., pp. 293–314). Boston, MA: Rowman & Littlefield.

Schultz, T. W. (1963). *The economic value of education*. New York: Columbia University Press.

Schweisfurth, M. (2011). Learner-centered education in developing country contexts: From solution to problem? *International Journal of Educational Development, 31*, 425–432.

Seidman, S. (2008). *Contested knowledge: Social theory today* (4th ed.). Malden, MA: Blackwell.

Sen, A. (1999a). *Commodities and capabilities*. Oxford, UK: Oxford University Press.

Sen, A. (1999b). *Development as freedom*. New York: Oxford University Press.

Sen, A. (2005). *The argumentative Indian: Writings on Indian history, culture, and identity*. New York: Farrar, Straus and Giroux.

Shields, R. (2013). *Globalization and education*. London, UK: Bloomsbury Academic.

Shiva, V. (2005). *Earth democracy: Justice, sustainability, and peace*. New York: South End Press.

Sidhu, R. (2006). *Universities and globalization: To market, to market*. Mahwah, NJ: Lawrence Erlbaum.

Silova, I. (2004). Adopting the language of the new allies. In G. Steiner-Khamsi (Ed.), *The global politics of educational borrowing and lending* (pp. 75–87). New York: Teachers College Press.

Silova, I. (2012). Contested meanings of educational borrowing. In G. Steiner-Khamsi & F. Waldow (Eds.), *World yearbook of education 2012: Policy borrowing and lending in education* (pp. 229–245). New York: Routledge.

Sklair, L. (2010). Transnational practices. In G. Ritzer & Z. Atalay (Eds.), *Readings in globalization: Key concepts and major debates* (pp. 184–194). Malden, MA: Wiley-Blackwell.

Sklair, R. (2005, March 1). *The silent qualifiers of globalization*. Public lecture given at the London School of Economics and Political Science. Retrieved from http://www.lse.ac.uk/collections/sklair

Smail, A. (2014). Rediscovering the teacher within Indian child-centred pedagogy: Implications for the global child-centred Approach. *Compare: A Journal of Comparative and International Education, 44*(4), 613–633.

Smith, S. R. (2012). Street-level bureaucracy and public policy. In B. G. Peters & J. Pierre (Eds.), *Handbook of public administration* (2nd ed., pp. 431–436). London, UK: Sage.

Song, S. (2015). Cambodian teachers' responses to child-centered instructional policies: A mismatch between beliefs and practices. *Teaching and Teacher Education, 50*, 36–45.

Soudien, C. (2009). India and South Africa: Diaspora and transfer. In L. Chisholm & G. Steiner-Khamsi (Eds.), *South–South cooperation in education and development* (pp. 226–240). New York: Teachers College Press.

Sparke, M. (2013). *Introducing globalization: Ties, tensions, and uneven integration*. Malden, MA: Wiley-Blackwell.

Spreen, C. A. (2004). Appropriating borrowed policies: Outcomes-based education in South Africa. In G. Steiner-Khamsi (Ed.), *The global politics of educational borrowing and lending* (pp. 101–113). New York: Teachers College Press.

Spreen, C. A., & Vally, S. (2006). Education rights, education policies and inequality in South Africa. *International Journal of Educational Development, 26*(4), 352–362.

Spring, J. (2008). Research on globalization and education. *Review of Educational Research, 78*, 330–363.

Spring, J. (2015). *Globalization of education: An introduction*. New York: Routledge.

Sriprakash, A. (2010). Child-centred education and the promise of democratic learning: Pedagogic messages in rural Indian primary schools. *International Journal of Educational Development, 30*(3), 297–304.

Steger, M. (2013). *Globalization: A short introduction*. Oxford, UK: Oxford University Press.

Steiner-Khamsi, G. (Ed.). (2004). *The global politics of educational borrowing and lending*. New York: Teachers College Press.

Steiner-Khamsi, G. (2009). Conclusion: A way out of the dependency trap in educational development? In L. Chisholm & G. Steiner-Khamsi (Eds.), *South–South cooperation in education & development* (pp. 241–258). New York: Teachers College Press.

Steiner-Khamsi, G. (2012). Understanding policy borrowing and lending: Building comparative policy studies. In G. Steiner-Khamsi & F. Waldow (Eds.), *World yearbook of education 2012: Policy borrowing and lending in education* (pp. 3–18). New York: Routledge.

Steiner-Khamsi, G., & Quist, H. O. (2000). The politics of educational borrowing: Re-opening the case of Achimota of British Ghana. *Comparative Education Review, 44*(3), 272–299.

Steiner-Khamsi, G., & Stolpe, I. (2006). *Educational import: Local encounters with global forces in Mongolia*. New York: Palgrave Macmillan.

Steiner-Khamsi, G., & Waldow, F. (Eds.). (2012). *World yearbook of education 2012: Policy borrowing and lending in education*. New York: Routledge.

Steiner-Khamsi, G., Silova, I., & Johnson, E. M. (2006). Educational policy borrowing in Central Asia. In J. Ozga, T. Seddon, & T. S. Popkewitz (Eds.), *World yearbook of education 2012: Education, research and policy: Steering the knowledge-based economy* (pp. 217–245). New York: Routledge.

Stensaker, B. (2007). The relationship between branding and organisational change. *Higher Education Management and Policy, 19*(1), 1–17.

Stenvoll-Wells, D., & Sayed, Y. (2012). Education decentralization in South Africa and Zimbabwe: The gap between intention and practice. In A. Verger, M. Novelli, & H. K. Altinyelken (Eds.), *Global education policy and international development: New agendas, issues and policies* (pp. 97–118). London, UK: Bloomsbury Academic.

Stiglitz, J. (2002). *Globalization and its discontents*. New York: W. W. Norton & Company.

Strange, S. (1996). *The retreat of the state: The diffusion of power in the world economy*. Cambridge, UK: Cambridge University Press.

Stromquist, N. P., & Monkman, K. (2014). Defining globalization and assessing its impact for knowledge and education, revisited. In N. P. Stromquist & K.

Monkman (Eds.), *Globalization and education: Integration and contestation across cultures* (2nd ed., pp. 1–20). Lanham, MA: Rowman & Littlefield.

Suárez-Orozco, M. M., & Qin-Hillard, D. B. (2004). *Globalization: Culture and education in the new millennium.* In M. Suárez-Orozco & D. B. Qin-Hillard (Eds.), *Globalization: Culture and education in the new millennium* (pp. 1–37). Berkeley, CA: University of California Press.

Suárez-Orozco, M. M., & Sattin, C. (2007). Introduction. In M. M. Suárez-Orozco (Ed.), *Learning in the global era* (pp. 1–43). Berkeley, CA: University of California Press.

Sung, Y.-K. (2011). Cultivating borrowed futures: The politics of neoliberal loan-words in South Korean cross-national policy borrowing. *Comparative Education, 47*(4), 523–538.

Tabulawa, R. T. (2009). Education reform in Botswana: Reflections on policy contradictions and paradoxes. *Comparative Education, 45*(1), 87–107.

Takayama, K. (2007). A nation at risk crosses the Pacific: Transnational borrowing of the US crisis discourse in the debate on education reform in Japan. *Comparative Education Review, 51*(4), 423–446.

Takayama, K. (2012). Bringing political 'bite' to educational transfer studies: Cultural politics of PISA and the OECD in Japanese education reform. In G. Steiner-Khamsi & F. Waldow (Eds.), *World yearbook of education 2012: Policy borrowing and lending in education* (pp. 148–166). New York: Routledge.

Tarabini, A. (2010). Education and poverty in the global development agenda: Emergence, evolution and consolidation. *International Journal of Educational Development, 30,* 204–212.

Teach for All. (2015). *Network partners.* Retrieved from http://teachforall.org/en/our-network-and-impact/network-partners

Thomas, G. M. (2007). Globalization: The major players. In G. Ritzer (Ed.), *The Blackwell companion to globalization* (pp. 84–102). Malden, MA: Blackwell.

Tikly, L. (2001). Globalisation and education in the postcolonial world: Towards a conceptual framework. *Comparative Education, 37*(2), 151–171.

Tikly, L. (2004). Education and the new imperialism. *Comparative Education, 40*(2), 173–198.

Tilak, J. B. G. (2007). Post-elementary education, poverty, and development in India. *International Journal of Education and Development, 27*(4), 435–145.

Tilly, C. (2004). Past, present, and future globalizations. In G. Steiner-Khamsi (Ed.), *The global politics of educational borrowing and lending* (pp. 13–28). New York: Teacher's College Press.

TIMSS and PIRLS International Study Center. (2015). *About TIMSS and PIRLS.* Retrieved from http://www.timss.org

Tomlinson, J. (2007). Cultural globalization. In G. Ritzer (Ed.), *The Blackwell companion to globalization* (pp. 352–366). Malden, MA: Blackwell.

Tooley, J., & Dixon, P. (2006). 'De facto' privatisation of education and the poor: Implications of a study from Sub-Saharan Africa and India. *Compare, 36*(4), 443–462.

Tummers, L., & Bekkers, V. (2014). Policy implementation, street-level bureaucracy, and the importance of discretion. *Public Management Review, 14*(4), 527–547.

United Nations. (2015a). *2015: Time for global action for people and planet.* Retrieved from http://www.un.org/sustainabledevelopment/

United Nations. (2015b). *Outcomes on education.* Retrieved from http://www.un.org/en/development/devagenda/education.shtml

United Nations. (2015c). *Transforming our world: The 2030 Agenda for Sustainable Development.* Retrieved from https://sustainabledevelopment.un.org/post2015/transformingourworld

United Nations. (2015d). *We can end poverty. Millennium development goals and beyond 2015.* Retrieved from http://www.un.org/millenniumgoals/

United Nations Education, Scientific and Cultural Organization. (2015a). *Education 2030: Towards inclusive and equitable quality education and lifelong learning for all.* Retrieved from http://www.unesco.org/new/fileadmin/MULTIMEDIA/HQ/ED/ED/pdf/FinalVersion-IncheonDeclaration.pdf

United Nations Education, Scientific and Cultural Organization. (2015b). *World Education Forum 2000.* Retrieved from http://www.unesco.org/education/wef/en-conf/participants.shtm

United Nations Education, Scientific and Cultural Organization Institute for Statistics. (2015). *Higher education.* Retrieved from http://www.uis.unesco.org/Education/Pages/tertiary-education.aspx

van Vught, F. (2008). Mission diversity and reputation in higher education. *Higher Education Policy, 21*(2), 151–174.

Vavrus, F., & Bartlett, L. (2012). Comparative pedagogies and epistemological diversity: Social and materials contexts of teaching in Tanzania. *Comparative Education Review, 56*(4), 634–658.

Verger, A., & VanderKaaij, S. (2012). The national politics of global policies: Public–private partnerships in Indian education. In A. Verger, M. Novelli, & H. K. Altinyelken (Eds.), *Global education policy and international development: New agendas, issues and policies* (pp. 245–266). London, UK: Bloomsbury Academic.

Verger, A., Novelli, M., & Altinyelken, H. K. (2012). Global educational policy and international development: An introductory framework. In A. Verger, M. Novelli, & H. K. Altinyelken (Eds.), *Global education policy and international development: New agendas, issues and policies* (pp. 3–32). London, UK: Bloomsbury Academic.

Waldow, F. (2009). Undeclared imports: Silent borrowing in educational policy-making and research in Sweden. *Comparative Education, 45*(4), 477–494.

Waldow, F. (2012). Standardisation and legitimacy: Two central concepts in research in educational borrowing and lending. In G. Steiner-Khamsi & F. Waldow (Eds.), *World yearbook of education 2012: Policy borrowing and lending in education* (pp. 411–427). New York: Routledge.

Wallerstein, I. (1974). *The modern world system: Capitalist agriculture and the origins of the European world-economy in the sixteenth century.* New York: Academic Press.

Wallerstein, I. (2010). The modern world-system: Theoretical reprise. In G. Ritzer & Z. Atalay (Eds.), *Readings in globalization: Key concepts and major debates* (pp. 205–209). Malden, MA: Wiley-Blackwell.

Ward, S. C., Bagley, C., Lumby, J., Hamilton, T., Woods, P., & Roberts, A. (2015). What is 'policy' and what is 'policy response'? An illustrative study of the implementation of the Leadership Standards for Social Justice in Scotland. *Educational Management Administration & Leadership,* 1–14. doi:10.1177/1741143214558580.

Weiss, L. (2010). Globalization and the myth of the powerless state. In G. Ritzer & Z. Atalay (Eds.), *Readings in globalization: Key concepts and major debates* (pp. 166–174). Malden, MA: Wiley-Blackwell.

West, A., & Pennell, H. (1997). Educational reform and school choice in England and Wales. *Education Economics, 5*(3), 285–305.

Whitty, G., Power, S., & Halpin, D. (1998). *Devolution and choice in education: The school, the state and the market.* Berkshire, UK: Open University Press.

Wildavsky, A. (1964). *Politics of the budgetary process.* Boston, MA: Little, Brown.

Wilkins, C. (2015). Education reform in England: Quality and equity in the performative school. *International Journal of Inclusive Education, 19*(11), 1143–1160.

Williamson, J. (2000). What should the World Bank think about the Washington consensus? *The World Bank Research Observer, 15*(2), 251–264.

Wilson, D. N. (1994). Comparative and international education: Fraternal or Siamese twins? A preliminary genealogy of our twin fields. *Comparative Education Review, 38*(4), 449–486.

World Bank. (2005). *Education notes.* Retrieved from http://www.un.org/sustainabledevelopment/

World Bank. (2011). *Learning for all: Investing in people's knowledge and skills to promote development—World Bank Group education strategy 2020.* Retrieved from http://siteresources.worldbank.org/EDUCATION/Resources/ESSU/Education_Strategy_4_12_2011.pdf

World Bank. (2015). *Updated income classifications.* Retrieved from http://data.worldbank.org/news/2015-country-classifications

Yearley, S. (2007). Globalization and the environment. In G. Ritzer (Ed.), *The Blackwell companion to globalization* (pp. 238–253). Malden, MA: Blackwell.

Index

© The Editor(s) (if applicable) and The Author(s) 2016

L.M. Portnoi, *Policy Borrowing and Reform in Education*,
DOI 10.1057/978-1-137-53024-0

T

U

Printed by Printforce, the Netherlands